CAPSIZED

Jim Nalepka's Epic 119 Day Survival Voyage
Aboard the *Rose-Noëlle*

Also by Steven Callahan

Adrift: Seventy-Six Days Lost at Sea

CAPSIZED

Jim Nalepka's Epic 119 Day Survival Voyage Aboard the *Rose-Noëlle*

STEVEN CALLAHAN

2013
New Street Communications, LLC
Wickford, RI

See page 284 for a complete map of the *Rose Noëlle's* four-month drift.

Map and Illustrations © by Steven Callahan.

New Street Communications, LLC
Wickford, RI

newstreetcommunicaations.com
newstreetnautical.com

To Richard James Hellriegel, who has found his place in peace.
Rick was my friend, my soulmate, and will forever be my brother.

- James Nalepka

But look! here come more crowds, pacing straight for the water, and seemingly bound for a dive. Strange! Nothing will content them but the extremest limit of the land; loitering under the shady lee of yonder warehouses will not suffice. No. They must get just as nigh the water as they possibly can without falling in. And there they stand- miles of them- leagues. Inlanders all, they come from lanes and alleys, streets avenues- north, east, south, and west. Yet here they all unite. Tell me, does the magnetic virtue of the needles of the compasses of all those ships attract them thither?

No man prefers to sleep two in a bed. In fact, you would a good deal rather not sleep with your own brother. I don't know how it is, but people like to be private when they are sleeping. And when it comes to sleeping with an unknown stranger, in a strange inn, in a strange town, and that stranger a harpooneer, then your objections indefinitely multiply. Nor was there any earthly reason why I as a sailor should sleep two in a bed, more than anybody else; for sailors no more sleep two in a bed at sea, than bachelor Kings do ashore. To be sure they all sleep together in one apartment, but you have your own hammock, and cover yourself with your own blanket, and sleep in your own skin.

Upon waking the next morning about daylight, I found Queequeg's arm thrown over me in the most loving and affectionate manner. You had almost thought I had been his wife.

— **Herman Melville,** *Moby Dick*

Introduction
to the New Edition

I first heard of the *Rose-Noëlle* when my wife and I were visiting a catamaran anchored near our own floating home in Grenada in early 1990. The cat's owner was from Minneapolis, and his sister had just mailed him a newspaper clipping about a fellow Minneapolitan who *supposedly* had drifted for an astounding one hundred nineteen days on an overturned, half-flooded trimaran. The clipping stated that some officials and members of the public now thought that the story was a hoax.

After drifting in a life raft for seventy-six days in 1982, I was more sympathetic with the *Rose Noëlle* crew than those officials and other sceptics. One such official in particular had made a similar claim, that my survival voyage was a hoax, when I had the bad taste to wash up still alive in 1982. Similar reactions to survivors are all too common. An initial euphoria, "He's made it! How incredible!" often is followed by, "I'm sorry, but this is impossible. He must have staged this for some reason." The reasons usually make no sense at all, actually. Who would torture themselves with months of starvation plus hundreds of painful sores and disposal of a lifetime's material possessions just to score an appearance on some surreality TV show? I suppose anything is possible, but if you've ever actually suffered these things, you'd know that staging a hoax is way more unlikely than actually doing the deed. Doubt is common enough because I think that people just can't believe the human animal can be as resilient as it actually is. More to the point, showing up alive can embarrass those who have either written off the survivors, or have screwed up elements of their official capacities. If, for example, they have made misjudgements or mistakes relating to search and rescue operations and you survive, they have not only failed but also have done so under the public's eye.

I had spent most of my life sailing all kinds of craft, which included multihulls since the 1960s. I'd helped build several trimarans, had lived on one, and had designed several other multihulls. Although by the turn of the millennium, multihulls would be better known and embraced by western yachting communities, thanks largely to their success in the America's Cup, they had been reviled by the yachting establishment for many decades, I thought completely unfairly. The critics had long chastised these boats as dangerous because, given enough wind or big enough seas, they could capsize, and once upside down, were virtually impossible to reright.

These critics tend to ignore a simple fact: Numerous traditional single-hulled working craft and pleasure boats, including most tall ships, will not reright automatically from a knockdown past 90 degrees. For the most part, the "self-righting" monohull is actually a relatively modern phenomenon. Furthermore, single-hulled monohulls are actually more subject to capsizes and pitchpoling because they have much less total righting moment for any given size; and although many monohulls will reright, with enough wave action to give them a boost, many others are very happy to remain upside down. Even some boats that might reright on their own if kept watertight actually fill with water and sink prior to rerighting.

Multihull stalwarts also have countered that multihull capsizes are about as likely as sinkings of single-hulled crafts, which can result from a wide variety of structural failures or collision with flotsam or other craft, and that the survival rates of crews from sunken boats are hardly reassuring. In comparison, virtually all multihulls are built with materials that will float, and they contain no ballast, so the vast majority will not sink even if they are badly holed. All the research I have done covering every known capsize for decades showed that the survival rate of crews on capsized multihulls, and even the salvage rate of the boats themselves, was staggeringly high, not something found with those who were on monohulls that sank or had gotten rolled over. In these studies, once the worst had happened on a multihull and it went upside down, even when a vessel had not been that well prepared, it appeared that multihulls still could serve as very stable, incredibly roomy, amazingly well-stocked life rafts.

So at base, the case of the *Rose-Noëlle* was extremely lengthy and might stretch believability, but to me, drifting for 119 days on an overturned multihull seemed completely plausible. After all, Maurice and Marilyn Bailey (*117 Days Adrift*, Sheridan House Publisher) had lived that long with only a life raft and inflatable dinghy as support. It should have been obvious that having a much larger platform filled with tools and food would make the oceanic struggle for survival infinitely easier. Over several decades, I have written several articles supporting the notion that multi-hulled boats (two-hulled catamarans, outriggers, and proas, or three-hulled trimarans) are among the safest of ocean-going craft, and the case of the *Rose-Noëlle* fits both that outlook and what seems logical based on numerous ocean-survival case histories.

When my wife and I returned from the Caribbean to Maine in the spring of 1990, there, among the pile of mail from our nine months away, sat a letter from Jim Nalepka, the Minneapolis native who had been aboard *Rose Noëlle*. I also learned that a friend of mine knew the skipper, John Glennie, decades ago and vouched for his competence. These serendipitous coincidences with which the story of *Rose Noëlle* is peppered were too much for me to ignore.

Jim Nalepka had written to me because, shortly after he landed, he had seen a copy of *Adrift*, which chronicled my own ocean survival drift. He thought I might help him write a book about his experience from the viewpoints of the crew, especially his and his friend Rick's. I knew just how important this event must have been for Jim personally, but I wondered what new dimensions his story would add to the small library of ocean survival books. I didn't want to repeat the themes and issues in *Adrift*, although I was sure there would have to be some parallels. I was keen to write about the *Rose-Noëlle*, if for no other reason than to stand testament to the ultimate safety of multihulls, but I also wanted this book to be more than a tale of desperation in which the good guys lived in the end.

Four months adrift is a very long time, but durations of survival experiences in and of themselves are only one of their many elements. Frankly, I had very quickly tired of reporters asking me if *I* had set any records (I had not, unless one multiplies the qualifiers to include "a person alone in an inflated raft"). I reminded the press constantly that survival is not a sporting event. I also had spoken with numerous other survivors, both oceanic and terrestrial, and found that all experiences are unique, and that some relatively brief survival experiences were in many ways more challenging than some lengthy ones. What is important about an event is not its duration but what survivors discover from the journey.

So I could find out what Jim had discovered, he agreed to travel to Maine. He called it "our blind date." We had no idea of what to expect, so we expected nothing from one another. Conversations flowed easily. I liked Jim immediately. Jim did not *look* like an ocean survivor, but then again, no one really does.

Survivors are rarely well-tanned rippling-muscle hunks or sore-covered corpses. Jim's face was somewhat cherubic, his hair thick, his smile shy, his voice soft. He appeared sensitive and easygoing. But two other things really stood out. One was Jim's complete candor. He had an amazing ability not only to see common human frailties in his mates but also to expose those he found in himself. The other was his wry wit, which often was self-effacing. Unlike the dedicated sailors I'd known who had focused their tales on dry facts of what happened when, Jim saw his experience largely through what he and his mates felt and how they all evolved throughout the journey, sometimes by surprising leaps. Jim's insights and personality give, in my view, his story more depth and realism than I find in most other survival tales that I have read. I can only hope I have done some justice to it.

I was a seasoned sailor when I found myself adrift. Jim didn't know what a cleat was. In heavy conditions, he had to look for signs of fear in his shipmates' faces to know whether he should be scared or not. Writing a story from the viewpoint of a complete neophyte would be fun for me. I did not anticipate how much Jim's story would challenge and enlighten my own perceptions of the sea, survival, and masculinity, however.

As I re-edited this manuscript for this e-book and paperback edition, first published by HarperCollins in 1993, one thing really jumped out at me: I laughed a lot. Jim has an infectious sense of humor, and his mates were not devoid of this gift either. Among survival experts, it is well known that maintaining a sense of humor is a critical component of survival. Someone who usually is quick with a joke but then stops even smiling at the most funny things, usually is on the precipice of doom. Survivors may be guilty of a kind of gallows humor, but if one disappears into gloom, if one cannot at least smile inwardly at some things, one has suffered a "sense of humor failure" and is lost.   I was amazed by how often the crew of *Rose-Noëlle* found things funny, approached elements of bad news with sardonic humor, and pulled practical jokes on one another.

Despite this humor, I do not expect this to be an easy book to read. Especially towards the beginning, the characters often exhibit behavior hard to take.   After the capsize, it takes them an extraordinarily long time to learn how to become a survival team, and it never works flawlessly. They are not varnished heros. At times they are fearful, weak, defeatist, petty, jealous, self-interested. Frankly, I believe how Jim reveals all the lesser but very normal human qualities that are impediments to grace makes this crew more believable than the characters found in many tales. If one studies other survival case histories, one will find that this crew is not atypical. In fact, even though I was alone, I was subjected to the same weaknesses and often the very same arguments within my own head. Reality is no Disney cartoon. This story is a hard look at the way real people really feel, think, and react in real crises.

Hopefully, this book also reveals the answers to the typical post-trauma questions: "What did you think about out there? How did you feel?" As Jim notes, thoughts, feelings, and character are not static. They may be plagued by inconsistency and contra-dictions, but overall, they evolve, as do surrounding events.   Jim was not only able to criticize himself and his mates, but he also shows what he gained from them and how each grew. Phil, for example, drove everyone nuts at the beginning but, by the end, had gained immense self-confidence and filled an indispensable role among his mates.

When one reads this tale, one can easily come down pretty hard on John Glennie, the skipper, but frankly, as a mariner, I have great sympathy for him. He may often have been overconfident and bull headed, and he proved incapable of effectively communicating or consistently leading his very motley crew. However, it's hard to understand the substantive challenges of voyaging with unknown people, especially those with no offshore experience, unless you've walked in those sea boots. Once the boat capsized, John may have lost his credibility, and it seems he did little to reclaim it, but I can relate to his depression at having lost all he had, including his dreams, and I can only imagine the effect of also having a bunch of novices with limited skills and decidedly selfish desires on his hands. In the end, John persevered, no mean task.

In the final analysis, I came to be very fond of the whole crew. I would not have been interested in Jim Nalepka's story if it had not appeared to be different from *Adrift*. I would not have been interested if Jim could not tell me the story. I may have shaped and juggled the words herein, but it could not possibly have come to life without Jim's eloquence, his candor, his objective views on the strengths and weaknesses of both his mates and himself. As he talked, I came to see that this was not a tale so much about survival afloat as it was a tale of mens' survival in contemporary society. Similar struggles could have occurred as easily within a jail cell or even suburban home as it did within the confines of their Pacific prison.

For six months, Jim lived with me and my wife, and we worked on the book daily. He'd sit in a chair and let me plague him with questions all day long. I'd organize and draft at night. After Jim left, I took a number of additional months to do further research, check facts, and come up with a final manuscript.

Skipper John Glennie wrote his own account of the incident, but *Capsized* significantly differs, not only in numerous minor details but also in overall themes and tone. In this book, you will see through Jim's eyes alone, as Glennie's related his recounting. We do not pretend that Jim's view is completely objective. Because memories are flawed, no doubt we, too, are guilty of minor factual errors. That said, Jim and I tried very hard to be much more inclusive of the entire crew's memories and perceptions.

Our purpose is not to replicate or denigrate Glennie's account but to paint another picture of the same scene. Interviews of John plus his own account helped me to establish a chronology and to understand a little of his feelings and thoughts during his survival drift. I give John thanks for his leadership during the event and for putting together his account.

We ventured further, however. We relied on a great number of resources unavailable or untapped by Glennie, who created his account much closer in time to the event. Conversations and style of speech are recollected to the best of Jim's ability and confirmed through our listening to interviews of the entire crew and feedback from those who knew them. Multiple sources also confirmed details of events or opened questions for further inquiry. Jim's close friend and shipmate, Rick Hellriegel, originally intended to help Jim with this book, but illness prevented him. Rick, Jim, and Phil, however, were interviewed in great depth by Bruce Ansley shortly after their escape to land. Bruce, a newspaper reporter at that time in New Zealand, kindly allowed us to use all the tapes and transcripts from the twenty-four hours of these interviews, for which we are incredibly grateful. We also tapped dozens of press articles, the New Zealand government's official inquiry into the event, and interviews of and other sources about many people who went through their own survival experience ashore, particularly Heather Hellriegel, who reviewed this manuscript and added to it.

Jim was certainly unfamiliar with survival and maritime history as well as with sailing. I have taken the liberty to add information about survival, history, and the environment where I thought it relevant. I've also inserted details about the search and rescue operation and lives of those ashore. Although Jim was not privy to these elements at the time of his drift, we have included them in order to put some of the events into clearer perspective.

To create our chart of the drift, we merged an approximated drift chart created by Greg Reeve at the Auckland Weather Office with details that we knew, such as the boat's actual landing position, as well as notable events along the way. In numerous cases, we knew details about the weather and wind direction as they related to events on board. As we placed in order birthdays and survival activities, like when the survivors caught fish or made specific tools, we could create quite a tight overall chronology to which our survivors could agree and to which with weather patterns observed both on board and ashore concurred.

In cases in which the crew maintained conflicting memories of chronology or details, Jim and I decided to rely on common sense and the majority view. Glennie says, for instance, that he tossed the first battery, but he had to be in the cave to get the battery. Why would he crawl out to toss it rather than just handing it to one of three pairs of waiting hands? Rick remembers tossing it, so that is our version. If Glennie thought about hooking up the EPIRB to the ship's battery immediately, as he says, why did he throw out the second good battery, and why did he later wait several days after the EPIRB died to try to resuscitate it with the remaining battery? Hopefully, minor differences in detail do not threaten the integrity of either account.

Jim wanted to emphasize how mutually dependent the entire crew was during their days adrift, a fact that he and Rick felt was downplayed by their skipper. Jim acknowledges Glennie's competence and the crews' dependence on him, but the rest of the crew remember that Glennie was hardly a flawless leader. He resisted their efforts to fish. He also resisted retrieving gas bottles to rig a stove. Fish and heat transformed their world. Phil Hoffman, on the other hand, was often treated as low man on the totem pole, but he created a valuable rain collection system and was the chief hunter of fish.

Our story requires no heros or demons. Like the voyage itself, all men facing all situations are complex puzzles. By examining the puzzle of this crew, the primary themes of *Capsized* emerged. There are moments of humor, of cynicism, of passion, of depression, of hope, and of hopelessness. There is both incredible selfishness and touching generosity. Each of the crew is a combination of diverse traits of character that in some situations proved to be assets while in others liabilities. All those aboard *Rose-Noëlle* were flawed, as all men are, but their virtues kept them together to survive and form a well-rounded survival team.

Frankly, I see the same flaws and rationalizations all around me in society. They are far less stressed than the crew of *Rose-Noëlle* was; however, a major attraction for me was how this case history reflects society at large, and how these very different individuals could both create a new society from scratch and learn to accommodate and even transcend their vices in order to achieve and witness what few others, if any, have before. Yes, this story often is testament to the darker side of mens' souls and my own good luck in having drifted alone, but I think it also is witness to the larger over-riding positive qualities of humankind, and in particular, to male aptitude, creativity, and determination along with a surprising amount of sensitivity, empathy, and generosity. And yes, all these things even when out of sight of women. Some readers, safe within the embrace of their armchairs or beds, may fantasize that they would show fewer faults under similar circumstances, but let's hope that the tale of the *Rose-Noëlle* gives us all pause to consider both the limits and capacity of our own characters.

For the *record*, if the survivors of *Rose-Noëlle* hold any record as such, it is that, at the time of the event, they tied with the Baileys for surviving the second longest time at sea after their craft was *fatally stricken*. During the second World War, Poon Lim drifted one hundred thirty-three days on a solid ship's raft. Among solo ocean survivors, he remains to this day (April 2013) the uncontested champ. In warmer waters, at the time of *Rose-Noëlle*'s capsize, there had been one case of a Costa Rican boat that drifted one hundred forty-two days after running out of fuel. That boat remained upright and intact, however. Since first publication of this book, a Mexican fishing boat drifted for eleven months across most of the Pacific. There is no doubt that the *Rose-Noëlle*'s crew are in a very special club, but in terms of maritime history and survival at sea, the greatest significance of their drift may be that they survived longest by far in such cold waters where hypothermia can kill in minutes. In fact, I have yet to find another case of survival offshore of more than a week in such high latitudes. This is the result of having both a reliable and commodious survival craft and a crew able to exploit its advantages over life boats and rafts.

Mere facts do not tell any story. We have tried to choreo-raph herein facts and impressions that tell a story worth reading, a voyage into the limitations and capabilities of men, which are as diverse and real as the waves on which they rode.

Steven Callahan
September 2013

Acknowledgments

by
Jim Nalepka
October 1991

Prior to our ill-fated voyage on *Rose-Noëlle*, I could not have imagined the unknowns of the sea or the adversity that we were about to face. During those days adrift, the only thing of which I was certain was that we were alive. Our family and friends, unfortunately, had no idea about what had happened. With the official opinion stating truly that our chances of survival were remote, those close to us could only rest their hopes on their confidence in our survival instincts and the strong force of their own faith. I realize now that what they went through was as equally, if not more, traumatic and painful as our own ordeal. I believe in the power of collective human spirit and feel that it played an important role in my own survival. To all those who were with me afloat and ashore, I give thanks for their continued faith and help without which we would not have survived.

I am forever grateful to my sister Cathy, husband, Tom Moynihan, and their children, Meg and Jack, for their unyielding faith and unconditional love and support. Also thanks go to my mother, my father, Doris, brother Mike, and their families for all their prayers and efforts to secure my safe return. Joe and Peggy Schierl, Mary O'Donnell, Pam Caldwell, and so many friends and acquaintances in Minnesota worked unselfishly with my family to obtain information, inspire action, and lend one another support during those trying times. I offer gratitude and friendship to them all.

I feel inadequate to express my appreciation to my extended family in New Zealand. To the patient and understanding staff at the Cobham Outward Bound School, thank you for your tender loving care when I needed it. I owe a special debt to Sue B. in New Zealand for her constant love and support, which has meant so much. My heartfelt feeling of indebtedness to Pete Brady and Jenny Jones, Martha Bell, Pete and Lee, Gino Rocco and family, Mary P., and all the people who create that strong, caring community in the Marlborough Sounds.

How does one put into words the experience and meaning of being at a close friend's side when he is dying? Heather Hellriegel's amazing spirit and intense love lifted Rick and us all. Her mother, Gloria Whiting, was nothing less than totally selfless throughout Rick's extended illness. Heather's and Rick's son, Matthew was inconceivably sensitive and aware, which strengthened all those he touched. Rick's parents, Peter and Helen Hellriegel, and sister, Debbie, showed extreme courage in the face of the inevitable. John and Nancy Stewart were superb, objective listeners and helped us all sort out our lives. Steve O'D., Frith O'H., and the entire staff of the Wairau Hospice gave so much of themselves because they love and care. All these people transformed what was a difficult process into a profound experience of the human spirit.

During the writing of this book, it was an honor and privilege to have worked with Steve Callahan. His talent, diligence, understanding, and just plain hard work (between naps) made the story come to life. What started as a blind date turned into a committed relationship and an honest collaboration. To his partner, Kathy, a personal thank you for her never-ending support and kindness. Both Steve and Kathy allowed me to be a part of their family during the endless months we suffered together in Maine.

Just kidding!

New Zealand writer Bruce Ansley generously provided taped interviews that he conducted with Rick and I, which helped a great deal in the writing of this book. Most importantly, they allowed us to recapture Rick's point of view and memories after he was no longer able to do so in person. Rose Young most graciously granted us use of her photos. Thanks to HarperCollins for believing in this story.

My deep and humble thanks go to my mates, Phil Hofman, John Glennie, and Rick Hellriegel without whom I would not have survived. Finally, an overdue tribute of gratitude and utmost respect goes to *Rose-Noëlle* who kept us safe, dry, and warm for one hundred nineteen days.

The crew of Rose-Noëlle *on their second morning after crashing ashore on Great Barrier Island. From left: Phil Hofman, Jim Nalepka, Rick Hellriegel, John Glennie.*
(Reproduced with permission of Dominion, *Wellington)*

Chapter 1
To Serve, To Strive, And Not To Yield

End of May 1989

Exhaling clouds into the crisp, late night air, I plod on, thirty-eight years and eight time zones from the time and place of my birth in Minnesota. For once in my life I wish I could clearly see where I'm going, but it is a quarter to six New Zealand time and still pitch dark. In the Southern Hemisphere, it is early winter. A gauze of snow rests upon distant mountain tops. My feet leave dark prints in the lightly frosted ground. I traipse along a trail carved out of the bush, follow a dirt road that aimlessly winds down the hill, and cross a small bridge under which a steaming creek murmurs as it empties into the end of Queen Charlotte Sound. The ocean rests as black and still as if covered with a thin sheet of ice. I walk past the jetty on the main road that leads me to good old Outward Bound, or OB, as we say.

Through the glass mullions of the kitchen's heavy wood doors, I see the dim purple aura of two Bug zappers inside. All is empty and still in the kitchen save the slow swing of the overhead exhaust fan. I wander about flipping switches, awakening my day with a stab of lights. To warm up the room I turn all the stove burners on high.

Within minutes I have slapped two ten-gallon pots onto the stove to get the porridge bubbling. Some days there is a third pot for baked beans, but today it is the eggs' turn. A battery of bread—thirty loaves at a whack—stands at attention on a wheeled cart headed for the toaster. Next I go to a thirty-gallon drum called the Zip and pour boiling water into my undersized cup, melting the megaspoon of instant coffee crystals in the bottom. Real coffee does not exist at OB. In the cold storage I grab a bottle of Silver Top milk, peel back the foil cap, scoop out the crowning inch of cream, and flip it into my coffee.

Three co-workers stagger in, mumbling in turn a comatose "G'd day," and join my morning coffee ritual. As they pry their eyes open, we discuss the Maori taboo against sitting up on kitchen benches, which we ignore with slight pangs of guilt as we hop into place and shoot the breeze until our cups are drained. That done, we break into our work gigs. One of us watches the breakfast porridge, another folds the tea towels, and the third organizes rations for the OB *watches,* or groups of students, who'll be heading for the bush, rivers, and sea.

Through the walls, we hear students outside grunting and counting, "One, two, three, one two, three . . ." as they stretch, bend, and leap about. A phalanx of warmed-up bodies in front of the school takes off on a two-mile run. The instructors who wait behind to record finishing times, drift into the kitchen, chatting us up, and drinking brew until the students straggle back and plunge into the sea for an icy swim. Next they hit the cold showers, which are warm compared to waters of the Sound. Finally the duty watch is ready for work, and crowds the kitchen to help. It's seven o'clock.

We in the kitchen crew wheel out a three-foot-diameter wok from Hong Kong. The metal crater rests on a cart rigged up with its own gas bottle and huge plumber's burner. A label on the side of the cart reads THE BIG GUN. Into the bowl I dump and stir 200 eggs and some rice left over from last night.

At seven-thirty, as the dinner bell clangs, students burst through the doors and flood the dining hall. Everybody stands quiet. Duty watch says grace. Then the masses throw themselves at their plates and dig in.

Our kitchen crew relaxes, eats breakfast, and talks to the instructors as they amble in and out, telling us about the schemes they'll impose on their watches for the next three days. "We're heading out on kayak scheme on the Pelorus today," says one. About a third of the students will wipe out in rapids on that one. "Out on Bush One," says another with a mildly sadistic smile. Bush One is a tramp over two- to five-thousand-foot "hills" covered with razor sharp gorse, a thorn-laden shrub that is out of control in the hills. "Up the Queen Charlotte," another adds. He'll cram fourteen people into an open twenty-foot cutter. They'll throw their aching backs at the blistering heavy wood oars until they are lucky enough to find a following wind.

Outward Bound: "To Serve, to strive, and not to yield." Learn how risk can become more nourishing than food. Place yourself in the hands of the unknown. Face peril with confidence. Overcome adversity by finding and leaning on the strengths that lurk within yourself and the strangers who are your mates. Trust is what it's all about, really. That and dealing with your own limitations, discovering when even your strengths may become a liability, learning when to back off. So much for theory.

The instructors seem more into who's in charge, what they'll prove to their students and each other, who will win out, and less into cooperation, what they'll find within themselves, and how everyone can win. Maybe that's what happens when adventure is contrived. They're not really out there on the edge, beyond familiar ground or into unknown waters. The instructors lead their charges like a line of baby ducks in an established, unchallenged pecking order on familiar routes with known risks. The uncertainties are limited and they'll all be back in three days.

Shit, I think. I still wish I was going along. Not sure why. Maybe it's because, even controlled risk might take me to the edge of my limits. A routine OB scheme is still no cake walk. Nature seems to have the capacity to spring nasty surprises on you. Sometimes danger lurks within the very familiarity with it. Three people have died doing their routines since I have been here. Even a small adventure might set the stage for me to discover something new. Then again, maybe I just want to go along for an OB tramp because I get to stay here and make thirty-six trays of flap jacks instead.

Did I move half way around the world just so I can cook two hundred eggs at a shot? Was I crazy to quit my secure city job? Just to get that job, two thousand of us shuffled along in line for three days carrying our Fooseball games, TV sets, joints, booze, hopes, and screwed up lives. I was one of the lucky two hundred who got work.

The few years I spent working a s a "turd herder" in the city's sewers were no fun, but then for over a decade I got to whack away at the pavement in the open air. The joyous sun beamed down. I liked the heft of the jack hammer, the sweat, the feel of my muscles as they grew taut against the pull of work. That kind of toil was as pure and unpretentious as the flight of a bird. It was simple. You did your job and at day's end went home and washed off the grime. You didn't have to think too much. Nobody expected much.

When November snows flew, the paving season ended. We threw our work boots into a fresh stretch of pavement. Giant vibrating rollers smushed them into the goop, though the tops sprang back up like sentinels awaiting our return in the spring. Until April we were supposed to be on call for snow removal, but the bureaucrats went to the next name on the list if you didn't answer your phone. Pay for twelve months, work for seven: it was the life of Riley.

Ah, the grand old days. But, now that I think twice, it wasn't all that grand. After fourteen years I tired of my own dull thoughts whirling round in the dust and the heat, the mindless chitchat about the new strippers down at BJ's or Zeke's Night Cap, the endless bitching—the boss was a jerk, nobody's wife understood them, someone's daughter was always ready to run off with some guy with purple hair, the police netted a three percent raise while we got only a lousy percent and a half. Life was a bitch. But we did *our* work; it wasn't *our* fault.

Each spring I returned to look at the increasingly tired faces, sagging bellies, and graying, thinning hair of guys I joined up with. For what? The better house, the only pool in the neighborhood, the best looking wife? The whole damned system had lobotomized us. Our dreams were no longer who we might become or what we could do. Our aspirations were no more complex than going fishing, hunting deer, the girls down at Zeke's. Sitting on the can down at the city garage, flipping through the mountain of raunchy porno magazines rooted out from the squeaky clean taxpayer's trash, I began to feel like the whole world was going nowhere. Even the porno magazines showed the very same breasts I looked at back in 1975. I swear they were. All my co-workers were only waiting for their glorious retirement. One guy spoke dreamily of kicking back in "Moosetown" in Florida. We were all beginning to sound like clones of Barney Rubble. Everybody was counting years, counting *decades!* In just sixteen more years I too could retire. Christ! I was only thirty-six.

Still, it was easier to bang my head against a familiar wall than walk around and face the unknown on the other side. At least until one lazy winter afternoon.

My friend Bobette and I gazed over downtown through the falling snow and moaned about the cold. I romantically reminisced about beautiful New Zealand, where I'd taken a bike trip. Bobette is one of those people who go on faith, the confident result of thirty years of the women's movement. "Just go" was her advice. "But I have this job," I complained, though I also was offered a job in New Zealand at Outward Bound.

"What!?" she yelled at me. "They offered you a *job* and you're sitting here? You're a nitwit, Jim Nalepka!"

"But I've got my pension, hospitalization, life insurance. We even got dental care this year." I just couldn't pry myself from the city's tit. She kept bugging me though; she made me make a list. On the positive side we cataloged "The opportunity to meet new people, experience a different culture, escape Minnesota winters and hot summer asphalt fumes, challenge myself with an interesting job, take a risk, trust my gut feelings, take responsibility for my own future . . ." All told there were about forty positive items. On the negative side I struggled to come up with "What about my cat Tony and who's going to shovel the sidewalk? You know there's a fine now if you don't shovel your walk, Bobette."

In the end, Bobette won, of course. So here I am New Zealand, but where's the risk, the challenge? I may be at Outward Bound, but I am not a part of the adventure. I may serve, but what am I striving for?

By nine the place is a ghost town. Alone, chipping last night's crap out of the ten-gallon bowl from the Hobart mixer, I look out through the bank of windows that face Queen Charlotte Sound. Blankets of verdant fields fold across mountain slopes that are rooted in the sea. From my perch I often see ducks, gannets, shags, and the occasional dolphin. Every year there is one white heron. Heading up the Sound, one of the school's distant cutters looks like a water bug slowly wandering across the surface as its oared legs rise, swing, fall, and swing back in slightly haphazard unity. As the boat passes beyond the edge of my picture window and I lose sight of the crews on their adventuresome quests, I turn back to my own routine.

Flap jacks done, mail call over, I head home for an hour. Back up the hill. Martha's gone for the week, as usual, but soon—next month—we get three weeks together. She's promised. By the time she gets home on weekends, she's worn out. Martha's great. She is. She's full of energy and enthusiasm. She writes letters for Amnesty International on behalf of tortured prisoners, organizes women to find themselves through adventure in the out-of-doors, but I yearn for things for which she has no need. She requires no growing commitment, desires no future family. I don't know if she really cares if we ever get time together. Just give her a desk and a million projects and she's happy. Sometimes, sandwiched between letters and proposals, I find that soft side of her. Sometimes, in carefully timed slots of her work schedule, she squeezes me tenderly. But those times are getting too rare. Hell, I'm considering sleeping with the damned Kiwi sheep. Don't think I haven't thought about it.

Rick strides through the door like a stag, says, "Is the jug on?" prances to the fridge, flings open the door and asks, "Anything to eat?" I pour him a cup of tea. Stuffing his square-jawed face with chocolate cake, crumbs falling out of his mouth, Rick mumbles something about sailing and Tonga.

"What? What are you talking about?"

'Tonga. I'm going to go sailing to Tonga."

Sun. Beaches. Warmth. Fruit. Adventure. "Man, I'd love it," I hint. "When are you going?"

"In the next few days. I'll find out today." Rick drains his cup and flashes back out the door. He never wastes time.

And what the hell do I get to do? Tidy up the cold storage and check the bloody mouse traps. Shit.

Mattie thrashes around in his car seat beside me, his hair blowing everywhere and his eyes wide with infant wonder as a perpetually new world unfolds in front of him. His dad, Rick, and mum, Heather, are in front, driving us both to our destiny. So call me James. Like Ishmael in *Moby Dick*, I think I'll "sail about a little and see the watery part of the world." I can't believe I'm actually going to Tonga, almost fifteen hundred miles to the north over open ocean. Okay, settle down. I've never been to sea before—hardly been in a boat. I guess it doesn't matter. Rick will keep me clued in. But have I got the right gear? Of course I've got the right gear. Martha went through all that with me. But what was all that about my sister's address? "In case something happens," she said. Give me a break.

Rick pulls into OB so I can give my farewells. There's good old Bill, always going to do some chore with an axe or wrench or something tucked under his arm like some overworked troglodyte. Rick slams on the brakes and Bill stuffs his handsome, bronzed, seventy-year-old head in through the window. "Where the bloody hell are you jokers goin'?"

"Bill, I'm going sailing! I just want to say goodbye to ya."

"Well Yank, if ya never come back I get that push-bike of yours, right?"

"Sure Bill. It's yours, mate!"

Rick weaves the Subaru up, down, and around the curves of Queen Charlotte's Drive for seventeen kilometers to Picton, our port of departure. Already I feel queasy. If I feel ill here, how will I feel once we hit the deep blue beyond? What am I worried about? Everybody knows I'm no sailor.

Rick and I have visited the boat twice now. The skipper, forty-seven-year-old John Glennie, seems like a nice enough bloke, even if he does have beady Jack Nicholson eyes set close to a chiseled beak. Like a proud bird of prey, he's taut and trim, maybe a bit high strung. "Bloody sea jock," Rick calls him. What else can you call someone who carries a business card that says:

John A. Glennie
Yacht *Rose-Noëlle*
Yacht Deliveries
Yacht Builder by Profession
Adventurer by Choice

But John told us he's sailed more than 40,000 miles, mostly back in the sixties when he and his brother sailed from here to California. Rick thinks he'll calm down a bit once we get offshore.

I couldn't tell a bowsprit from a yardarm, but this is definitely a flash boat. And from laying down her backbone to laying on the bright yellow and white finish that glows like glass, Glennie has created her. He's obviously talented. Rick is clearly impressed.

Rose-Noëlle has descended from Micronesian outrigger canoes. Unlike Western boats with one hull, *Rose Noëlle* is composed of a main hull set up like a bloody apartment with everything but a microwave, and two smaller outer hulls, which John calls floats. From each side of the main hull a pair of long tapered arms stretch out and curl down over the shoulders of the two supporting floats.

Rose-Noëlle *being launched. (Rose Young)*

Unlike a monohull, John's three-hulled trimaran has no heavy keel to keep her upright. Her stability relies on her wide stance. A monohull with lead keel is like one of those lead-weighted, inflatable clowns that kids knock down but then rights itself. *Rose-Noëlle* is more like a table—tough to push over. Some folks snipe at multihulls because, like a table, if they flip, they won't reright themselves. John is quick to point out that, without lead to pull the boat under, a boat like *Rose-Noëlle* won't sink if she's flipped or even run down by a whale or a ship. Glennie says a modern design like his can't flip anyway. All sounds good to me.

Cresting the final hill over Picton, we face a great panorama of the harbor where our ship, the *Rose-Noëlle* awaits. Since ancient times men have embarked with unknown shipmates on whom they must depend for their very lives. I suppose centuries of seafaring haven't changed things much. In *Moby Dick,* Ishmael embarked on *Pequod* in search of whales. Captain Ahab took his crew after Moby Dick and doom. By his own admission, our captain "holds a short fuse for fools." Like skippers throughout history, our captain will test his crew and find out only too well of just what we are made. And vice versa, I figure. Rick warned me not to mention that I cook at Outward Bound, but I had to open my big mouth. So Glennie showed off all his pots, pans, the stove, oven, even the damned flour. How will I cook out there when I can't even keep my stomach in place here on the pavement?

What about my other mates?

Look at Rick with both sinewy, finely sculpted hands perfectly situated at ten and two o'clock on the old steering wheel. Definitely in control. Plays strictly by the rules. At thirty-nine years old, Rick has been a cop and OB instructor, and now runs his own sea kayaking business. He's independent and bloody tough. Three years ago doctors diagnosed a terminal tumor nesting in his head. The docs gave him a sixty percent chance to live two years. After twenty-five radiation treatments, Rick and Heather went home and forgot about it like it was a broken leg that needed only to be set.

The medical profession said radiation miraculously zapped the tumor, but I figure it just couldn't beat Rick's brute stubbornness and tough hide. I admire his fearlessness and his drive.

Rick is well traveled, well read, and doesn't hesitate to let you know just what is right. His business partner's home-brewed beer was never quite perfect until one day the partner covertly handed Rick a bottle of premium store-bought beer. "Now you've got it," concluded Rick. He *knows* what is right and he won't compliment you for less.

When he goes out, every hair must be in place. He keeps his body as lean as a lion. The way to frame a photo, the way to hold a paddle, every nut and bolt of existence must be just so for maximum efficiency or effect, even when it doesn't matter. Drives me nuts sometimes, but I can't help but like him.

Sure the son of a bitch stormed into the house, got me drooling over Tonga, and didn't even ask me to go along. He's always testing people, seeing how they'll react, which bait they'll bite. He is confrontational but not mean. He did come back. He knew I wanted to go and how much it meant to me. He's anxious to help us mere mortals up a rung toward the same perfection at which he aims with fearless pursuit. Inside that iron man is plenty of compassion. Rick pulls through for you in the end and I trust him. That's the important thing.

That leaves Phil Hofman. The second time Rick and I visited the boat to check out the scene we found Phil hovered over a bowl, popping every other walnut that he shelled into his mouth. He looked up, casually greeted us with a firm hand, and went back to shelling as we chatted amiably. Don't know too much about Phil yet, but he seems like a regular New Zealand bloke, an affable Humpty Dumpty with thick dark eyebrows that stand in stark contrast to his pale, round, mostly bald head. The hair that remains forms a rim from ear to ear, wispy and white. In some lights he has the look of a pudgy baby, in others a man in his fifties. Phil's forty-two, just three years older than me, but beneath his overstuffed shirt is already a long scar from open heart surgery. He still takes heart pills. With his sweetheart from his teenage years and two kids, Phil lives aboard a ferrocement boat with no name. Seems to suit him somehow.

John Glennie (left) and Rick Hellriegel prior to departure.
(Rose Young)

Phil knows how to sail, but he's never been to sea before, and rarely wanders further from his wife and children than to the pub. He has never set foot outside of New Zealand, but since his boat has been moored next to Glennie's, the wanderlust in Phil's eyes has been stirred. To Phil, Glennie has been everywhere and done everything. Phil could use a serving or two of that. Glennie tells Phil over and over, "Going with me to the islands will be good for you, Philip." Glennie also berates Phil's "stone boat," but Phil continues to dog John's heels on *Rose-Noëlle*, probing him with questions, talking boats, the sea, the horizon beyond.

When we first met Phil, across the table from him sat a beautiful and affable Rose, John Glennie's current Ms. Special and soon to be ex-special. "Oh," I said to her, "the boat's named after you!"

Rose stopped dead, looked up at me with the gigantic, teary, cow eyes of one of those little girls on a velvet painting, and said, "No. He named it after one of his *old* girl friends."

There followed a stony silence.

The night before our departure, Phil took his usual place in the pub. His mates shared farewell drinks and banter. One turned to Phil and said, "You should want your head read for sailing off in a trimaran."

"Well, what can go wrong?" asked Phil.

"Trimarans are renowned for turning upside down" was the overstated answer.

Phil shrugged. "Oh well," he said, "a boat like *Rose-Noëlle* won't sink. A boat like that would just float around the Pacific for months."

As we swoop down to the harbor, Heather and Rick banter back and forth in the front seat. All seems smooth between them for a change. Maybe it's because he's going away. Rick can be a real pain. He expects Heather to serve up his meals, do his laundry, care for Mattie, keep all the details of his existence in proper order. He might not admit it, but his family and his home are like shackles on him. As she labors under mountains of diapers, Rick even refuses to hook water up to their laundry shed. Heather has lashed him with accusations of selfishness. He hates it, but he has not changed. Rick has so many years ahead of him, but he feels driven to do so much more with his life. He must plan and adventure, write a book, kayak the sea, roam Africa, roam free. In a recent rage, he returned Heather's fire with, "I'm selfish. I've always been selfish. You knew that when you married me." Like unstable atoms, they have parted and recombined many times. Rick knows that he must try harder to make things work for them, but he has too much yet to prove. Today, in the wake of a really good talk, Heather is happy. He's really going to try to make things smoother. So Heather sends him off with her blessing. This voyage is something he needs to do. And maybe, when he returns, things will be different.

When we wheel down to the wharf, *Rose-Noëlle* looks like a beehive with Phil, Rose, John, John's sister, and her husband buzzing about, stowing cabbages, apples, kiwi fruits, and other food into the bulging hulls. I take my pack below and set it next to the navigation station. John catches me. "You can't put that there. Get out what you need and put it in the outer hull," he commands as he rushes off. What will I need out there? Well at least I'll wear my $180 Salopettes—warm, synthetic pile bib overalls that all the gear junkies at OB think are essential for mastering mountains, wild rivers, and raging seas.

From left: John Glennie, Jim Nalepka and Rick Hellriegel prior to departure. (Rose Young)

For another hour I follow people about like a lost puppy, not really knowing how to be of service, listening to orders like "put this out in the port float" or "fetch that from the lazarette." Port? Which way is that? "No port *left* in the bottle." Okay, port is left. But lazarette? So I watch the drones fly about and note which holes they probe. They talk about a trampoline and I wonder if we're going to an oceanic gymnastics meet until I see they mean the netting that stretches over the open area between *Rose-Noëlle*'s hulls and the forward and after beams that tie the three together.

Two yachties from the boats in the harbor stand away from the bustle with hands on hips. They share mumbled pronouncements of observers everywhere who believe they know more about doing something than the people actually doing something.

Just as I get the hang of the departure bucket brigade, the fire seems to be out and all activity around the boat ceases, except for the butterflies in my stomach.

I understand that the weather prognosis is also a bit shaky. One of the yachties on the quay is Jim Bramwell, a buddy of John's who will soon depart New Zealand with his family, following our wake. Bramwell reassures Glennie with a weather chart that indicates that light northeasterlies will assist us offshore where a southerly will push us rapidly north to Tonga. John is satisfied and that's good enough for me. Let's get out of here.

We bid farewell to those who've gathered. I touch Rose's hand then reach up to the jetty and grab Heather who wears Mattie like a part of herself. She bends down to give me a final female hug.

"Wait a minute!" Everyone looks up to see John on the dock. With a towel draped across one arm, an animated finger in the air, elfin face, and mouth screwed into a lopsided smile, he turns and shuffles off. Rick, Heather, and I, even Mattie, seem perplexed as our lifted brows quiz each other for some explanation.

In five minutes John reappears. After his brief shower, he set up a secret ham radio schedule with Jim Bramwell. The plan is for Bramwell to receive the latest weather maps and radio the information to us. John will acknowledge Bramwell's call, but will not identify us because John has no ham radio license, so it is illegal for John to use the ham radio except in a situation when danger to life and limb is imminent. Although we will never receive any weather information from Jim Bramwell, he and his son, Daniel, will play an unexpected role in our future.

Finally we cast off. *Rose-Noëlle* pulls away so fast that in the moments it takes us to coil and stow the docking lines, Heather and Mattie have shrunk to a distant dot on the end of the jetty. The outboard motor drones on for about a mile. Rick and I chat as the lush panorama slides by and we feel the unfamiliar dance of the boat bouncing lightly across harbor waves. Phil and John raise the mainsail. I wait for orders that do not come, so instead I absorb all the sights and sounds. John unrolls the big jib with a rumble, which snaps in the light wind. The winches emit a staccato click of well-greased metal on metal like huge fishing reels spinning to the tune of a hooked behemoth. When the sails are yanked into position and filled taut with the breeze, *Rose-Noëlle* leans slightly away from the wind and glides. I am awed by the floating sensation, disturbed only by the hissing wake that leaps about at our stern and runs away back to port. Sailing is all I dreamed it would be.

As we proceed down the cliff-lined final leg of Tory Channel, John finishes preparing the boat for the open sea— securing the last loose stores, hoisting Rick in a fabric chair so he can stick a piece of rope through something at the top of the mast. We are ready for it, I think. The narrow chute of the channel suddenly widens and the mountains retract like curtains from a stage. *Rose-Noëlle* enters the swirling, current-tortured waters of the infamous Cook Strait that opens up before us. Our only audience is the North Island that sits ahead, a brooding sole witness to our debut.

John makes VHF radio contact with the secretary of the Picton seaplane service. This is the last contact we'll have with terra firma while aboard *Rose-Noëlle*.

Unshielded by the hills, *Rose-Noëlle* flies across the north-westerly wind into the late afternoon. She runs at twelve to fourteen knots; the speedometer sometimes touches sixteen knots— eighteen miles an hour. I did not know boats could sail so fast. *Rose-Noëlle* cleaves the chop so smoothly that, from my spot beside Rick, the expanse of deck seems almost motionless. Only when I see the land slipping quickly behind and the rushing wake do I sense our speed.

John doesn't like single-hulled boats and makes rude comments about them. Without all that lead ballast to drag around, three-hulled trimarans like *Rose-Noëlle* and two-hulled catamarans are really light and easy to push. Their width makes them so stable that they can carry more sail too. In John's eyes Western monohulls are barges that plow through the water while multihulls are birds that skitter across the surface. When Captain Cook first visited Hawaii, he noted how the native catamarans and proas literally sailed circles around his ships. The Pacific Islanders settled islands over millions of square miles of open ocean, while Europeans dared not venture outside the sight of land for fear of falling off the edge of the earth.

I know nothing of such matters. Nor do I realize the significance of sailing at forty-one degrees South Latitude, edge of the roaring forties, realm of the albatross. Here winds whip around the world unhindered by continental land except at infamous Cape Horn. At these latitudes, even in summer, the earth wears a rotating necklace of storms. Forty-foot breaking waves are common. The color of these roaring, liquid mountains is so dulled by gale-scudded skies and streaks of windblown spume that they are called graybeards. Leave harbor in southern New Zealand in winter and you enter some of the most notorious waters in the world.

I'm only a passenger. Ignorant. Trusting. Inadequate. I don't know what I can or will ever be capable of doing. Should I be sitting here? It feels okay, but am I in the way? Well, nobody is screaming at me. I should do *something*. Inspired by memories of the city road crew, I lapse into an old Roids Rodgers trick. Roids was supposed to rake asphalt, but by age sixty had mastered busywork. When volunteers were called he was always ever so occupied moving barricades or a shovel only to move them back an hour later. So I bend over, untie my shoe and methodically retie it with precise detail so I can appear like I'm doing something useful. Rick, Phil, and John trade places at the helm as clouds crowd over the sky and the green tinge of dusk dims our world.

Wind streaks across the darkening sea, pushing it into a steep chop. The ship jumps and crashes. Clouds of spray waft aft. My senses are restricted by the coming night. Each lurch of our ship, each snap of Dacron hits my nerves like an unexpected electrical shock. Phil follows John forward to drop the mainsail and reduce its size. Phil is like a neophyte tightrope walker on the pitching deck, stumbling, falling, getting up again. As Phil and John work on the sail forward and Rick steers, I glance aft at a small dot on the horizon emitting a twinkling pinpoint of light. In minutes the light grows to a steady dot. "Hey Rick, you see the ferry?" I ask.

"Yeah, mate." He waits until John and Phil finish taking the reef and yells up to the deck, "Hey John, the ferry's behind us."

John doesn't respond. Buffeting wind fills our ears and carries our voices away. Rick yells out several times to John as the ferry closes but John doesn't respond except for a glance aft. He turns and begins to take another reef. Has he not heard Rick or is he ignoring him?

The ferry grows, its outline becoming clear and its light now a steady beam. Rick's hands grip the wheel as tensely as in the car on the way to Picton. He keeps gazing aft, then forward. I look up to Phil who struggles to help John with the sail. Rick yells again. "John, what the hell is going on with this ferry!?" Phil looks aft at the brutish grey form as it begins to rise above us and says to John beside him, "Hey mate, do ya see the ferry?"

"Yeah, yeah, I see it."

Everyone but John seems to be edgy so I get even more tense. Rick is now frantic and screams forward, "John! Are the bloody mast lights on?"

I am astounded by the gigantic shape that looms above us. Blazing lights from the cabins, meeting places, and deck stab the near-black night. The ferry seems to pause there above us, silently, like a beast in the final moment before it pounces and crushes us. John leaps down the hatch and flips on the lights. The ferry seems to veer suddenly. Maybe it's Rick at the wheel or maybe John grabs the helm and turns us away. I don't know; I am too busy holding tight. I only know that the monster slides by a hundred yards off.

We collect around the cockpit, all eyes but John's as round as frisbees. With a brief diabolical guffaw, John dismisses our apprehension with a mutter: "That was my good old buddy Brownie up at the helm. He wouldn't have hit us." It is as if our skipper feeds off our anxiety.

The ferry shrinks again to a pinpoint of light as rapidly as it came, and I am left wondering if it really happened at all.

With *Rose-Noëlle* squared away, we beat northeastward, slipping along and edging away from the North Island's coast to confront the Pacific and even larger unknowns.

Chapter 2
Never Underestimate the Power of Water

I'm behind the wheel, actually steering a boat in the open sea! A light wind fills the sails and we're cruising, man! Nice and smooth—like driving down the interstate in a big American bulge-mobile: a '59 Caddy with great white shark fins, or maybe a '53 Buick with the decorative portholes down the side. Basking in the compass light's soft red glow, the hash marks on the little compass card merely waver to verify that we're stuck in the slot with cruise control engaged. This lasts about thirty seconds before the boat slides away, with the compass going wacky and wheeling around. I yank the wheel and the boat careens back on course, past course, and shoots off the other way. I spin the wheel to pull her back. Zoom—off she goes the other way. Spin the wheel again; here we go; slew city.

John leaps to the cockpit, grabs the wheel, and steadies us back on track. "I told you to do it slow," he instructs. "Don't oversteer." Okay, I nod. We're all right now, back on course, so John ducks below again.

I feel like a kid trying to drive his daddy's car, knowing how much fun it is to whirl the wheel but not really understanding the consequences. Another minute at the helm and I get *Rose-Noëlle* to career down the waves like a starship swerving through a meteor belt. John vaults from below again. "Haven't you ever steered a boat before?" he yells at me. I feel about 1.2 millimeters high. Some men forget that even *they* learned once upon a time. Some men have no tolerance for those who are unable to steer straight toward our worthy destination, toward *their* worthy destination. After he gets our course together again, poor John collapses on the floor in front of me like a coiled, sleeping dragon.

God, I'm nervous. My jaw hurts from grinding my teeth. And this wool balaclava is so itchy. No scratching allowed. Don't let go. *Can't* let go. So, let me see—pull the wheel this way and the compass goes that way. Or is it the other way around? Meanwhile the stars wheel in unison with the compass; or do they rotate opposite it? Oh, God that itch. I'm stripping this damned thing off.

By the time I get the hood yanked off, we're heading back to Picton, *Rose-Noëlle* does her best to buck everyone out of their bunks, the sails complain with loud flagging, and John erupts. "You really don't know how to steer a boat!" he scolds, nudging me aside. I fall on the seat under the weight of his rebuff. The puny residue of my self-confidence melts and silently flows out the scuppers. Should I slink away? Should I ask him to show me again? Should I just sit here? Do I deserve to go to sleep? What do I do? No telling from John. I know he sees me, but apparently I am a ghost.

An hour later I slither below to wake Rick and relieve John. "I still have another hour off watch," complains Rick. I confess to my failures so he takes pity on me and accepts his fate with only a mild grumble.

Stars are out. Wind light. Music on. John Lennon croons "Imagine." Rick and I bask in a feeling of pervasive peace. Here, on a ship at sea, there *is* no country, *are* no possessions, only shared space.

Next we accompany Bo Diddley as he sings about the way he spells—M-A-N. Rick and I rock and roll to the tune as I wonder, how do *I* spell MAN?

Maybe I spell it like this, right here, right now. Unlike when I was on deck with John, I feel amazingly relaxed. Rick coaches me patiently as I try to steer. Together we chat about Minnesota, hum along with the tunes, and share the possibilities of this adventure. Our reasons for undertaking this voyage may differ as much as any group of mens' reasons for doing anything, but adventure is the one inescapable commonality that draws us on. I smugly wonder what all those chumps back at OB are doing? For once I'm being a "real man." I chuckle to myself.

By the end of our watch, the wind is virtually nonexistent and we often put the boat "in irons'" meaning she stops, drifts backward, spins in circles. It is unbelievably still. The only sound is the occasional clank from the rigging as the sail wags side to side. The sea has evidently had enough of us, so we go below to sleep.

Privacy in a boat is a relative term. As the boat works over the waves, its front and back rise and plunge the most. Sleeping in the ends would be like sleeping on the ends of a seesaw. John has designed the interior with all of the beds—I mean the berths—in the middle of the boat for the most comfortable ride. His space is a nook behind the galley and close to the cockpit—under the cockpit actually. Phil takes a berth on one side of the main cabin/living room. Rick and I take the double berth on the opposite side. Our berth and Phil's are high up, housed within the cabin where it flares out from the hull and over the water. Sometimes waves that sweep by underneath tap on the bottom of our beds. Only the floor or one of the dinette seats could also serve as a bed, but one would get stepped or sat on there. As is, we can hear everything anyone else says and can see all but John. Our beds are our only private space, and they're obviously not all that private. I'm sure that by the time we get to Tonga, we'll know everything there is to know about one another. I hope that we can stand each other's little secrets and foibles.

In the army I slept with plenty of guys but never really racked out close enough to touch. Rick and I have been friends, but I realize that I have yet to fathom his intricacies. Yet as I slide in next to Rick, I begin to understand the shape of him. I do not want to, but know I must lean on him, and he lets me. For now it feels reassuring, comfortable enough.

June 2

Rick, John, and I are silent as a bright orange sunrise frees us from our first night at sea. The brilliant yellow hulls and snowy sails of *Rose-Noëlle* seem to vibrate with light as we glide over pewter water that clear skies transform to a crystalline aquamarine. Rugged, folded, forested mountains of the Wairarapa coast still lay within sight, but a light, crisp, winter breeze eases us away from our homes and our past. Each of us knows what we have left behind, but I wonder how our expectations of our destination differ.

Tonga—the last true kingdom of the Pacific—where a sovereign reigns supreme. Captain Cook called them the Friendly Islands. Many of the 150 or so isles are little more than coral reefs. All together they compose only 270 square miles. For Rick and me, this voyage is an end in itself. It really doesn't matter if we're headed for Tonga or Timbuktu. We seek only a foreign environment, to go farther than we have gone before. It is Tonga in particular that John seeks though.

John is half again Rick's age and a decade older than Phil. As he listens to old Eddie Fisher tunes, John tells us of those bygone years when he first voyaged farther than he had gone before. In the early 1960s, John turned from racing bicycles toward sailing the sea. He and his brother David wended their way across the Pacific, logging 35,000 miles and fulfilling their dreams, which John defines as "earning our reputation as playboys of the South Pacific." Following that epic voyage, John got together with a journalist friend to log his various conquests in an as yet unpublished manuscript actually titled *Playboys of the South Pacific*. "It was *almost* published," says John, but it was refused by a female editor because "You know how *they* are." A highlight of John's dream voyage was a beautiful French Polynesian teenager, a Miss July. After their trek, John and his brother began to build twin trimarans, living like bachelors in run-down digs, the walls papered with Playboy pinups, when John got the tragic news that his teenage queen had been killed in a plane crash. In her honor, this ship now bears her name: *Rose-Noëlle.*

John does not seem happy settled on land. He is leaving the tumult of the past two decades ashore—a string of relationships, two children from two different women. John talks about the islands where "women treat you right."

For nineteen years John designed and built *Rose-Noëlle*, sanded, painted, saved money, bided his time. He has spared no expense or effort to fine-tune every detail, has poured every ounce of himself into this quest. It is as if there is no room for error if he is to recapture the archetypal swinging-sixties male dream that he left behind while Rick and I were still kids. Out here he is in command, free of the confines of other peoples' expectations, free of the give-and-take of relationships from which I, too, have fled. We are on a voyage to Tonga, Pacific paradise, with crystal waters and waving palms under which topless women with grass skirts dance and wait on the pleasures of the great white gods who come from across wide waters.

I must confess that there was a time in my youth when John's dreams were not all that different from my own.

Our voyage seems as much through time as through space as we journey to the land where men are still men and kings are still kings. I wonder how far we will voyage into John's good old days. Will we bypass John's birth entirely and fall back to more ancient times when men relied on each man's special skill for the hunt, when they depended on one another so much for mere survival that they could not afford the luxury of mutual destruction? Or is even that a myth? Each of us holds dear a different time, a different dream. Perhaps John needs a place where an outdated political system reigns, serving as a beacon for ideals and cultures that are more familiar and comforting to him. John often begins or ends sentences with "When I get back to the islands" or "Just get me back to the islands."

Despite the light winds and calm sea, my stomach feels increasingly queasy—like a hangover without the throbbing head, but daylight reveals a familiar reality to which I can relate and in which I can feel a bit more at ease. The interior of *Rose-Noëlle* looks like a yuppie bachelor pad full of the latest gadgetry. In the kitchen—*galley*, I mean—there's a stainless steel sink, an ideal collection of posh cutlery and other cooking hardware, even a four-burner stove with oven. Great! I can make bread. There's a dining space like a restaurant booth with a scenic overlook of the whole Pacific. There's even a color TV. Phil, Rick, and my berths are on the outer perimeters and above this space. Forward is a bathroom that the guys call a head for some strange reason. I have to go, but don't know how the damn thing works yet. John crawls through a hole beneath the galley counter into his big bed under the cockpit. *Rose-Noëlle*'s interior is tarted up in bright colors. Like a kid's sugary breakfast cereal, we have a choice between lime green and lemon yellow, which are offset by a cherry-red plastic parrot on a hoop overhanging the sink. The decor includes a whole garden of poly-propylene and vinyl flowers. Like a timeless memorial to his youth, resting in the galley is even a garland of plastic flowers that was given John in the islands. Plastic flowers from Polynesia? Who am I to criticize? At least I don't have to water them.

Looking forward from galley to dinette, head (bathroom) just forward of bulkhead.
(Rose Young)

A sailor's eyes might be drawn to the efficient use of space, the integrity of *Rose-Noëlle*'s design, her lithe lines, and the first-class quality of her construction and equipment. John has two radios—the ham radio for long distance and VHF for short distance—solar panels as well as a wind generator for charging batteries, radar, and a SatNav, which can fix our position from the signals it receives from orbiting satellites. Of course, John is still trying to fathom the directions for the SatNav because virtually all of his sailing was done back in the sixties with his brother when a sextant was high-tech navigational gear, but we are getting fixes. It's clear, even to me, that John is as well prepared as any mariner can be to face the hazards of the sea, and that *Rose-Noëlle* is a beautiful and capable ship, even if the interior styling is not my scene.

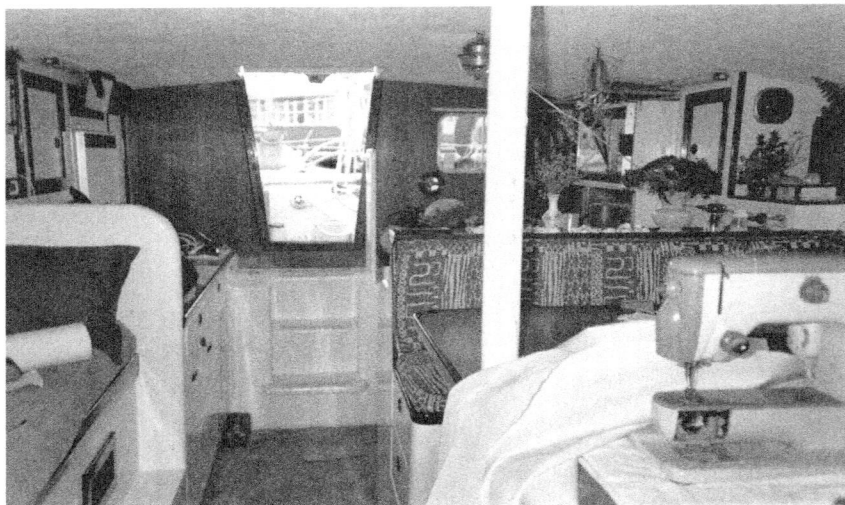

Interior looking aft from dinette toward galley and cockpit.
(Rose Young)

Now that the weather has allowed me some down time, I hop on deck and probe my crewmates about how I can be more useful rather than a seasick slug, but there is nothing to do so I gravitate to the galley and more familiar surrounds below. On deck, I still feel like I'm walking on eggs around Glennie. Will I ever fit into his idea of a good crewman? I drag out my favorite Cadbury—a half kilo (1.1 pounds) chunk of chocolate called the Energy Bar—slap it down on the dining table, and invite my mates to help themselves. Not much of a contribution, but something. It takes no time at all for Phil to amble by and snap off a slab. If you looked up "Easygoing Bloke" in a Kiwi dictionary, it would say "See Phil Hofman." We spontaneously lapse into unpretentious conversation. Nothing heavy; but there are no hidden agendas when you talk with Phil. A landlubber most of his life, Phil was a caretaker and maintenance man for a government power station. When his job was automated, Phil was laid off, but the government continues to send him enough redundancy pay to buy his cement boat on which he lives and from which he met John. He never plans to go back to a steady trade, is happy enough on the dole supplemented by the odd job as long as it doesn't burden Friday afternoons after four o'clock, which is exclusively reserved for the Terminus Pub. Phil seems calm and satisfied; yet he's driven to study Glennie's manifesto. Phil knows how to sail, but seems a bit unsure and unsteady on his feet. He's keen to please John, often following at his heels, pumping him with countless questions about how to do this and that, discussing the mysterious ways of boats and the sea, and probing into John's aura of freewheeling adventure.

I come up on deck again and John asks, "Hey, you want to hear the tape again?"

"No thanks, John. Maybe later."

Early last night, after cruising to the tunes of Eric Clapton, we asked John what he wanted to hear. His eyes lit up as he handed me one of his tapes. "Here, try this."

Out of the speakers emanated a distorted, eerie voice in a molasses-thick accent that sounded like a sedated Dr. Ruth. She lectured her audience on the god within each of them. She called this god something like Ramtha. Maybe it was Rambo. I don't know. Her haunting, solemn voice droned along, soft, smooth, and deep. Then her dirge is shattered by sudden, shouted, cheerleading chants in a language that I could not identify. The refrain builds to a crescendo before the lecturer went on to talk about each person's capability to control his or her own destiny, which also was rudely interrupted by another wild chant. I believe in the lecture's basic precepts, but the cacophonous chanting and bizarre production stood in overwhelming contrast with the sublime, simple beauty of the surrounding sea and stars. Rick and I just exchanged looks of bewilderment. Phil, leaning on his elbow on his bunk, rolled up his long forehead into a field of furrows and cocked his head in one of those "Don't look at me" looks.

We returned to rock and roll for a bit and then John pumped in another Rambo tape. Then some Van Morrison followed by another tape from the *Twighlight Zone.*

I still can't figure out how John's inspirational tapes, his avid reading of Shirley MacLaine and other New Age interests square with his playboy, rugged individual ideals.

The day wears into a peaceful afternoon. Just when I begin to feel at ease aboard, a massive gray army of clouds rolls up from the south. Within an hour, frigid Antarctic southerly winds reaching thirty-five knots attack. Gust-driven needles of rain rake the boat. Phil and Rick reduce sail by tucking in a reef and then another. John finally drops the mainsail and rolls up the jib completely. He tries to set the storm jib, but when Rick raises it, nobody secures the ropes that control it. In a second, the storm jib becomes a maniacal monster, cracking before the gale, grabbing the ropes and winding itself up in them until it is bound as if in a straight jacket. Rick and Phil get the sail back down and John stuffs it below. Grumbling at his crew's incompetence, he surrenders and unrolls a tiny triangle of cloth from the regular jib.

By nightfall the wind blows forty knots. Rick is not terrified, but he is anxious at the helm as *Rose-Noëlle* accelerates down the face of rising waves like a jet on a runway. He's never sailed so fast before and is worried that he might stuff-up. With one wrong move of the wheel, she could fling herself across the wave, tip onto her side and flip. The sky is coal black. He can't see anything. As the compass bounces around, Rick's best guide is the wind that he must keep striking the side of his face, so he pulls off his balaclava to keep touch.

I remain below, poking my head out on deck now and again to find that it is absolutely raging out. Two of my mates remain on deck all the time. The noise and motion seem so awful and strange, but I do not know if I should be scared or not, so take my clues from my mates' faces as each comes below in turn, dripping and shivering. Each grabs a chunk of the Energy Bar that remains on the table, and sits down to rest. I am shocked as they brush by me in their wet, frigid, plastic clothing, and I am ashamed not to be able to assist. Phil seems increasingly on edge and is no longer able to control our flight when it's his turn at the wheel. Rick seems okay, though tense. John maintains his face of stone.

Phil and Rick urge John to set the Squid to slow us down. The Squid is a plastic cone from which blades flop to serve as a kind of brake as it trails from a line aft. When John deploys it, we slow a bit, but still run off like a cut cat. The shrieking wind pushes us north.

Dishes and glasses in the sink clatter. Water rumbles as it shoots by under us, sucking air down the drain noisily like a bathtub whirlpool emptying the final quart. Our gear bags fly off the bunks and roll around on the floor. I keep picking stuff up for something to do. There is an increasing amount of stuff to pick up.

John wants to untangle and set the storm jib to move faster, but Phil and Rick keep telling him they're mucking-up steering as it is, and urge him to take all the sail down instead. During Phil's next turn, *Rose-Noëlle* broaches and slews sideways down the chests of breaking waves. The boat heels heavily. Things fly around. Even the chocolate bar ends up on the floor.

John stops talking about putting up sail and takes a long stint at the helm himself while the rest of us hunker down below. We wonder how long John can carry on. What happens if he passes out or falls overboard? Without him we're stuffed. We keep yelling out to him, "John! Why don't you lash the helm and get down here?" He seems not to hear our pleas.

I ask Rick, "Are we okay?"

"Yeah, we're okay."

Phil, nervously munching on another piece of chocolate, reassures me with, "Never underestimate the power of water. The sea takes no prisoners."

"Thanks Phil. I needed that."

After several hours, John is too exhausted to carry on. He

lashes the helm, strips the boat of all sail, and comes below. While peeling off his foul weather gear, he says, "Boy, a hot cuppa would be good about now." When I serve him the tea, his eyes drill right into it, he grabs it with both hands and says, "Oh lovely." He sits there calmly sipping it while we gather around like Plato's pupils.

We throw questions at him. "How bad is it going to get?" "How long is it going to last?" "How big a wave would it take to flip us?"

John says nothing for a bit, but remains focused on the steaming cup in his hands, smirking at our worries. "Look," he says. "This isn't the Roaring Forties."

What does that mean?

"I've sailed 40,000 miles and this is just another blow," John says.

Yeah, twenty years ago you sailed 40,000 miles, thinks Rick. Rick wonders if John's current ability matches his confident memories, but even Rick must trust John's judgement. John is the expert out here.

"This boat will never capsize. It *can't* capsize." John is so confident in his boat that he hasn't installed an escape hatch to cover such an eventuality.

"Here, Rick, take a look at this. See if you can figure it out," Phil says as he slides a sheet of directions across the table and reaches for some of the shards of the Energy Bar that remain. Rick is the next to try to decipher the instructions to our emergency parachute anchor. When tethered to the bow, the parachute is supposed to fill with water and pull the boat's nose face the wind and dangerous waves. If it works, it should keep *Rose-Noëlle* from turning her side to the sea and prevent a capsize. Completely unimpressed by the din of the storm, John calmly reads how the parachute sea anchor consistently saves sailors' asses as they make their way around Cape Horn. Even improves fishing profits! But the directions seem to have been written by someone fired by the IRS for their inability to communicate clearly, and the photos of people being rescued by helicopter do not inspire much confidence.

Phil climbs up on his bunk, pulls back the curtains, and peers out at the sea for what seems like a half hour, muttering, "Bloody hell, John, it's blowing a mighty blow out there." John ignores him and Phil lays down for a bit.

Each wave towers above us, pauses, and then tumbles down. The head of one thirty-five-footer curls over us and breaks on the boat with the crack and boom of a bomb. The sea is mostly white, tinged green, veined with road maps of foam. The storm blows wave crests flat and drives the strafing downpour into horizontal streaks.

With each crash, Phil leaps, thumps his head on the ceiling, tears back the curtains, and peers through the small ports out at the chaos. *Never underestimate the power of water. The ocean takes no prisoners.*

Everyone but Rick has been sick. In good weather, if someone gets sick, there are usually jokes about the technicolor yawn, the liquid laugh, the big spit, but our mood is too somber. Our minds fill with the din, the jumble of falling gear, the swerving bucking ship, and welling vomit. Each time we perform the ritual and make love to the toilet, we are granted a reprieve from the paralyzing nausea. Immensely relieved, life, even under the attack of the sea, holds promise. But slowly, like the storm itself, things worsen again, our minds become hazy and depressed with noise and sickness. Moving about on this runaway train is an effort. Even sitting still is exhausting. How long will it go on?

Phil keeps nagging John about setting the sea anchor. Rick agrees. John bursts to his feet, "Okay," he says, "who's going out there with me?" There is one long silence.

Now's my chance, I think, sitting here on my dry bunk. Something I can finally contribute. At last I can prove my worth, especially to John. And to myself. John begins to pull on his soggy wet weather gear. Leaning outboard, I peer out the port. Oh my God! My heart virtually stops. If I go out there, I could be blown overboard. I'll *probably* be blown overboard. My body goes stiff as a frozen side of beef. Fortunately, Rick gets up and starts to get his gear, saying to no one in particular, "I'll go mate." What a relief. And what a piece of shit I am.

For an hour and a half Rick and John are lost in a blurry wild jumble of spray, rain, and sixty-knot gusts of wind. They work with their backs turned against the attack, perched precariously on the boat's sharp nose. They overhang storm-swept seas that *Rose-Noëlle*'s bow splits like an axe. Water leaps from the impact in sheets of rumbling froth that glaze her decks and fall in cataracts, sliding along her sides as she skitters down waves at ten, twelve, fourteen knots, running from the waves, fleeing the storm, slicing north. Although they are hooked to the boat by their safety harnesses, John and Rick must move carefully and slowly, keeping a firm hand on the boat lest they be swept away. Even with the harnesses, they are not safe. If they go over, they will be pummeled against the surging hulls, dragged under frigid water, frozen, snuffed.

Like looking through a wiperless windshield in a hurricane, Phil and I see only the occasional movement of smeared shapes through the ports. The sirens of the storm are so loud we can hear nothing of our companions' work. We nervously wonder if they will ever return.

Although the wind pushes the sea into moving mountains, waves themselves do not move water forward. Yes, the overall influence of the wind slowly coerces the ocean into currents. The storm also decapitates large waves and sends the heads rolling down upon us. Still, the immense torsos of those waves merely rise and fall, resting largely in one place. We will drag the hemispherical parachute, which is almost twenty-eight-feet in diameter. Towing 183 tons of water will essentially anchor us to the sea that leaps but only ambles onward as current.

When John and Rick put the parachute overboard and *Rose-Noëlle* races forward, it takes but a moment for the sea anchor to submerge, pop open, and fill. The warp zips out behind. It is as if Rick and John have harpooned a whale swimming in the opposite direction. They hold on, taking care not to let any fingers or toes get in the way as the line comes up as hard as a bar of steel, yanking *Rose-Noelle*'s bow around. She shudders, swings, and faces the oncoming waves. Rick and John ease out the stretchy nylon rope in measured bits—*zzziip, tunk*. They give the line more scope as it shakes furiously from the load, *zzziip, tunk, zzziip, tunk*. Finally it is done.

Below, the motion becomes calm. Phil and I just look at each other for what seems like forever. Finally I ask him, "What do you think Phil?"

"Bloody hell, mate. You got me." We sit in silence, re-breathing the confined atmosphere that is laden with hints of grease from a sink full of dishes, sweat, urine, and vomit.

The hatch bursts open. A frigid gust rends the dead, humid air of our cave. Rick flings the doors back with a cue-ball crack against the cabin. He leaps down with John practically falling on top of him. Water cascades from their foul weather gear. Rick mutters, "Bloody hell." Through John's elfin smile he says, "Shit, oh dear, it's blowing," and sort of dances about, shaking off spray like a dog that's just climbed out of a stream. Phil and I are relieved to have everybody below. "Spot of tea would be nice about now," says John.

As we settle down again below, *Rose-Noëlle* rides much more smoothly, but the gale continues to grow. Phil paces, peers out, mutters, "I don't like it John. I really don't like it." John says nothing. After a couple hours Phil says to John, "What do you think about letting somebody know where we are?"

"No!"

Phil's anxiety increases my own, but the fact we can talk to people ashore is reassuring. On the other hand, the SatNav tells us that we're 140 miles east of Castle Point. Who the hell is going to come out here, no matter what happens?

As we slide into another night, John replaces the hope of sunlight with sunnyside-up eggs. The brilliant yellow yokes leak across brown mounds of chile pap. It looks like puke. John hands a plate to each of us. "Here, eat this," he says. We push it around our plates a bit, or close our eyes to swallow, and then toss the plates into the sink and escape to our bunks.

Boom! Rose-Noëlle lurches, pitches up, and I am in the air. I slam down on the dinette table, and roll off onto the floor. Something is deadly wrong.

John knows the sea anchor is gone or fouled. He readies himself to check it out. Rick turns to me, "You want to give it a burl this time, mate?" I am in shock, unable to respond. After about fifteen seconds Rick climbs out of the bunk and gets his gear on.

John and Rick disappear into the tomb-like dark that gobbles up the feeble light from their torch. While they are out, Phil mutters, "We're going to flip. I really think we're going to flip."

The sea anchor is completely useless now. The tripping line that is used to retrieve the chute has instead wound around and collapsed it. One of the trampolines has also been ripped loose. John removes the tramp and tosses it into the cockpit before coming below.

As we gather below again, Rick says that he considers John the total expert out here while he's the novice, but he still thinks we should get rid of the sea anchor, that it helps to keep us sideways to the seas. John points out that an error in trying to retrieve it could be disastrous. It could easily pinch off a finger, yank off a hand. Rick thinks we should cut the anchor away, but John resists. It's new and expensive gear, and it's too dangerous on deck. Finally Rick assents to John's decision, as if the captain requires his blessing. With the collapsed sea anchor dragging, *Rose-Noëlle* is left to her own, sliding down waves sideways, exposing her flanks, revealing the full depth of our fears.

Wham! Another breaking wave heaves me off the bunk. I try to break my fall, but it happens so quickly that my efforts are useless. My Salopettes have ripped. I struggle to my knees like a punch-drunk boxer. Phil is really beginning to go nuts and I find even myself trying to calm him down while wondering who's going to calm me down.

There is no pattern to the attack of the waves. Rick and I are tossed across the cabin a half-hour later and then twice in ten minutes. I wait for the next monster wave and it doesn't show. I relax only to find myself auditioning for a spot with the Flying Nalepka Brothers again. I'm pretty bloody pissed off. Pissed at everything.

John is secure in his little nest behind the galley and under the cockpit, just yards away where we can't see him, but we know that he hears everything. Phil is on the downside, away from the waves, so when we go flying, he merely gets thrown more securely into his bunk. We hear no offers of assistance from either of them, although Phil won't shut up. He is claustrophobic yet hemmed into a coffin-like berth on the other side of the boat. With each crashing wave he vaults toward escape, whacking his bald head on the ceiling so often that his forehead is now smeared with blood. "Never underestimate the power of water. We're going to flip. I've got to get out of here," he groans again and again. Why doesn't he shut up?

Maybe we *are* going to flip. I don't know what to think. John is so totally cool, like this is just routine. But each bad wave sounds like a howitzer going off. It lifts *Rose-Noelle,* and sends her scooting across the water with a shudder and a kind of *dooga-dooga-dooga* sound. Rick says that he's not really frightened, but these conditions are on the limits of what his imagination can take.

John finally gets up, thinking it's time to lighten the mood onboard, and sticks a tape in the deck. "Ladies and Gentlemen, let's welcome Kevin Bloody Wilson." The Aussie barroom troubadour belts out one bawdy song after another. A typical tune questions why men should waste time with women, worry about their sensitivities, or show interest in their inner selves when all a man really needs to know is stuff like "Do you fuck on first dates? Does your dad own a brewery? Will you show me your tits?" John's just about keeling over with laughter. I hear a restrained occasional chuckle from Rick. Phil continues to peer out his little window. He is oblivious to everything but the blow outside.

Contrasting with Bloody Wilson's gig, we next listen to the radio and BBC news—something about thousands of students being run down by tanks in China's Tiananmen Square. That's followed by a sappy John Denver love croon. Nothing fits together. If you took a snapshot of this interior it would just look like a cushy condo, but it is closer to a room in a war zone undisturbed but with a tank just about to smash the walls flat. The potpourri of contrasting stimuli comes at me too fast—news of solid shore on this raging sea, sickness, sick looking eggs, fear, love songs, student protests, Phil's protestations, the god within, Kevin Bloody Wilson, who I can certainly do without. . . . Riding this surreal merry-go-round, I feel as disoriented as if I had taken some psychedelic drug. I am so tired. I just want calm, rest, a blank mind.

How many people the world around are completely absorbed in their own surroundings, oblivious to the intense realities of those who are crushed in China, starving in Africa, overwhelmed by the Pacific? We are not concerned with any of the others, only with our own necks.

Another wave strikes. Rick and I fly like loose change in some giant's pocket and crash to the floor.

Phil is up again. "I can't take any more of this!" He grabs the mike of the VHF radio and calls out for anyone who can hear. There is no answer. He repeats. Silence. Again. John tells him that we're too far out for all but a passing ship to hear the short-ranged VHF. "Bloody hell, John! Well, tune in the ham radio and call for help. I want a helicopter and I want it *now*, John!" John chuckles at him and refuses. John says he has no ham license, so he won't radio unless it's an emergency. "This is no emergency."

"But we're going to flip."

"We're *not* going to flip Philip. This boat will never, *never* flip."

Phil's fear is contagious. We ask John where the emergency equipment is. Rick digs out the EPIRB (Emergency Position Indicating Radio Beacon), stuffs it in a waterproof bag, and lashes it to the table. He lays flares out on the table top. I grab our two life jackets and put them on our bunk.

We all return to our berths where we remain awake and tense. But as daybreak nears, the storm distinctly calms. The booming attacks of the waves cease. The clattering of pots, pans, and glasses uncannily disappear. All is amazingly peaceful and I become aware of my sore muscles as they relax their grip. I am floating as if on a waterbed. Even Phil's fear seems to have evaporated. I look about the cabin that is bathed in the reassuring, warm, orange glow of the SatNav light. It is like a constant rising sun, bringing with it all the hope of a new day. We have made it.

Rick keeps looking at his watch and outside. The white streaks and foamy crests have disappeared, leaving enormous round-backed waves over which we float like a roller coaster car. John is up. Rick and John look at each other for a moment and Rick says, "So today we can go sailing again." John nods and goes back to rest on the dinette seat. It is about five-thirty.

For another half hour we await daybreak. *Rose-Noëlle* seems to pause for a moment, a long moment. It is eerily quiet. My mind snaps back to memories. May 6, 1965. I am fourteen, huddled with my brother and sister in the basement. The house shakes. The air roars. The roof is ripped off as the tornado passes and flattens three blocks of houses just down the street.

Now an avalanche of water consumes *Rose-Noëlle* with a tremendous rumble and crash. I feel the boat twist and shimmy. I am airborne. I look up to see the table on a rocketlike trajectory above me. Bodies, sleeping bags, dishes, books, television, all rain down. I think we're upside down.

Cold and wet. Water on my back. I leap up, now standing on the cabin top. The water is up to my ankles, rising to my shins. Where's Rick? Where *is* everybody? Phil's yelling something, trapped in his berth with the water rising. Rick calls out, "Jim! Jim, where are you, mate!?" I reach toward him, find his hand, and grasp it. Each of us gives a firm but gentle squeeze. The water bubbles up, rising to our knees. "Rick, how high is it going to get?"

"I don't know, mate."

The orange light of the SatNav blacks out, leaving us in utter darkness.

Chapter 3
Cave Men

Phil was dead right, after all. Our beds are under water. Our table and toilet dangle in the air. Sinks and countertops hang from the ceiling. The sea continues to rise. How do we get out of here?

From the dark chaos I hear Phil's haunting groans and curses. Through the trap of advancing icy water, Phil thrashes, thumps, and squeezes out of his coffin and under the overturned table.

I am shocked, almost paralyzed by the cold. I would not be surprised to see icebergs float by in the water that continues to rise up to our waists. Dawn's gunmetal-gray filters down from the surface of the sea outside and into the cabin through the capsized boat's windows. Inside, undulating surges of water now wear a sequined silver sheen. Pale white outlines of my mates' faces emerge. John asks, "Is everybody okay?'

"Yeah, yeah, we're okay." The water is now midway up our torsos and we do one of those seashore dances in which one wades on tiptoes, vainly delaying the inevitable shock of the total plunge. John assures us again that the boat won't sink, that this is as high as the water will go. I accept his word. Rick grumbles, "What a bullshit artist. He also told us we weren't going to flip." Phil's worst nightmare has leapt from his head into reality and in so doing appears to have killed his fears. He calmly awaits orders.

An unlikely looking flotilla of apples, plastic flowers, sleeping bags, books, directions for the sea anchor, the wrapper to our *Energy Bar* sail by, headed for the entry hatch that has somehow come adrift. John rails at Phil for kicking the hatch out in a panic, but Phil denies it. There goes a raft with all my precious tapes. Bye-bye Muddy Waters. Ciao Eric Clapton. Later Stevie Wonder.

Oh, and Bon Voyage Kevin Bloody Wilson!

The gears are obviously grinding in John's head. He instructs me to sink even deeper in the water by the companionway to grab everything I can before it floats out. Thanks a lot. Sunken treasures sweep by. Some bump against my legs. Jars of peanut butter, flares that Rick left on the table, plates and cups, my OB gear bag . . . all are sucked out and swept away. John positions himself in front of the entrance to his berth nook that rests under—now over —the cockpit. The mouth is now a cave opening *over* the kitchen counter, fortunately resting like a little beachhead a few inches above water. At John's direction we scramble to recover anything that floats, which we hand to him and he tucks back into what was his lair and now belongs to us all.

As clutter builds in the aft cabin, John climbs in. He meets an acrid stench and finds one battery hanging by its lead wires, its sulfuric acid solution mostly drained. Mixed with seawater, the solution forms poisonous chlorine gas. John removes both batteries and hands them out. Rick biffs the leaky one out the hatchway and I prop the other on a shelf over the table. There is a third battery forward to run the anchor windlass, which John later rights and secures, but he remains worried about the fumes.

The uneven contours of the cockpit are now the floor of the aft cabin. They fill with water. To create a flat bed above water on which we can rest, John first establishes a foundation from loose drawers and then continues to build and even out a surface with wet-weather gear, sleeping bags, a couple dozen rolls of toilet paper. John completes the platform, leveling the surface with the entry hatch doors. After a couple hours we've retrieved most of the flotsam and John has it stowed into overhead bins in what was the base of his old bed, which now is the ceiling of our cave. The lockers are sealed with screw-caps.

Shivering and numb, we crawl through the box tunnel entrance, about two-feet square and eighteen-inches long. But as we reach the more open, innermost confines of our sanctuary, it is dark, dark, dark and the air is completely dead. Claustrophobic Phil freaks out at the prospect of being trapped against the hull farthest from our den's entryway, so John settles there. The mouth of our cave is like a TV set through which we view a reassuring light and cropped picture of the main cabin forward.

The aft "cabin" is six-and-a-half-feet long, plenty long enough to lay upon, but it is only four-and-a-half-feet wide at the shoulder, giving us a whopping 13.5 inches of width each. It narrows even more at the foot to less than three feet. After a lot of shuffling and bumping, we get settled. Squeezed in flat on our backs, our shoulders are jammed together and the two bodies on the outside are pushed up onto the sides of the hull. Eighteen glorious fun-filled inches span the space between our noses and the roof. Our mattress of boards is softened just by twin, quarter-inch-thick foam camping pads that Rick and I brought. They are only big enough to span our sumptuous bed from our shoulders to waists. I now know how it felt to be stacked up like chord-wood in a slave ship. Phil was wrong about one thing: The sea *does* take prisoners.

Our only refuge from the frigid sea is this jumble of wet, cold, bodies packed solid. We fit best when we rest on our sides like nesting spoons. When one turns, we all must turn. It's like Simon Says with each of us taking our turn as Simon, announcing our intentions so we can all react as a unit. But we are all so tired and cold that we collapse and pass out, hugging ourselves but sucking the warmth from each other.

In the pitch-dark, farthest away from the mouth of our cave, rests John. Next is Phil, and then me and Rick. Phil is a furnace. I have the right spot.

John, Phil, Rick, and Jim crammed into the cave-like compartment which became the only habitable space inside the Rose-Noëlle *after she capsized. During their four months adrift, the crew spent all of their nights and most inclement days together in this twenty-inch high, twin-bed sized space. (© Steven Callahan)*

Tunk! "Bloody hell!" Phil has smacked his head again. It's still rocking and rolling outside when I awake. Waves inside the hull occasionally slop through the entryway and break on its foot-and-a-half-wide beach that separates us from the flooded main cabin. The wash from these breakers spill a gallon of shockingly frigid water over the head of the berth where Rick and I rest. At least we have some fresh air and light here, unlike John on the otherside who sleeps as if in a tomb. In this prison there is no great po-sition in which to exist.

Propping ourselves as best we can, we slice off chunks from a turkey-sized mutton ham and kilo block of cheese. I see a convenient jar of horseradish mustard bobbing by, so I pluck it out of the water. I stuff a piece of mutton into the jar then into my mouth. John follows and says, "Lovely. Isn't it a pity we don't have one of Christabel's [his sister] scones?"

"Scones!? He's worried about scones!?" grumbles Rick, clearly pissed, as if John himself threw the boat upside down.

Well, maybe John's right. I feel oddly snug and secure. Each bite is a relief, a step away from the reality of our cold surrounds. I'm actually enjoying it. Between the tornado-like capsize and this bizarre picnic, it's as if we were lifted out of normal life as in *The Wizard of Oz* and landed in *Alice in Wonderland*.

Phil asks John about the EPIRB. When will we turn on the emergency transmitter? How long before a plane will hear it? How long before rescue? John answers that the signal might not carry through the hull, so we'll have to first cut a hole to the outside. After that, maybe five days, "provided that the pilots are listening," he adds, but I hardly hear his proviso. My mind only echoes, *Five days! I'll never live like this for five days.*

Phil and John slosh through the four-foot-deep water forward and step up from the bottom of the cabin top to the bottom of the foredeck, where it is only about knee deep. With chisel and hammer they beat four holes through *Rose-Noëlle*'s inner fiberglass skin, middle foam core, and outer fiberglass shell. They slide a keyhole saw through the pilot holes and connect the dots.

Rick and I remain aft, munching on apples. We have a lot of apples. We harvest them as they continue to bob up from the deep. Despite the fact that Neptune has hoovered out a lot of our gear, *Rose-Noëlle* has resisted a spotless vacuuming. Everyone but John has lost everything except the clothes on our backs, but John has an amazing amount of gear tucked away in various nooks and crannies. Everything John owned was on board when we began. He still has a locker full of clothes. There's a whole shop of tools, from a plethora of hand tools to drills and a grinder. Under our makeshift berth is an insulated chilly bin," or ice chest. We have the bottom half of a fishing rod, a reel, paper, pencils, a set of signal flags, a spotlight, a stainless steel barbecue grill, and a host of other useful items, including the boat's built-in basic equipment. The forty-foot structure itself is a mine from which we can prospect a wide variety of raw materials. We also discover such *practical* items as John's bicycle competition medals, the recorder-like stem to his bag pipes, and his champion's garland of plastic flowers.

We have the great fortune of a substantial food stash. John stocked *Rose-Noëlle* with a year's staples. I supplemented that with a hundred bucks worth of cruising stores before departure. Even without exploring all the lockers in which food may be trapped, we have collected three pound of rice, ten cans of baked beans, five each of corned beef and soup, four each of beets and mackerel in tomato sauce, a few of creamed corn, and a half dozen of assorted fruits. To spice up our fare we retrieved John's Tupperware case chocked full of spices. The Granny Smith apples will eventually total about fifty.

For liquid we begin with a five-gallon jug of water, a bunch of tinned condensed milks, reduced creams, and coconut milks, and fifteen to twenty liters of pop in plastic bottles. John nabbed a few liters of orange juice and a couple of milk as well, which we guzzled to wash down our picnic and get the salt out of our mouths. John also tells us that all three of the boat's tanks are full with a total of 360 liters of clear fresh water.

We may be cold and wet, but we won't starve to death or die of dehydration in five days. We eat and drink freely whatever we want. It occurs to none of us to ration.

John still worries about the batteries, so he and I toss the one forward. It thumps on the hull and disappears in waters three miles deep.

Phil and Rick use one of John's C-clamps to secure the EPIRB to the side of our access hatch. We all stare at the silent little box. A red light flashes. Our spirits are sparked. I do not wonder if we will be saved. I wonder only when.

Before our departure, when John arranged to receive weather information from Jim Bramwell, John told Jim that he would not identify us, but would only report our position. Jim would then return the weather forecast. John understood that contact would be at eight-fifteen. Bramwell thought it to be eight-thirty. This night, as we float around upside down, Jim hears a message, interrupted frequently by Japanese fishing boat conversations and so dim he cannot recognize the voice. Position: 34 degrees South Latitude, 179 degrees 45 minutes East Longitude. To him it seems about where *Rose-Noëlle* should be, so he marks his chart. The position is, in fact, more than 300 miles north of us. Multihulls, it seems, even upright ones, move a good deal slower than he expects.

About June 6, Day 3 Following Capsize

Stuffed into our cave we remain fearful of the ocean's power as *Rose-Noëlle* slides across the Pacific's heaving chest. The boat lurches and pitches. What if? we wonder, What if she flips us right-side up again? If that happens, we will be trapped by an avalanche of the gear on which we rest and the water that surrounds it. In the moments before we drown, in the dark, we'll have to fight our way up through the trash pile and find the opening. Those in front of the cave entry will have some chance, but those deeper inside, well. . . . Phil continues to refuse the innermost berth. He claims that he just can't handle it. Never will he sleep in that corner. Every time a big wave cracks on the hull, he leaps toward the entrance right over whoever is in the way. We curse at him and push him back in place.

John tells us our concerns are ridiculous. "This boat will never flip rightside up again."

If he's so fucking smart, what are we doing out here upside down? I think to myself.

Rick is more blunt. "That's exactly what you told us about capsizing in the first place." In Rick's mind, John blew it and now we're all up shit creek in leaky gumboots. To Rick, John is no longer the expert, no longer our captain. We're not sailors any more. We're survivors. That's Rick's territory. After the capsize, everything changed. John does not even suggest that he should maintain command.

With the rumble of each large wave rolling down on *Rose-Noëlle*, with every crash, our muscles tense. Rick and I grab hands and squeeze. It's all we have. We have Glennie's worthless assurances and we have each other.

About June 7, Day 4 Following Capsize

I love coming to work. Sure, some of my cohorts are first-class male chauvinist jerks, but hey, I can't deny the pleasure of our comradery. Sure it's the women in my life whom I've admired most and who've done the most for me, but I'm always drawn back here where everything is simple and straightforward. What is best is being out here in the sun, just working. Across the wide head of my push broom is branded THE BULLDOZER. I bear down on the inch-and-a-half-thick handle, sweeping up rubble from a pavement patch job, stirring up whirlwinds of dust that mix with the sweat that drips down my muscles as I dance back and forth between the passing cars. I love the whole feel of it: the strain through my shoulders, the sky, the heat, the dirt, the exercise of my own, albeit small or merely personal, potential for power. A bald fat guy walks up to me with another BULLDOZER, lifts it, and pushes it into my face, shocking me awake from my dream of being back on the road crew in Minneapolis.

Uuh! What the . . . I screw up my eyes against the attack of Phil's wispy hair as he backs his head into my face, inhales deeply, and then vents a groan followed by a deep belch. Meanwhile his toes are doing their irritating curling dance on the top of my feet. "Ah, Phil. God!"

"Oh, sorry mate."

"Your hair was right in my face!"

"No, it wasn't. You put your face into my hair."

None of us are gentlemen, but Phil is really rough as guts. Thank God this cabin isn't an inch tighter or any of us a pound bigger. We can't stand it when one of us is out on watch because we desperately need each other's warmth. We can't stand it when we're all in here together because it's as tight as hell.

Our muscles ache from resting on our hard platform. Each of us has explored every topological detail of our minuscule domain. We keep careful track of the positions of stringers on the hull, the edge of openings in the furniture, the hash marks that compose the calendar that we've drawn above us. Our eyes measure angles and trajectories between these ledges, valleys, signposts, and our bodies. We have set up our boundaries, built guard posts, developed early warning systems.

Rick and I smile at each other as we spread out our shoulders and arms, pushing across borders into enemy territory, testing, waiting for the counterattack. John's monotone firm voice issues the challenge. "Well, I don't know what's going on here, but all of a sudden I don't have any space."

"Bloody hell! And it's not coming from this end either!" adds Phil.

Rick and I feel like chuckling. Rick teases them further, "It's not us mate." I know how pissed they are. I get pissed when they do it to us, but it's something to do.

Phil grabs the indelible marker that we use to make our calendar. He rises and makes a slash of ink overhead. "There!" he says. "This here is my space, mate! That's your space." He cooly tosses the marker up into the bin. It falls down again and bounces off his belly. Rick and I smile, holding back a laugh. Phil snatches the pen again and tosses. It bobbles out. He grasps it firmly and shoves it securely away. We shuffle around and resettle for a while.

None of us makes too much effort to get along. We'll be out of here soon enough, so why bother with treaties and compromise? The fact is, we are coming to despise our neighbors.

Phil takes the brunt of our frustration. His attitude of resigned doom bugs us all. As long as we're all dumping on him, nobody will be dumping on us. John continues to nag him: "Wouldn't it be nice if we just had this or that? We wouldn't have lost it if you hadn't kicked the companionway doors out Philip." And why can't Phil get on the inside just once? Rick thinks the rest of us get a bum deal, especially if the boat re-rights itself. Phil's claustrophobia is just a load of crap. Anybody on the inside feels claustrophobic because they're suffocating. Only a little waft of air even makes it into the cabin, and then it has to cross three bodies to get over to the dark side. Sometimes we have to yell out, "Give me some air, give me some air!" Our mates shift a couple inches and we feel the tiny bit of fresh breeze and suck it in. Phil refuses that inside spot just because he wants more air and a position of easy escape. We try to sleep twelve hours a day, but it feels like we're hiding in a trench with the ocean's bombs going off all around. Phil's a loveable knucklehead, but in this tight space his belching, toe curling, and tickling hair, take on the stature of war crimes.

It's not just Phil, though.

John grunts whenever he tastes or smells anything good. Especially when he cracks the bottle full of garlic from his sister, he oohs with orgasmic ecstasy. We know he will ooh every day; it is just a question of how often. Maybe John is just showing appreciation for what we have or nostalgically acknowledging his sister, but for us, especially for Rick, it is a painful reminder of what we have not, and it sounds as if he is enjoying himself. We want him to be as miserable as we.

As Rick and I expand our friendship, we discuss everything from Mexican food to how we react to the women we know and their need for independence and self-reliance. We talk about the complex and we talk about the simple.

Rick wants to know what baked, sauce-covered, cheese- and meat-stuffed tortillas are called. I tell him they're enchiladas.

Out of the dark John pipes up with "tamales."

"No John. They're enchiladas," I say.

"Well, when I was in San Diego, they were tamales."

That's John. Always butting in. His answer is the only right one. He's always done it bigger, better, and before anybody else. If he hasn't done it, it ain't worth doing or it can't be done. This comes from the guy who assured us that his boat could not capsize.

Rick confronts John directly. "John, you wouldn't know shit from chewed dates."

And Rick. I love the guy, but he can be annoying too. He springs old OB mind games on us. His various logistical problems include such stuff like, "The world is going to end in two weeks. Which ten people would you bring with you?"

Come on Rick! Too close to home. No one answers him, so he thinks our cerebral gears are grinding away. Finally I tell him, "Look Rick, nobody wants to play that game." We all go back to watching our positions, checking our border patrols.

As for me, well, I'm sure I'm extremely irritating at least to John. I'm the ignoramus out here, just dead weight. I don't know how to do anything, was no help before the capsize.

John grieves for his boat and the loss of everything he owns. That grief is only enhanced and complicated by our presence. Our cave, everything around us, is listed as belonging to one John Glennie in the record of deeds within John's head. But they are old deeds made by a man's past that we do not know and to which we cannot relate. We no longer, if we ever did, recognize John's interests and command. He is irritated by Rick and I as we help ourselves to whatever food we want, but he makes little fuss. We would probably ignore him anyway, but we take extreme advantage of his inept communication as he relinquishes command by default. Phil, Rick, and I are interlopers in John's domain, ignoring his rights to and feelings for his ruined material world, using his stuff, challenging his control, yet demanding that he keep us alive.

When John mildly objects, as we help ourselves to food, Rick is quick to point out his failure. John assured us that the boat would never flip, but here we are. Rick lashes out at John again and again with, "Everything changed after the capsize."

John may not suffer fools gladly, but he is soft compared to Rick. Rick is really tough, maybe too tough. He does not sit passively by and wait for orders but takes control. We need more air, so tomorrow we'll cut another hatch. We need to set priorities, so let's do it: Stay alive, stay healthy, learn to get along with each other. As soon as the weather lets up, we'll begin to figure a way out of here. If you don't like what somebody's doing, don't let it fester within. Confront them head on. In a lot of ways, I envy his direct approach, though it can get peoples' backs up. John says nothing, but you can feel the tension between them.

I am not even sure what attracts me to Rick. Maybe I'm drawn to his vigor and determination. I need him for the hope he inspires. He's been on the edge before and survived. When you get down to it, however, I cannot justify my attraction to Rick. I can't dice up, clone, bottle, or scrutinize my feelings under a microscope. Feelings and faith seem their own justification. No matter how inconsistent, confusing, or inconvenient, our emotions are no more wrong than the waves and no less of a factual force to deal with. Both are moving us by their mere existence. Our sins sprout only from how we rationalize how we impose those feelings on each other. Here, on *Rose-Noëlle,* our sin grows in the sour soil of our mistaken belief that, if our feelings or ideas are not wrong, they must then be right.

Rick seems to believe that he can force his way out of this situation. John believes that we must have faith in our own godlike power, live in the now, make the best of what we have. If we have sufficient faith, our needs will be provided. I envy John's acceptance and wish that I could feel at ease here, but if carried it to it's logical end, such acceptance could lead to one's death without a struggle. I'm not ready to die.

I need John. I trust his knowledge of the sea and the boat, but I also need Rick. This is my opportunity to be more of an achiever, to work with Rick to get us out of here. If I don't try now, I may never get the chance.

Without Rick, I would likely just do as John tells me, but with Rick, we have the strength to challenge him. John may resent us for helping ourselves to whatever *Rose-Noëlle* holds, but Rick and I feel justified as we pillage John's belongings while clinging to the little each of us have left. What is ours is still ours and what is John's is also ours.

It's my turn to do watch, which means poking my head out for a couple minutes to look for a ship. I slosh through the cabin forward, take a piss, check the EPIRB. Still ticking. Thank God. We'll get out of here soon. I peer about at the seas that continue to calm, but that Antarctic air still blows upon us from the south. It's too frosty to be outside.

When I get back to our soaking slimy cave, I crawl in next to Rick who nests next to Phil under the one wool blanket that we all try to share. Waves have sloshed through the entryway so routinely that our platform virtually floats. We're drenched. Bilge water, our dripping clothes, our breath, and our sweat evaporate, but the 110 percent humidity is as trapped as we. A heavy coat of water varnishes the ceiling and ripples from side to side as the boat rocks. Drips grow fat, fall, form again; drip, drop, drip-drip . . . I yank the blanket over me. It's yanked back. "Come on. Give me some blanket."

"Quit pushing," complains Phil.

"Hang on, hang on, hang on. I'm not into your space," replies Rick.

Phil flips over, facing Rick and warning, "Hey!" Poking his finger into Rick's chest he commands, *"Stay Outt'a my space!"*

Rick explodes, grabs Phil's lumberjack shirt collar, pulls his head up and raises his fist, yelling, "Don't you ever point your finger at me!"

Both John and I blurt, "Hey! Hey! Knock it off!"

Rick lets Phil go. They say nothing and settle down. I pull a corner of the blanket across my shoulder, glad not to have reached my limits yet, more glad not to feel as bad as both Phil and Rick now feel. But five days; can we make even one more day?

About June 8, Day 5 Following Capsize

Like a monkey, John hops out the access hole in front of me. "Come on! Let's go!" he says.

I poke my head out. Holy shit. *Rose-Noëlle* rests in a valley between rolling hills of waves that lift her up, up, and up until I look out on a vast plain of empty Pacific. The blow has finally calmed. A cold light breeze rustles in my ears. Smaller waves glaze the overturned hulls with a hollow *ca-tunk, blush, ca-tunk.*

Electric-blue skies stand in stark contrast to the blazing lemon hulls capped with dingy white bottom paint. *Rose-Noëlle* looks like a mother whale flanked by two babies. Unsteadily I clamber out of the hatch and ride the mother bareback. The soaked surfaces of the boat appear as slippery as melting ice. I wonder if I should wear a safety harness.

John chuckles at my fears. He nonchalantly wanders along the wing deck. The wing decks used to serve as extensions of the cabin that overhung the water, but now they look like sidewalks stretching along each side of the main hull, lifted a few inches above a street flooded with water miles deep. The forward and aft beams intersect the wing deck sidewalks at right angles like outstretched arms, and hold the baby hulls in position flanking the mother. They also serve as walkways slightly above the water but are partially convex and sloped like shorelines slipping into the sea. The trampolines between the hulls and beams have been washed away, leaving a rectangular pool on each side of the boat. Smaller waves slop up on our sidewalks as John finishes fastening some horned thingamajigs to the boat's bottom.

Someone from below hands up the two- by four-foot plastic V-sheet. I stuff it under my arm and nervously shimmy up the keel and aft to the middle of the boat while John urges me on: "Come on. Hop to it. Let's get it up." We stretch out the orange signal sheet with a big black V that spells HELP to search and rescue patrols. The wind slaps it around.

"Hey, John, uhh, what do I do with this end?"

"Just tie a bowline to those cleats and she'll be right."

Cleats? Oh, they must be these horned things he's screwed down. Now a bowline? Well, wing it. If you can't tie a good knot, tie a lot of 'em. No grannies allowed. I manage a half turn and about ten half hitches. So there! John seems satisfied.

Looks good. They can't miss us now. When I creep back down the hull to that foxhole of security, Rick reaches up to give me a hand. He gives mine a squeeze and I give one back.

The weather quickly closes in again.

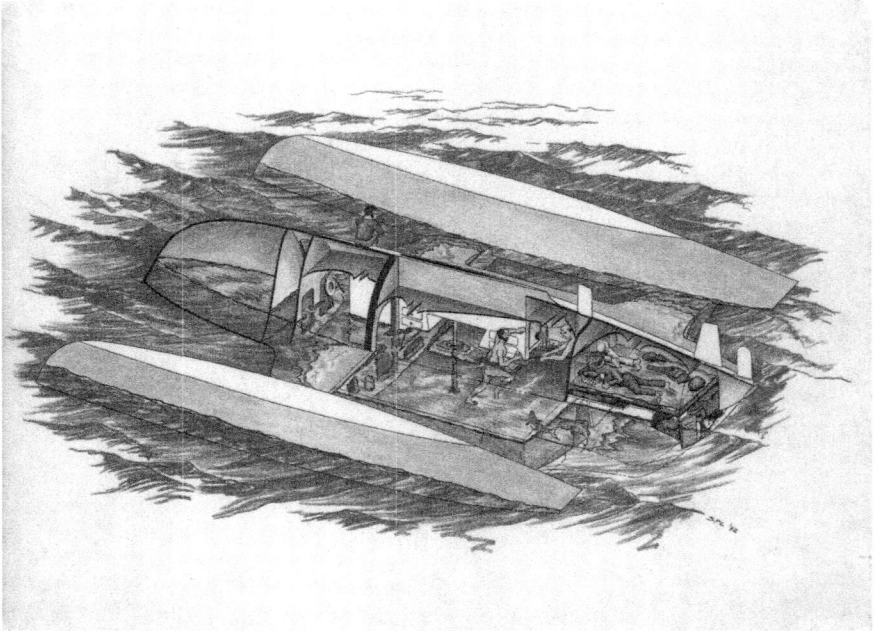

Cutaway view of Rose-Noëlle *interior shows Jim cooking in*
aft cabin; Phil crawling out of cabin on the plank into the galley area;
John gathering food in the forward cabin beside the dinette; and Rick
keeping watch on the hull just aft of the forward hatch cutout.
(Note: The starboard side hull skin and portions of the cabin sole [floor]
and starboard side furniture are eliminated for clarity.)
(© Steven Callahan)

Chapter 4
Just Another Day at the Beach

June 9, Day 6 Following Capsize

Kicked back, naked, the sun burning through the closed eyelids on my upturned face, I wish only for a cold brew at hand. This could feel as good as being racked out on a Maui beach. The sea is finally flat calm, the air warm, the sky clear. Our clothes are spread out on the hull, drying for the first time.

Opening my eyes I am confronted by Phil's short, fat, pink body. Like the rest of us, he suffers from saltwater sores. Our shoulders, thighs, buttocks, and biceps—all the pressure points where our drenched bodies were pressed against our saturated bed —are now covered with a red burning rash sporting thousands of pimply heads. Running from diaphragm up his sternum is the rope of Phil's bypass surgery scar. On his right arm he wears an industrial, generic, tattoo: Printed in faded uneven letters is KAREN. "Hey, Phil, who's Karen. Old girl friend?"

Phil turns to me, looking really serious, a piercing somber stare. Finally he says, "No. It's my wife."

I feel like a jerk. What did I have to ask that for? What must be going through Phil's mind? Will he ever see her again? Maybe I left a girl behind; maybe I *want* that relationship to be more than it is, but it is not. Maybe it never will be. Rick may have a wife and child, but he and Heather haven't exactly floated on smooth water. Rick's been too busy pushing himself to find the limits of what he can do rather than to work at what his relationship with Heather might become. And Glennie . . .what can you say about him? For some reason women seem to gravitate to him, but it doesn't seem long before they blast off again. As John talks about this one and that one, I get the impression that women are like those little silver spoons with enameled insignia on the handles that people collect to show how many places they've been. *He* certainly doesn't have any-body to get back to. We've all squandered any right to claim a piece of anybody's heart. All but Phil. He tells me that he's been with Karen since she was fourteen. Of us all, he's the one who really has something to lose.

Into my dim brain sinks the thought that this moment of sun might be the only warmth I'll ever feel. Bad weather is bound to return. I might never again share a lover's flush, will be lucky to capture a few calories through the tough hides of these guys here on this boat. This isn't Maui. This isn't just another day at the beach. The horizon is empty, but this is not a sought after solitude. This is no OB contrived adventure. It is the real thing and these men compose my sole world. The sun and calm are only a rest, a reprieve, a cease fire in our war with the sea and the skirmishes between us. Must it be this way between men?

John dives into the hull and retrieves his first aid kit. We spread antiseptic cream over our sores and wounds. Rick has a gash on his ankle that looks particularly bad. Over is entire ankle bone the skin is missing and, in the center, from a pencil thick hole, puss and lymph ooze. Bruises, small cuts, nothing too drastic dot the rest of us. We have no serious injuries, *yet*. Relieved by the cream, we are already healing. At least our bodies are healing.

Naked, we are made equal on the surface, but we are very different men. John is so matter-of-fact about stuff, like he couldn't dream up a better adventure. Rick now yearns to be with Heather and his son. Phil exudes an inexorable sense of doom. His Glenniesque myth of men confronting and overcoming the ocean wilderness has been demolished. As for me, before this voyage I had just started to make something of my life, just begun to honestly explore the wilderness within myself. Right after the capsize, like Rick, I blamed Glennie for putting us here, but now I accept that John didn't twist any of our arms. I'm pissed off at myself for following that primordial urge to seek the edge. Now I find that edge is too sharp. I'm not ready to die. I won't accept it. That EPIRB is going to work.

About June 11, Day 8 Following Capsize

The EPIRB has been emitting its silent cry of help, five days are long gone, and the only thing that has found us is another rising howling wind.

From now on I'll have to think of things as they are rather than as they were before the boat capsized. What was down is now up; what was the bottom is now the top. Anyway, we did finally saw out a second hatch through the top of the boat just to the side and behind the keel.

I sit on the cutout that we have clamped below the hole as a kind of cockpit floor, peering out at the windswept night. The ragged fiberglass edge of the sawn hole catches my clothes, so I work on filing it smooth as I look around. What's that? A ship? I grab the spotlight that John rigged up to our remaining battery during our vacation in the sun. The battery rests on what was *Rose-Noëlle*'s floorboards by the hatch. On the same shelf, nesting in a plastic ice cream box, the incredibly bright spotlight is always ready. It reassures me, as if I command my own lighthouse. John has even rigged it up with a switch. I've got to respect the guy's ingenuity.

I know we couldn't make it without him. Maybe his dogmatic attitude is more the result of his position as our captain than it is the result of any inherent maleness. Maybe the role makes a man as much as the man makes the role. Maybe men have been as controlled by history and society as have women, repressing the softer, more generous, more acquiescent parts of ourselves in order to survive in our ordained roles.

In any case, the night has not provided a ship. It must have been a mere flash of night sky reflected off of that icy sea. Rick will always hold Glennie responsible for us being here, but the sea, the bitchy, cold, endless sea, not Glennie, is our enemy. There is no question about that.

I drop down the hatch, twisting in order to stick my foot into a locker when there is a crash on the side of the hull, like a glass factory collapsing. A column of solid water falls through the hatch, pounding me down. After the initial battering, a cascade continues for thirty seconds while the bins and shelves in which the battery and light live empty out. "Aauhhh! Fuck that water's cold!"

I hear my comrades from the cave laughing. As I crawl in, dripping all over them, Rick says, "Ghoulie got you, eh mate?"

"What do you think!" I settle next to him, waiting with relish somebody else's turn, but the next couple turns at the watch are more benign. Because the drenching rogue waves that we call ghoulies are totally unpredictable, you never know when you'll get soaked during a look around, so I call our turns at the watch "rolling the dice." Sometimes you win, sometimes you lose. Sometimes you get screwed five times in a row. Just like life.

Rick is worried that *Rose-Noëlle* won't be able to withstand another storm. He's worried that the loads of the sea on her flooded body will soon begin to break her up. John dismisses this idea with hardly a thought. But Rick's worry is another nail in Phil's emotional coffin. All but John are worried that the boat will re-right and we'll become trapped, or that she will fall apart and leave us floating alone in freezing seas. "This boat is never going to break up," John insists, but that hardly reassures us.

As the seas build outside, so they build inside the coal black hull. Rick and I accordion a small mattress and hold it like a shield against the opening to our only refuge. We hear breakers bash the hulls and ghoulies crash through the hatches we have cut through the hull forward. Each wave builds inside the hull and tumbles toward us like a bowling ball rolling down an alley. Even in a dazed slumber Rick and I work together, subconsciously aware of the noise and waking just enough to push the cushion tight across the entry. But each wave that bursts on the three-inch-high breakwater at the mouth of our den finds faults in our defense. Streamers of shimmering water, alive with bioluminescence fall around us, sparkle, disappear. Some of the tiny animals remain on our skin and in our hair, glowing like microscopic fireflies.

We just begin to raise the cushion when a tsunami, all out of proportion to its warning noise, overwhelms us. A torrent of water and flashing light drive us back. Even John and Phil who are tucked in behind the bulkhead get wet, but not as wet as Rick and I. The bioluminescence covers us, making us look like we've been dipped in gold dust. "Crikey Dick!" says Phil. "Never under-estimate the power of water."

"Shut up Phil," I say. "I am bloody tired of being cold and wet. You guys want to switch places with us so we can dry off and get warm?" There's no response as Rick and I begin to shed our clothes. "Well how about it?"

Phil answers, "Don't be a wuss. You Jokers should be there now. We were there yesterday."

We have been regularly rotating. Usually, when someone gets up to take a watch, the rest of us shift, but until now there's been no regular order. So Rick protests, "Look, we're wet. We might get hypothermia. We've been holding up this damned mattress for hours. Let's switch." There is absolutely no response from John or Phil.

Rick rips right into a sermon. A good sermon. He covers all the bases. He talks about how we have to work together as a team, how we really need some help right now that our mates could give us, how we need to be able to depend on each other, and he adds that we never asked to be in this situation. Sounds good to me, but they aren't buying.

Desperately, we both beg Phil to just get in between us so we can get warm. He agrees. Like a beneficent blast furnace, Phil rotates so that each of us in turn can give him a bear hug. John lays as if dead in the corner.

Later, Rick and I talk about the flooding and John's apathy toward our plight. "Can you believe that guy?" I say.

"Yeah," says Rick. "I guess we know what he's made of. John's a dickhead. That's why we have to stick together—you and I, Jim. We have to."

Capsized
85

Rick and I are hardly angelic. In another day, with another wave, we chuckle to ourselves as we watch John and Phil vainly fend off surge after surge. Do we volunteer to switch places? Hell no. And do we volunteer to dive down into that bitchy, cold, black water to retrieve food and other gear? No. We leave it to John. We all have enough flaws to go around.

On the other hand, thank God for Phil's warmth on cold, wet days. And John hates getting wet even more than the rest of us, but he continues to dive for food. Maybe he dives so we do not pilfer what he feels is his, or maybe he just thinks he's the most qualified. Nonetheless, thank God for John too. The truth is, I need everybody.

About June 12, Day 9 Following Capsize

"Where are we John? Where are we going?" I ask.

John says, "You sure you want to know?"

"Yeah, John."

John reaches down to the foot of our bed and pulls out a fat roll of charts. He shuffles through them and yanks one out. This one takes in the whole Southern Pacific Ocean. New Zealand is about the size of Japan, but on the chart it rests like a capsized doll's boot near one corner. A few dots represent the Chatham Islands that lie 500 miles east of New Zealand. On the far right hand side of the chart, 5,000 miles away, rests the coast of Chile. John tells us that the prevailing winds and currents will sweep us east southeast toward South America and the infamous Cape Horn. I gaze at the chart, dumfounded. Between here and there it is completely empty.

After the initial shock of finding our position, we grasp at straws, at anything that floats. "We could hit the Chatham islands," suggests Phil.

Pinpricks in the Pacific. Right.

"Not likely," says John, but he suggests his own dim hope. We could bump into the Maria Theresa reefs or drift close enough to them to be sighted by fishing boats. "I saw a Japanese fishing boat, once. It appeared from nowhere," he says. He lifts our spirits then lets us down as he mutters, " 'Course that was twenty years ago. Haven't seen one since."

"Maybe we'll run into a ship or another sailboat," I suggest.

Almost before I can spit it out, John says, "Aren't any ships out here. No reason for anybody to be out here." I don't want to believe him, but I look at the map again. There *is* nothing out here. It's not on the way to anywhere. The only place on the planet with emptier waters is down in the screaming 50s where the winds of the world whip about unhindered by any land mass whatsoever. The closest land to us is something like 15,000 feet straight down.

The EPIRB gives us our only real hope of attracting rescuers. We have moved it, wedging and lashing it into a long deep slot in the middle of the boat's back in which the centerboard lives. The light continues to flash. Yes, there is always the EPIRB.

Jim Bramwell tunes his radio on once again and calls for the *Rose-Noëlle*. After a little while, he hears an extremely weak, scratchy voice. All he can make out is "twenty-eight degrees." When he asks if that is a latitude, there is no response.

Sometime during the night our EPIRB quietly passes away.

Chapter 5
We're Not in Kansas Anymore

Once again I say to myself, "Just click your heels together three times, Jim, and say, 'There's no place like home,' click, 'There's no place like home,' click, 'There's no place . . .' " Shit! What am I thinking? This isn't a damned movie. We *are* the movie. Nobody can hear us now. Nobody is ever going to find us. There will be no happy ending.

The EPIRB's death hits me like a hammer over the head. I feel dazed and fearful of the next blow. There is nowhere to run. My panicky brain is assaulted by confused ricocheting worries. We've eaten too much food, drunk too much water. We'll run out. What are we going to do? How could I get myself into such a mess in the first place? It was just supposed to be a nice sail back to the islands. That's what Glennie said. It would be good for us. Right. My anger with John eats away at me until I burst: "I hold *you* responsible for this mess we're in," I spit at him. I want him to react, to lash back, even to strike, but he just shuffles away.

We take the dead EPIRB and cradle it like a stillborn child. Reverently we transport it into the aft cabin and tuck it away into the bin above us where we can look upon it, pay homage to it like some monument to our hopes.

No longer do we think about when we will get picked up. Now we wonder only if and how we can survive.

We settle in for the long haul. We've taken a board that normally fends the boat off docks and propped it between our cave entrance and the galley counter as a gangplank. Each end rests in vacant drawer holes. At the entryway end, the plank securely stuffs into the drawer slot the mattress that we use as a dam against invading waves, leaving a tongue that we can flip up to fend off surges. No longer do we need to wade and hoist ourselves up to our escape hatch. Instead we can crawl out of our hole onto the plank, put one foot into an open bin in the navigation station, and boost ourselves to the cockpit platform while standing. We don't even have to get our socks wet while taking a routine leak or look around. Phil is surprisingly agile in the maneuver, his body shape somehow perfectly suited for the awkward task.

A small sea still exists among the drawers and other gear that fill the cavities under our bed platform. In our cave, we rest on a jumble of hard flat surfaces that are floating. As *Rose-Noëlle* yaws and pitches over the sea, water erupts in little geysers through the surface faults.

Except for the ghoulies and water seeping up from under our berth, however, the simple pleasure of a plank of wood transforms our world. As we move in and out of the hull, we are able to stay dry and warm.

We continue to urge John to make his almost daily dives to retrieve anything he can find in *Rose-Noëlle*'s private recesses with which only he is familiar, allowing him to maintain the secrets of his old domain and building our reliance on his wizardry. It would be generous of us if it weren't for the fact that only John volunteers to face the cold, wet unknown.

The sea temperature at these latitudes varies between fifty-four and fifty-nine degrees Fahrenheit (twelve to fifteen degrees Celsius), similar to North Atlantic waters off New England. Surface waters cool even more when icy southern winds sweep across them. The body loses heat to water twenty times faster than to air, and the average person in these waters will die of hypothermia, or exposure, in less than a few hours. It's estimated that hypothermia killed two-thirds of those who perished in the Royal Navy and British Merchant Marine during World War II.

After only minutes in the water, John emerges shivering. We are at least generous enough to offer our bodies for the hours it takes to re-warm him when he returns.

John is not a communicator. He does not ask us to do this or that. Maybe he thinks that we should know what to do and how to do it. But we don't know where things are and we don't know what to do, so we don't volunteer. We still believe that this survival gig is largely a waiting game. John seems to withdraw more, resentful of our presence, pissed off at himself for carrying such an inept crew, people with whom he cannot relate. Though we do not have faith in his reassurances, we continue to rely on him. I wonder what we would do if we lost him.

Another day, another dive. I crawl out on the plank behind John and sit on a small, square blue cushion while he slips into the water. He pulls his mask and snorkel over his face and submerges. My eyes follow his vague outline as he swims around in the dark, cavern-covered lake. As John kicks into the deep, there is an occasional flash of light skin, like fish darting at food. Because anything can swim out and in at will through the open entry hatch, I wonder what other creatures might be down there with John. Another flash of leg or arm—I don't know which. Total emptiness. Where has he gone? I put my face close to the water and peer around. He wouldn't swim out of the hull would he? Where are you, John? Johnny boy, here Johnny. Come on, John. *John!*

Bwush! A long neck, capped with gooey gloppy strands,

flies up from the sea at my face! I fall over backward and fend it off as it attaches itself to my hand. As the explosion of spray falls away, I see the ropy muscles of the monster's neck lead to an elbow, biceps, and then up to John's smiling face. A sea-soaked, putrefied box of spaghetti. I have been attacked by spaghetti from the deep!

About June 13, Day 10 Following Capsize

Phil and I are particularly keen to help measure the food stock. We unscrew the round inspection ports that seal the five lockers above us. Our arms snake around cans, dehydrated food packets, sacks of rice, and bottles of soda, and yank them out. The occasional lump falls on us as we combine our stores with the remaining apples, a few kiwifruit, some cereal stuff, and a tub of rolled oats from the cupboard. John's diving expeditions have contributed jars of jam, peanuts, more soggy rice, even a bottle of Chinese barbecue sauce. And let's not forget our drying spaghetti monster. We sort the loose heap on Phil's belly. At first glance it looks like a mountain, but we all realize it amounts to meager pickings for a 5,000 mile drift to South America. John's dives have been quite successful, but who knows how much more there is to retrieve?

Until the EPIRB died, we drank relatively freely. Now the juice and milk are gone and the water jug is nearly drained. Time to tap into *Rose Noëlle*'s liquid reserve. John wades forward to fill the jugs from one of the two water tanks that now reside above, between the ceiling and the boat's hull. He wonders how he will recap a tank once he pulls the plug without letting all 140 liters drain. We hear John say, "Oh, no!" What's going on? We hear him splash aft again and then nothing for a while. He crawls back into the aft cabin looking dejected.

"What's going on, John?" we ask.

He says nothing as he rolls over the top of us toward the pantry, into which he reaches and unscrews a cap to a third water tank in the ceiling of our cave. "Oh, shit. Oh, dear," he says. "Huh. Fancy that. Not a drop."

"*John,*" we urge, "tell us what's going on."

"Tanks are empty." He expounds in detail about how they must have drained through the open vent pipes of the tanks, but I don't really understand, care, or even hear him. I only hear over and over again, "Tanks are empty."

Men can live only ten days without water.

June 14–23, Day 11 to Day 20 Following Capsize

Nobody will know we're missing until about June 24, which was our ETA in Tonga, leaving us with another ten days to reach that date. So now we pin our hopes on a search. How much wishful thinking can fit on the head of such a pin?

With the black marker in hand, John reaches up to the overhead and crosses four bars with a diagonal, after which he places a big X over 14 June, the forty-eighth June 14 in his career as a human being, and maybe his last. "My, it's my birthday today," he says matter-of-factly.

"Happy birthday, mate," says Phil.

"Yeah, happy birthday, John," I add.

Rick mumbles, "Happy birthday."

Except for our day at the beach, the weather has been consistently raucous and frigid, so day after endless day we remain entombed. Taking a turn at the watch is a relief, and I sometimes boost myself up on the keel to fill my lungs with fresh air, or pause on my return and just sit on the plank for a bit, but always I am drawn back to the warmth of my mates. "Comin' down!"

Those left behind automatically react to my warning and shuffle over. Rick and I are on the dark side today. I enter on hands and knees, feet first, face down. Phil grabs my feet and guides me in a twisting shuttle while my mates hunch as far forward as they can to let me pass aft of them, urging me on.

"Come on, mate. Let's go."

"Get your arse in gear."

"Hurry up."

Once I'm inside and settled again, we ready ourselves for breakfast: one ten-inch-diameter bowl full of mueseli, oats, cornies (cornflakes), sultanas, and a sliced apple. We will share this bowl and later a spoon of rice each. It is not enough, but it is what we feel we can afford. Usually I prepare the mix while the others stare at every flake and nut. I mix Vitafresh fruit drink or powdered milk with a bit of water in our handy plastic bicycle water bottles and squirt it over the mix. The air is thick with anticipation and our mouths are full of saliva as I cap our meal with a spoon of brown sugar.

One by one we take the bowl, load the soup spoon, and shovel it in. In the old days when food was plentiful, we paid little attention to one another, but now we watch carefully as each of us uses the spoon like a steam shovel. When it's my turn I prospect for nuts and sultanas, twisting the spoon subtly to probe the depths of a promising claim. As it emerges from the hill, food spills over the jaws of the spoon, and I delicately balance that walnut and sultana that rest tenuously on the edge. It teeters, it totters. Quick, steady, but get it in! My mouth is a cavern stretched as wide as I can get it until the load has landed and my teeth come crashing down to scrape the shovel clean before it retreats. With bloated cheeks I try to swallow without choking when I see Phil's face, his eyes as bulging and round as boiled eggs and his nose practically pushed into the bowl. "Bloody hell, mate! Save some for the rest of us!"

John takes up for me. "You'll get your turn, Philip. You obviously aren't missing too many meals."

"Hang on, hang on, hang on. This isn't a fair way to do this. You guys are getting more food than me," interrupts Rick.

"What do you mean, Rick?" asks Phil.

"You guys are getting more food than me. My mouth just isn't as big as any of yours." As I choke down the last of my bite, Rick methodically explains what he calls "a better way." He says we should all have our own bowl, cup, and spoon.

"But who will get what food?" challenges Phil.

"We'll decide what we'll have and dish it out in front of everyone," somebody says. Yes, we'll vote on it.

Food, warmth, and other simple needs have become the focus of our ethics, emotions, and politics. If necessity is the mother of invention, this morning's bite of breakfast gives birth to democracy and a system of private ownership.

In the evening John asks if he can have an extra ration of water with which to celebrate his birthday. The legislature says "No way." We say that there is not enough water to waste when we have so little left and our only hope of calling for help is dead. John realizes that a few ounces of water will not make the difference between life and death for any of us. Our denial is merely another vote against him. The rest of us tell ourselves it is all perfectly rational.

Every day each of us gets angry at somebody else, or everybody else. If it isn't focused on Phil's moping or volcanic belching or scratchy toe-curling, it centers on something else no less trite. An elbow in the wrong spot, clashes over territory, over who took the last watch last night, or whose turn it is to rest on the dark side. We still believe someone will search and find us. We still believe that all we have to do is put up with this asshole a little longer and we'll get out of here.

John now wraps his finger around the edge of his bowl to scoop out any remaining food—that is, if he can't get his face right into it to lick the bowl. It drives Rick nuts. Rick thinks John is just like a little kid.

Within a couple weeks, we'll all be licking our bowls.

The EPIRB rests on the operating table of Phil's torso. Screwdriver. Knife. Off comes the head, exposing the patient's nerves, tendons, and guts. We discuss the prognosis. Is it dead?

Can we revive it? The batteries look pretty normal but are wired together and bound in shrink-pack plastic. We don't have enough flashlight batteries to replace them or to build up enough voltage. What is the voltage? Twelve. Well, Jesus, mate, what about the boat battery that's hooked up to the spotlight? "Might do," says John. All right! The twelve-volt boat battery will give this sucker life support until the second coming! We''e really excited. Maybe we won't have to ration food anymore.

John leads a long wire from the operating room out and up to the hatch. "Is it on?" he yells to us from the deck. Yeah, the wires are hooked up, but nothing from the EPIRB. We shift the wires.

"How about now, John?" Still no go. After a bit, John returns. To protect the spotlight, John put it in an ice cream tub, but ghoulies slowly filled the tub until the electrical leads drowned. The battery was very happy to spill its power into the water. Rick can't believe the attack of the ghoulies has killed our only remaining battery and robbed us so quickly of renewed hope. He thinks John must have done something wrong up there, so he ducks out to give the EPIRB a try himself, but he has no more success.

There is no more hope of calling for help. The only signals that remain are a flash light and two small strobes. Or maybe we can spark something off in the barbecue with our matches and kerosene if it's not too windy. Another week passes with little to disturb our rationing routine except a little wildlife, a fishnet float, and mounting hunger and thirst.

We drift as aimlessly as the giant albatross that I see gliding along within a foot of the waves, dipping and disappearing into the valleys and shooting up over the peaks. The largest species may stretch their wings over thirteen feet from tip to tip and glide for thousands of miles. Like glider planes, albatross use surface effect, air turbulence, and updrafts along the ocean's liquid hills. To gain altitude, they sweep around in circles, build speed in descent, and then shoot up over a wave crest, gaining height on the wave's air thermals, inching forward, steadily working against the winds of the roaring forties and screaming fifties. Sometimes they turn to run with nature's forces in the only latitudes of the world where land does not disturb the run of the wind. They love wind. Rarely does a bird from one of the nine Southern Ocean species make it to the north Pacific because it cannot glide across the windless doldrums. Man is proud to have created engineless birds of tin and plastic to soar on the currents of the air. Human pilots have even glided over a thousand miles before touching down, but that may be nothing compared to the elegant albatross. Rarely flapping a wing, they may whirl around the world without stop. No one knows how far they go before coming to roost. Albatross are not into keeping records.

From our cockpit on the top of *Rose-Noëlle*'s bottom, in a silver sea under grey clouds, we spot several black backs. They blow and submerge and then come up again forward. For an hour the pilot whales lead us deeper into their domain. Then the sea is empty. Where are they? Where are we?

The grey and blue of our universe are rent by a spot of orange. *Rose-Noëlle* drifts with its side to the wind and waves. The orange float, with less to drag, drifts towards us as if drawn to a bright yellow big sister. When it gets close, Phil dives in, swims a few yards, and hauls the inflated rubberized plastic fishing ball back to the boat for later use. The soccer-ball–sized globe is reassurance that other people still exist on the planet.

On June 23, our twentieth day adrift, the medical kit vanishes. Our water and half of the soda are gone. We've allowed ourselves three to six ounces of liquid a day. It's so little that Phil merely calls it moisture. "Give me my moisture," he says. I've never been this thirsty before.

On my way out to take watch or a pee, I pause before the galley. Three one-liter jugs of vinegar are stored there along with some pans. We've not thought of a use for them. Guiltily, keeping my back to the cave, I grab one jug, pull it to my chest as if I'm holding a baby, open the cap, and tip it up to my mouth. It's wonderful, difficult to stop. It is like sucking on a sweet lemon. But within a minute my throat feels even more parched, like the morning after drinking too much wine. Maybe it doesn't help my thirst except for that moment of sheer joy as I drink. Should I suggest a drink of it to the others? Nah, they probably wouldn't like it anyway. I take another long pull on the bottle and put it back in place. It is the first act that I perform in secret, with guilt, but it will not be the last.

By June 24, those we have left behind in New Zealand are aware that we have not shown up in Tonga and report it to the Marine Division of the Ministry of Transport. The authorities begin to call around the islands to see what they can find out.

Aboard *Rose-Noëlle* the liquid situation is desperate. It feels like a wad of cotton fills my throat. I lick my lips, but there is no moisture to wet them. All I think about is water. When will I get another sip? When will I be driven to drink seawater? It frightens me. I know it will kill me, but I also know that soon I may no longer care. The temptation will be too much, the self-destructive pull as strong as any addiction. Water is our drug of choice.

Rick pours soda from a bottle into a three-ounce olive jar that we call "the vial." One vial apiece per day; maybe two max. When we get a second, it feels like we've won the Lotto. With the liquid shimmering to the brim, Rick gingerly grips the vial between two fingers like handling nitroglycerin. Rick passes the vial to me and I take it in both hands. I turn and relinquish it to Phil and Phil gives it to John, all the while our eyes are glued to its every quiver. It is too painful to watch someone else get his fix. I look away, trying to think of something else, but am too aware of the noise of such minute consumption. Each of us has our own style. There is the squirt-around-the-mouth swallow and the gargle swallow and the greedy gulp. John finishes and concludes, "Lovely."

Rick pours another, but *Rose-Noëlle* lurches slightly and he spills a few drops down the side of the vial. "Hey!" shouts Phil. "That's my moisture you're wasting there." After he dumps his quota down his throat, Phil says, "Aahh. I could go for ten more of those right now."

"Be thankful you have anything to drink, Philip," scolds John.

"Well, what about another one today?" probes Phil. "I don't think I'm getting enough liquid. Let's vote on it."

Well, I know how this is going to end up. Phil always votes for more. He'd eat and drink everything on the boat if we'd let him. Rick, on the other hand, will vote to conserve. Always conserve. Discipline. Play by the rules. Survival mode stoicism. That leaves John and me. If it's a tie, which it rarely is, we'll go with the conservative approach. John volunteers, "Okay, Philip. I think we've had plenty today, but I'll go for another one." Great, John, thanks. If I vote no, we won't have another and Phil will blame me.

Rick and Phil verbally leap on me like jackals. Phil pleads, "Look at what we've done today. We cleaned off all the cans and rearranged our whole space. We've all done watches. I think we deserve it."

Rick says, "Look, we've only got five bottles of pop left and you want another drink, Phil. There's no sign of rain yet and we don't know how far we have to go."

God, I want another one, but Rick is right. Since the EPIRB died, Rick has really gotten into the survival mode. He's convincing too, always logically setting our priorities from staying dry to conserving food and water. He constantly outlines the realities of where we are—in the middle of nowhere—where we're going—halfway across the planet—and what we've got to keep us alive until we get there—not much. He reminds us of our priorities—staying alive, staying healthy, getting along—while we can afford no luxuries, no waste. Since the capsize, John has led by example but has never fought for any kind of formal command. He just doesn't communicate, allowing Rick to exert an increasing influence over ordering our lives.

Phil jumps in with a final plea though, "Well, I'm bigger than you jokers. I need more liquid than you do."

"Phil, the vote's over. Case dismissed. Next case!" I conclude.

Phil is clearly depressed. He thinks to himself that there's no hope. We're goners. We sent no radio message. There are no flares. He prepares himself for his final days, lying down flat and staring up at the ceiling, saying nothing. He remains on "ceiling patrol" for hours every day. We all worry about him. He just doesn't seem to care about anything except the immediate gratification that food and water provide. I'm sure he thinks, *If we are all doomed anyway, why not a last splurge?* We begin to guard gear because he carelessly drags it out of the cave and drops it in the hull where it is sucked out to sea. Socks, hats, the watch, a suit of foul-weather gear disappear. As Rick, John, and I debate how to survive, what we can do to catch water, how we can live off of the Pacific, Phil remains completely disinterested.

Phil's depression gets on everybody's nerves, but everybody is getting on everybody's nerves. Rick and I wonder if we can catch fish out here. John says flatly, "No."

"Why not, John?" I ask. "It's worth a try isn't it?"

"I've never caught fish out in the sea."

Phil speaks from John's shadow, "No, you can't catch fish out here."

Rick just ignores Phil but argues, "Because *you* haven't caught fish, John, doesn't mean there aren't any fish to be caught."

"Suit yourself, but you'll never catch any."

"Yeah, mate, you'd just be pissin' in the wind. Give it away," echoes Phil morbidly.

Spicy enchiladas, hot women, or cold fish—John thinks he knows everything about all of them. I just don't get the guy. One minute I look up to him. He *does* have all the experience, all the answers. He brings us food from the depths, comes up with brilliant ideas. The next minute he says we can't catch fish in the ocean. Where *can* you catch fish? The Himalayas?

John is confusing, all right, and his timing remains impeccable. Phil looks like he's ready to slit his wrists, we're all so thirsty that we'd eagerly drink blood, and John comes up with, "You guys are going to be famous." He is enraptured with a plan to write a book about this gulag, which I have come to think of as Glennie's Floating Shit Barge. He says he'll make us famous. I suppose he thinks that will perk our spirits. We might all die out here and he spends his time thinking about the Phil Donahue Show. What a jerk.

But my irritations pale before Rick and John's mutual resentment. When John tries to command, Rick asks him who the hell he thinks he is. When John says "Yes," Rick says "No." When John talks about women, Rick calls him a chauvinist, despite the fact that Rick has treated Heather like a sow for years. The answer is usually somewhere in between the two of them, but it doesn't seem to matter to them.

After we've taken our usual watch on deck and are ready to duck back into our cave, we yell "Coming down!" so our mates have a chance to shuffle around and make space for us. But after John ducks out and we stretch out, the unlucky one in front of the entrance is often suddenly assaulted by one of John's big feet jammed straight into the face. Rick lashes out. "You fucking wanker, John! How many times do we have to tell you to warn us when you're coming down?!"

"Oh," says John as if totally surprised. "Oh, my. I'm sorry. I didn't realize." He continues to ignore such common courtesies, pissing us off even more.

John rearranges our sleeping space, removing some of the packing from one side and putting it on the other where he will spend the day. We all get back in the cave and lie down again. There is a surge. Water boils up under Rick and me. We're floating, soaked. Rick is as mad as a stuck bull. With flaming eyes he roars across my chest at John, "You took stuff from under this side and put it over on your side, didn't you?"

John does not look at Rick. His bony long nose remains pointed straight up. "Well," he says calmly, "it was low over on this side and high over there, so I just leveled the space out. So why are you getting so bloody excited?"

"Look, mate, I'm wet! You're not! I don't like it."

"Well, you don't like it. What are you going to do about it?"

Rick fumes but only grumbles, "You don't care as long as *you're* dry." He lies back down and we give each other's hand a squeeze. "He only thinks about himself," he mutters to me. John just looks straight up, his snout in the air.

How long we can live like this? This voyage goes on and on. We go nowhere. We are all so tired. I have had enough. My mind runs from one irritation to another, and then back to my raspy, parched throat. My only relief is in dreams. There, I always find liquid. There, I actually get to drink. Fantasy may be as close as you can get to the real thing sometimes, but it is far from fulfilling. I hate the damned vial. I hate this place, these ridges and boards under my back, my aching bruised bones, the wet, the cold. And I wonder how long it will take before I really and truly hate everybody around me. Above all, I wish I had a drink. For the first time in my life I can really understand drunks. Soon I too will say, "I'd kill for a drink," but I'll probably really mean it.

June 25, Day 22 Following Capsize

"It's raining!" I see nothing in this deepest darkest corner in the middle of the night, but there is no mistaking the tap dance of water on the hull above me. "It's starting to really come down."

Phil is out like a shot with a white plastic sheet tucked under his arm and John at his heels. Phil launches himself onto the hull and stands with arms outstretched like an angel with plastic wings, his face turned to the sky in thanks. The sea is flat. The torrent comes straight down. John in the cockpit stretches the bottom of the sheet into a pot. It fills. He hands it down to Rick on the plank. "Here! Take this!"

"What?"

"The pot! The pot! It's full of water!"

Rick grabs it. I flick on the flashlight so he can see as he begins to pour it into an empty plastic bottle. He is careful, but some still spills.

"Here's another one!" shouts John.

"Hang on, hang on, hang on." Rick quickly spills the rest of the first pot over the bottle and exchanges it for the second pot coming down. I give him a new bottle and a flash of light for a moment; and then I take the full one from him.

The bottle is cold. It's wet. It's full.

I think for a second about taking a hit out of it, but things are happening too fast.

"Down she comes!" shouts John as he exchanges pots with Rick. *Now,* when it's to his benefit, he issues a warning cry.

Rain slaps on the hull like gunshot. We can hear Phil whooping and hollering.

Rick pours the water into the jugs with amazing accuracy.

"Down she comes!"

As quickly as I can, I hand Rick the next pot, give him another flash of light to get the next bottle started, and store the full one in the cave. There is another. Yet another.

The rain stops. Just like that. Gone. Phil remains on deck, waiting, John looking up.

Rick hands me the seventh and last bottle and tips the remaining water from the pot into his mouth. I think for a nano-second about the guys up on deck. "What the hell," I whisper to Rick, "they've probably been guzzling." I put the bottle to my lips and let the liquid flow. It's amazing what excuses you make and liberties you take when it's dark and no one else can see.

Chapter 6
Check and Mate

Our eyes begin a three-week search for rain clouds. We probe the sky for signs of planes, scour the sea for a puff of ship smoke or the splinter of a sailboat's mast. Nothing. As the days roll by, I am reminded of late fall back in Minnesota when the trees are skeletal. Crisp mornings are just short of frost. Sunny dry skies. Early nights. June is the dead of winter in southern latitudes.

New Zealand is no tropical island. The palm-covered atolls and islands of Polynesia rest a full 1,200 miles closer to the equator than to Picton. We're as far south as Philadelphia, upper California, or Japan is north. Here, sea currents swirl around Antarctica and migrate north and east, unwarmed by continental land masses. Day after day the wind sweeps up to us from the southern ice cap.

Wool has an ageless reputation for warmth. Even when wet, wool far excels the insulation provided by other cloth, particularly soaked cotton or synthetics. Only recently has wool been superseded by polypropylene artificial fleece, which dries quickly yet remains warm, dry or damp.

Rick and I are thankful for the clothes we've rescued. We both wear a suit of artificial-fleece long underwear. Over that I wear all-wool biking pants, a singlet with a sweater over that, socks, and hat. Rick has wool long johns and top and borrows an acrylic sweater from John.

John's cache of clothes is mostly light cotton stuff. He manages only one wool sweater that he has turned into a pair of pants by shoving his legs through the arms and tying the loose waist with a chord. He also layers himself with a variety of cotton and synthetic shirts, pants, and sweaters.

Phil is worst off. He has only a wool lumberjack shirt called a Swanndri, a synthetic insulated shirt, a pair of sweatpants, and white plastic rainpants. He also borrows clothes from John. Phil, however, has one thing we all covet: a synthetic winter jacket. Also from the packing under our berth, we recently pulled Phil's missing sheepskin coat, suede on the outside and fleece on the inside. It no longer resembles a coat, however, but a soaking leaden lump. It encroaches on our space and smears it's cold slimy skin against ours. We don't quite know what to do with it, so Phil wrings it out as best as he can and bundles it up as a gigantic, grotesque pillow — a pillow for Godzilla, maybe. "I'm going to dry it out. It's going to keep me warm, mate," Phil swears. Maybe when it's dry and warm we'll want it, but for now we can't wait to get away from it, so we treat it pretty much the way we've been treating Phil.

To augment our wardrobe, we also rip a synthetic tartar blanket into four scarves.

Even as insulated and dressed as I am, it takes little time on deck for the cold to make me shiver. Perched high up on the back of our mother whale, I see nothing on the horizon. Conditions are mild for the open ocean. Only three- to four-foot waves pound against the hull facing the weather and wash over the sidewalks around the boat. For the best visibility we keep watch from our cockpit. To keep our feet dry, we rarely stroll the wave-swept walkways. I can hardly feel my fingers anymore, so I shake my hands, rub them together, and stick them under my armpits. Despite the constant flamenco of my feet to stave off the cold, they too begin to hurt. I've had enough. Time to retreat. We still spend ninety percent of our time huddled in our cave to wait out the winter.

It's like entering a different world inside. It's damp here, but comparatively warm. Ah, warmth. We care about warmth, staying dry, the next meal, and the next daydream. Little else matters. We've found a toothbrush and soap, but we do not wash, do not shave, rarely brush our teeth. It doesn't make any difference. Our teeth feel amazingly clean. I can't smell anybody. Such time-consuming complexities of shoreside existence now seem like a vain waste of time, an unnecessarily complicated diversion from the important stuff of life.

One might think warmth and a dry bed are simple pleasures. One might consider a daily ration of three tablespoons each of rolled oats and cold rice, plus half an apple and a quarter kiwifruit washed down with three to six ounces of water or pop as meager nourishment. But even simple pleasures and meager nourishment are more complicated than they appear. They are only possible because of the complex play of the past and the present. When *Rose-Noëlle* capsized, anyone on deck would have been swept away. In another hour or two, we would have set sail and two of us would have been on deck. Would the surviving two have found food at all? Would we be able to keep each other warm? We have the luck that we survived together on a mother craft with life-nurturing stores. The ocean is brutal, but our bodies are just tough enough to withstand it. If it were a few degrees colder, if *Rose-Noëlle* had sunk just a few more inches, if she had been designed or built a little differently, we would already be dead of hypothermia. Millions, if not infinite, instruments of fate allow us to carry on, provide us with *just* enough.

My hand spontaneously fondles my Saint Christopher's medal. At first my prayers, if you can call them that, were vague. I merely wished for water and it came. But slowly I've come to formalize my thoughts, to thank whatever powers that be for our small fortunes, and to ask for more.

Rick sees my hand go out to my medal. He has long been an atheist. He asks me about the medal and my beliefs. I tell him about the chaplain with whom I worked in the army. "There are no atheists in foxholes," he was fond of saying. Rick latches onto that, huddled as we are in our own foxhole with the Pacific's waves crashing down all around. He too begins to talk to God. At first Rick feels like a jerk just thinking about it. He thinks to himself, *I'm a hypocrite. I know it, and God, you know it.* But after a while he feels more at ease as he thanks forces greater than we for the moderate weather of the last few days, and as he expresses his hope for more rain.

It is not just the past and outside forces that compose our complex drama of simple needs and simple fulfillments. I need Phil's warmth. I need Rick's logical approach to problems. I sure as hell need John with his intimate knowledge of the sea and our house on it. They seem to need me as I invent daily menus that become the focus of our mutual nourishment.

If we fall apart, if the complicated play should fail, we'll all be toast. Dead cold toast.

Thump-thump-thump . . . thump-thump . . . What is that noise emanating through the cabin as *Rose-Noëlle* flops on the swells? John slips down the side of the hull to the sidewalk and reaches under one wing deck. The end of a spinnaker pole is adrift. The five-meter-long aluminum pole normally serves as a kind of boom to hold out an edge of a billowing downwind sail called the spinnaker, which looks kind of like a parachute and is often called "the chute" or "the bag." John takes a pair of snips, reaches under the other end of the sidewalk, and clips a wire that retains the attached end of the pole. He pulls the pole out and we lash it to the keel.

The essential outside job done, we retreat again to lay on our backs day upon day like four sardines. Phil and John talk endlessly about boats. They are like two motorheads discussing the intricacies of fuel injection, overhead cam engines, and four-barrel carburetors. I never knew that the aluminum stick and bits of wire that compose a boat's rigging could be so intricate. There are evidently numerous species of that wire, all kinds of shapes to masts, and countless ways to combine them to create the spars across which the fabric wings of a sailing machine stretch.

Rick and I turn our attention to other realms. We often ask each other, "What do you think Martha and Heather are doing right now?"

"Do you miss Martha?" Rick asks with a smirk on his face.

"Sure. Sure I miss Martha. Yeah, I *do.*"

"Well, what do you miss about her?"

"What do I *miss* about her?" Do I have to explain? Rick has never understood my relationship with Martha. He has his own history with her when they both were instructors at OB in Minnesota. Though I didn't meet either until I got to New Zealand, Martha introduced me to Rick. But their's has always been an uneasy friendship. Martha is, well, a *strong* feminist. She founded a program that promotes womens' participation in outdoor activities. I like that, except for the fact that men are strictly prohibited. She's always jumping on somebody's case about any remark that could possibly be construed as sexist. She always makes sense, lays out her reasoning with impeccable detail, but she leaps on the unwary like a spider. Some are drawn to her strength while others approach her web with caution. Rick and Martha are male and female sides of the same fearless, capable, competitive coin, always ready to duel.

"Well, Rick, Martha's great. She *is*." I can tell he's skeptical. "Maybe I see another side of her that other people don't see. There *is* a soft side. Maybe she doesn't want to get married, doesn't want kids, doesn't want what most other women do, and I want that stuff, but it's okay for now. I like her, Rick. I *do*." I'm sure he remains unconvinced. "You know if you don't expect her to be like some woman from 1900, Martha has a lot of affection and warmth."

Glennie jumps in with, "I don't understand women like that. Just get me back to the islands. That's where women will treat you right." Then he lapses back into his conversation with Phil about rudders or helms or something.

Rick nudges me with his elbow and gives me a look that denotes *Get a load of this guy*. We forget about John. "You were married before, right? What was she like?"

I tell him that Pam was completely different from Martha. She was petite, wore makeup, jewelry, the latest styles, was the mother of two. Pam loved men. Unlike Martha, she never made any bones about womens' roles. She had come from a poor family and had been on her own since age fifteen. She was a survivor and I think she survived because she could face and express her feelings. She might get hurt, but she wasn't afraid. She had nothing to prove. Maybe her apparent vulnerability was actually her strength—it kept her honest. And when she stuck her foot in her mouth, she was able to laugh. I loved her. I still have a lot of that love left.

"Well, if you loved her, why aren't you with her?" challenges Rick.

"It was like living with Lucille Ball: it was one zany scheme after another. I often called her Lucy. Loving somebody, being their friend, doesn't mean you can live with them."

"You're still friends?" Rick asks incredulously.

"Sure. When I met her I was full of anger, confusion, insecurity—all kinds of stuff that I just didn't want to look at, like maybe if I ignored it I'd be cool, together, secure, brave. . . . But it wasn't like work—I couldn't go home, wash off the grime, and get five months off a year. I had to be a dad to her kids. Christ, *I* still needed a dad and I had to be somebody else's. All the fear and frustrations kept poking out of me like some huge frost-heaved rock in the road. I didn't want to deal with it, so I just kept laying on the pavement. I numbed it with drugs. I hung out with the guys so I didn't have to talk about it. I projected. I got mad. I'd drive around it or bury it instead of digging out the rock and fixing it right. I was really good at throwing a quick patch on stuff. Then it was Miller Time. The next year it was right back again. But she kept after me. When I had to help an alcoholic friend move from place to place at weird hours of the night or retrieve his car for the fifth time from the impoundment lot, she coerced me to confront him with his problem and deal with the possibility that he might reject me. My whole life I'd slipped, slid, bent the rules. I 'borrowed' shovels from the city and traded them for barbecued ribs. My garage was stuffed with the taxpayers' tools, but I told myself there wasn't anything wrong with it because I freely handed them out to neighbors. Pork-barreling politicians did the same stuff every day. I wasn't a thief; I was Robinhood! But Pam changed all that. She got my head spinning, questioning everything. How could I square my weaknesses with my need to feel like I'm not a bad guy? When I looked in the mirror, I began not to like what I saw. She changed me, Rick. She started teaching me the language of emotions. But it was too much too fast. I wasn't as tough as she was."

Rick flips over. After a while he turns again to face me. In a low disgusted voice he says, "Jim, I think I've been a real jerk. I've left *everything* on Heather's shoulders. She does the washing, the cooking, the cleaning, taking care of Mattie, changing his nappies: everything. I wouldn't buy her a new washing machine. I would''t even run the bloody water out to the washing shed so she wouldn't have to carry it." Rick wonders why he was always off in the mountains or kayaking or something and left her to pick up the slack. And he worries that now, because of this damned boat, she may be picking up the slack forever.

It is a new tack for Rick, to question himself this way. He has always been so concerned with what he does and how he does it rather than what he is. "I feel so good right now, Rick," I tell him. "I've just begun to live. Rick . . . I . . . I don't want to die Rick." We look at each other. Our eyes are glass.

"We're *going* to get out of here. It's just a matter of time," he says. My hand finds his. Our fingers and thumbs bend across one another's and squeeze hard.

About 27 June, Day 24 Following Capsize

Phil sticks his head into our nest and says, "Hey, there's a fish out here!"

Rick and I scramble out after him, plaguing him with questions. "How big? What kind was it?"

"I don't know. Big and black. Just cruising around."

We line up on the plank and search the water like three monkeys on a limb: See No Fish, Hear No Fish, and Smell No Fish. Nothing. "You sure you saw a fish, Phil?" asks Rick.

"Hey, mate! I know a fish when I see it."

I think to myself that Phil *wants* to see a fish. He wants a fish like he wants a roast lamb dinner. It was probably just a piece of gear floating around. "Well, whatever it was, it ain't here now."

Three of us climb out onto the hull. It's just another sunny, icy day in paradise. John remains below, too cold to come out. His diving routine over the past several weeks has taken its toll. He's tired, weak. He began this journey thin and now looks haggard. It's no time to push him. We need him too much. For once, Rick and John have cooperated, planning our task in detail. The spinnaker pole awaits erection, six lines already secured to the top. We have volunteered to rig a signal mast and Rick has reassured John that we can do it right.

We remove our socks, roll up our pants. Phil saddles the keel that runs down most of the length of the hull like a square-edged spine six inches high by almost the same wide. He waits over the box-shaped hole cutout of the keel in which the centerboard lives, and grasps one end of the pole. While painfully saddling and scooting along the back of the hill, Rick and I pick up the other end of the pole and push it up as if we were raising the flag over Iwo Jima. We wonder how much the pole will waggle about once vertical. We wonder if we can hang onto it until we get it tied down. We wonder if we can beat the clock to hypothermia.

Fortunately, the pole's tapered butt neatly drops about six inches into the centerboard trunk and stops dead tight. It stands on its own.

While Phil lends it an unneeded but reassuring hand, Rick and I turn and drop down the side of the slick hull, our clothes wiping up the spray like sponges. We slide on our butts with a half twist while trying to keep a grip on the slippery ridge of the keel or in the centerboard slot. I blow it, tumble, and crash down on the drenched sidewalk. I'm frozen already. Fortunately, John has fastened cleats about the boat so Rick and I need only scramble around, grabbing the ropes that drape from the pole and pulling them out. The wind snaps at our clothes, steals the feeling from our fingers and toes. I yank while Rick ties one forward, one aft. *Come on, come on. Let's get out of here.* But we cannot leave the job so unsecured. Putting our backs to the wind, we protect our faces from the lash of the Antarctic whip. Once the pole is secured fore and aft, we stretch lines to ends of each cross street that leads to the baby hulls. The entire operation takes an hour.

We are done and out of here. Like submariners escaping the deck in a crash dive, we plummet down the cockpit hole. I glance back as I drop. The pole looks great!

As we make our way back to our refuge, we're beaming. We chatter like a bunch of kids about how the chances of a ship seeing us now must be a hundred times greater. No longer do we ride a barge awash. We have a mast! We have a proper boat again!

Back in the cave, John looks mummified, completely wrapped up in a blanket with just his head poking out. Although weak, he seems really excited. "Oh, oh, fabulous! That's wonderful. That's great, guys." We're all so pleased with ourselves that we only hear him in the back of our minds, but then he hits us with words that catch us completely off guard. Stuttering and uncertain, he says, "Thank you. Thank you, mates." I look at him. He really means it. "I just couldn't make it up there with you guys today."

Phil gives John the stop sign with his hand up and head down. "Don't worry about it, mate. It's up."

"Yeah, John, you've done plenty," I add.

For the first time we've bungled our way to complete something as a team.

Jim Bramwell calls Kerikeri Marine Radio and reports the positions he believes he's received from *Rose-Noëlle*. Two days later Captain Gibb of the Ministry of Transport interviews Bramwell, who confirms that these messages were from *Rose-Noëlle*.

Bramwell also reports that a friend of his has seen us in Tonga. Heather and Martha contact a friend in Tonga who looks for us and finds no one who has seen us. The Picton rumor mill next churns out a story in which Heather has received a postcard from us basking on Norfolk Island. It is as grueling for our loved ones to keep the facts straight as it is to promote a search.

My friend, Pete Brady, is constantly bothered by Jim Bramwell's reported positions. We shouldn't be near the Kermadecs. He, Heather, even Rick's parents check with Bramwell. When Heather boards Jim's boat, she is not impressed. "Beer," he mutters. His wife scurries to fetch him one. Heather feels like Bramwell dismisses her as a total ignoramus. "Yeah, I talked to them," he confirms again. "They were up by the Kermadecs. They could be anywhere. They're probably off on another island having a party." She does not believe him. Rick would have called.

Armed with our supposed position and launched by pressure from our family and friends, on June 30 and July 1, an Orion aircraft roars off the runway and spends sixteen hours at a cost of a quarter million kiwi dollars ($150,000 U.S.) searching 20,000 square miles of ocean. They find nothing. It is not surprising. The closest they come to us is 330 miles to the north.

Sometime in July, About a Month Following Capsize

The ship is dressed, as they say. With our mast up, moving about on deck is much easier. On top of the rounded summit of the hull, we clutch the pole to steady ourselves standing, extending the range of our eyes. Around the base perimeter of the rope stays that secure the mast, we have added horizontal hand lines, giving us lots of handholds as we move about our ship. We have strung the stays with John's brilliantly colored signal flags and have crowned the pole with our bright orange fishing float, making our rigging appear like a celebration of our on-deck security. Somebody has got to see us now! The ropes also become our laundry line. All sorts of shirts, socks, pants, and other debris flag in the wind. We say to each other that we look like a Hong Kong, liveaboard, patch-sail Chinese Junk.

The mast supports a rain-collector device. Rain collection gutters run along the bottom (now top) of the hull. Signal flags festoon the rigging and a fishing float tops the mast to enhance the boat's visibility to passing ships. Jim is coming out of the cockpit just above the galley while John sits atop the hull cleaning fish. Phil has gaffed a fish while Rick runs along the wing deck "sidewalk" leaning on the spinnaker pole handrail ready to scoop the fish into his net. Normally, the barbecue, generator, more clothes, and drying fish would also be on deck, but have been eliminated for clarity.
(© Steven Callahan)

Phil's sheepskin coat, which we all call the "Bear," now hangs drying, crucified on a line from our mast. As it dries, Rick admires the Bear. "Sure is a nice jacket, Phil."

"Too right, mate," answers Phil.

Trapped in one of John's personal gear lockers in the aft cabin are a few roles of film and an automatic 35 mm Olympus Trip camera with the F-stop stuck on 22. Rick appears on deck like some reporter, snapping time slices of our existence on the ultimate Olympic trip. He records our signal mast, routines, sunsets.

Back in the cabin, Rick and I rack out on the dark side. Phil rests in the full light with eyes wide, ever attentive on ceiling patrol, recording every ding and scratch, always on the watch for enemy movement. What does he think about? He tells Rick that he's just trying to come to terms with the fact that he's out here and that he's going to die. The rest of us try to divert our minds from the next bite of food, the next sip of liquid. Will we ever get another rain?

John is in another world between us. He spends his days dreaming of the future, fame, and fortune. With a rescued pen and sheaf of paper, he begins to crowd a folder with boat drawings and musings. He logs the events of each day right down to my recipes, recording each nugget of his wisdom in a manuscript that will no doubt become the sea classic of all time. What will this one be titled? Four Men in a Boat? Moby DICKHEAD? Naw, that one's been used. What about Wet Dreams of the South Pacific, a sequel to the original classic Playboys of the South Pacific?

Actually, our minds are far away from sex. In these conditions, such urges seem the first to die. Instead, Rick and I talk about the roster of restaurants we will haunt when we get out of here. We talk about the menus, what the waitresses wear, about MacDonald's french fries and chocolate shakes. John interrupts us. "Uh, Jim, what spices did you mix with that rice last night?"

"Uummm, tandori . . . some cumin, and . . . ah, yeah, peppercorns."

"Aaah," he gently groans as the ecstatic memory is sparked. "That was lovely," he concludes as he madly scribbles down each detail in his memoirs.

Rick's eyes focus on John like an eagle. John pays no attention. Rick feels like John interrupts us just because he wants to be a part of our club, that he'll try anything to get into it. Who can blame him? John's options are the morbid company of Phil or stark loneliness while crammed together with three other men. But whenever John tries to climb in through a window of our conversation, Rick slams it closed on his hands. "I think it's bad karma what you're doing, mate," Rick lectures.

John doesn't look up, doesn't say anything. Rick is clearly perturbed. His sparkling eyes are full of fire; his barrel chest heaves. He is used to people fighting back. He desires the chase, the takedown, the kill. Rick masks his need for an emotional attack and triumph with quasi-logical argument. He accuses John of tempting fate by planning for the future. Our planned restaurant spree is no different really, but Rick and I prefer to ignore this.

"Tempting fate" is just one rationalization we throw at John to cover what really bothers us. Although I know it is unfair, we blame him for our demise. Why did he leave New Zealand with such a novice crew? Why couldn't he have radioed our position? Why was he so overconfident in his boat? Why did he let the water in the tanks drain? When it comes to cutting a hatch, rigging a plank, raising a signal mast, John is brilliant, but his good ideas are not the ideas of our captain, rather just one of the four crew. He is not leading us anywhere. He does nothing to get us out of here.

Our anger is blind to the fact that any boat can be overwhelmed by the sea. We overlook the fact that both Phil and

Rick knew how to sail before departure and that Rick had even been offshore before. We give John no credit for having such a well-conceived, well-built boat that, no matter how Spartan, is far superior to any life raft and contains a huge amount of stores for which John dives in dangerously frigid water. It's not his fault that the rest of us are oceanic imbeciles.

John's boneheaded egotism, his stoic indifferent stare, and the way he ignores our resistance, criticism, and suggestions bury any charity we might show him. We are blinded by our fury. Not once has he admitted that he was or might be wrong. He has never said, "I' sorry, mates." And now, he not only accepts but seems to relish this debacle. Maybe John doesn't have anything better in life to do than to float around out here, completely content. John is *safe* out here away from people, especially from all his complicated and demanding women. But the rest of us have real people, real relationships, real living that await us ashore.

"Hey, Rick, forget about him. Let's play chess." The capsize has revealed numerous items that John stowed away and forgot during ten years of living aboard, including a plastic baggie stuffed with games. I pull out a six-inch-square cardboard checkerboard with little cardboard pieces like one might find in a cereal box.

On our hard, ridge-filled bed, Rick and I lean on our elbows facing one another in just enough light to see. One brief game is enough to physically exhaust the players. Our pelvises, shoulders, and elbows ache. Our limbs fall asleep. We compete with John and Phil for space while constantly lifting and rolling our bodies to ease the pressure on our bones and needle-filled slumbering limbs. The bed undulates under our acrobatics. The board jumps about. Pieces fall off or slide into new squares. We argue. Our games are fairly matched, but Rick takes forever to make a move. "What's the big deal, Rick? Come on, let's move." I suggest a time limit.

Rick objects, telling me that he should have as much time as he wants to make a move.

"What do you take this so damned seriously for anyway?" Rick stares at me with the same panther eyes with which he stared at John. Why is he so obsessed with winning, with being the best? Why do *I* want to win? Do we go through life just exchanging one addiction for another—give up drugs to take up accomplishments? Donald Trump has proudly claimed that he "collects quality trophies." Do people like him ever consider *creating* anything of quality? John collects his women, Rick his conquests of mountains. Are these trophies any different from the addict's high? Maybe I walked away from drugs, but how do I deal with the most dangerous intoxicants of power, control, security? How much of each do I need; how much does it take to get hooked? Who will help me walk that fine line?

I bounce around to relieve my elbow. Phil says, "Hey mates, how about some space? Come on."

"We're trying to play chess," I answer him. "This is our escape. It's the one thing we enjoy. This is important to us."

John speaks up. "We *all* should play chess. Rick should play with Phil next and then I'll play you."

What?! I'm not going to be forced to give up quality time with Rick just to play with these ratbags any more than somebody is going to command me to go out on a date with somebody I don't like. I snap out. "Look John, you're not going to tell me who I'm going to play chess with. I want to play chess with Rick. I don't *want* to play chess with you."

On July 6 thirty of our friends and relatives, as well as concerned sailors, meet in Picton. Chaired by my buddy Pete Brady who remains skeptical of Bramwell's reported positions for *Rose-Noëlle*, the impromptu group has gathered extensive information about our vessel, her equipment and crew, and the weather. If we were where Bramwell reported us to be, we could have paddled the rest of the way to Tonga by now. And why did *Rose-Noëlle* sail 600 miles in the first four days and then sail only 360 miles in the following seven or eight days? The group develops four scenarios to describe what could have happened to us, including capsize. They suggest a new search area. They send a full report with the scenarios to the authorities and mail a formal request for a new search to their member of parliament.

Because the new search area is at similar latitudes to the old, the government declines any further expenditures on our behalf until new information comes to light.

Brady and the community won't let it go. Peter thinks that they might send up a private plane to search. Heather receives calls from people offering money. Rick's parents think about selling assets. In the end, however, no one really knows where to look. All anyone can do is wait.

It will be another three months before Jim Bramwell makes it clear that the positions he received could have been from vessels other than *Rose-Noëlle*.

About July 11, Day 38 Following Capsize

Rose-Noëlle pitches across choppy waters through yet another night. Rick lays against the dark windward side of the hull when he sounds the welcomed alarm, "It's raining. Starting to come down hard." It feels so good to hear the sound and broadcast the good news.

Again Phil and John are near the entrance and leap out with the plastic sheet while Rick and I organize our empty water bottles. We're ready and turn to crawl out. I lead. A wet foot smashes into my face. "Hey! Hey, what's going on?"

"Coming down!"

"Thanks for the warning, John!" He and Phil plunge back inside, drenched and shivering. We can still hear the rain pelting down on the hull. This time, our water collection routine is a complete and utter bust. Phil stood on the hull as before, but this time *Rose-Noëlle* slued and rocked in the rising seas. He held the sheet out, but the wind caught it and snapped it out of a hand. It was all he could do to keep hold of the sheet and the boat. John helped retrieve it and pull it out again, but the wind was still too much. The sheet was a billowing, flapping monster that pulled away from the two of them time and again. They were unable to collect even a spoonful of water.

We know that we must create a reliable water catchment system. John scours his mind for raw materials that can serve the purpose. In a valiant but vain effort to collect something, John takes a pan and puts it out in the cockpit. It fills with as much spray as rain.

Rick has long been keen to turn our raft into a sailboat. Why can't we rig a sail on that mast? He and Phil talk it over almost every day and now Phil also urges John to give it a go. It is the only hope Phil can find. If John will retrieve the sails from the outer hulls, we can rig them to our signal mast. Sounds good to me too. Why not?

John remains adamant. "This boat will *not* sail upside down," he says chuckling sarcastically as if we are all fools. He says we should concentrate on survival and wait to sight land or be sighted by a ship.

Rick points out that any boost, no matter how small, will push us more rapidly to wherever it is we are drifting. "You're so bloody one-eyed, John. Everything can only be your way." He stares in anger at John as if the very force of his will and his constant nagging will change Glennie's mind, but John just turns away, ignoring our ideas as if they are the idle whims of infantile minds.

Rick is right. What have we got to lose? Why is John so determined to resist? What's Glennie doing to promote our survival on which he says we should concentrate? He adamantly denies that we can catch fish. *I* think that John doesn't want to retrieve the sails because Rick's idea is a challenge to Glennie's omniscient command. We're overstepping our bounds. Each time we help ourselves to a piece of *Rose-Noëlle*, it is like carving a piece of Glennie's own flesh. Or maybe he's just enjoying himself too much out here. He's determined to prove himself and determined to carry on until fate delivers us ashore or to the hereafter.

How extreme will John get as this journey lengthens? The trimaran *Triton*, which capsized off the coast of California, was skippered by a Seventh Day Adventist so consumed by fanatic belief that he began throwing overboard the crew's food, water, anything that could help them help themselves. His refrain? If God wanted them to survive, God would save them. After it had been seventy-three-days adrift, rescuers found *Triton*. Her skipper was barely alive and died soon after. His brother lived, but his brother's pregnant wife did not. Did not God provide them with the tools to save themselves? How does one draw the line between faith and fanaticism? How does one determine when a man, especially a captain, should be followed and when he should be restrained?

John finally concedes to Rick and Phil's desires. He dives to explore the outer hulls and retrieves packs of gear, sails, and supplies with which to make a water catchment system. He emerges, telling us that the hatches on the outer hulls have been washed away. The sails and packs are gone, but other equipment remains. He retrieves a couple of buckets full of rags and epoxy and ties a line around a Honda generator that we haul aboard. The generator is probably useless, but if we can get it going, we might be able to charge the battery and revive the EPIRB. John is also able to fetch seven pieces of PVC conduit pipe about two inches in diameter and fifteen feet long. Finally, he passes us a few one- by four-inch strips of wood.

By the time he is through, John is completely spent and shivers for several hours. I do not think he can continue diving much longer. There is little left in the hulls to find anymore anyway.

As we stuff the pipe and wood into the centerboard slot and tie it down wherever we can, I glance through our access hole into the hull. Something is moving down there. I give a closer look and see a dim shadow slide out of the hull again. As we complete our tasks on deck Rick pipes up, "Hey, Jim, I think Phil was right. There *is* a fish down there."

About July 12, Day 39 Following Capsize

If it's possible, Phil has been more withdrawn than ever. Between our miniature meals and drink breaks, his mind seems to inhabit another world. Staring at the flat frigid sea or up at the ceiling, Phil appears oblivious about the necessities of our survival. He just doesn't seem to care.

Anything that is within reach of the water in the cabin is soon swept away. All of us use a heavy wool balaclava to ward off the cold on our heads during our watches. Phil drags it out of the cave and lets it fall. He drops a knife in the cabin. We urge him to retrieve it, but he ignores our rule: "You drop it, you fetch it." Phil's always poking around and, in the process, drops a screwdriver as well. When we first capsized, Phil retrieved a wreath of garlic. John asks where it is and Phil tells him in a bin forward. But did he tie it in? No. It too is gone. We all lose stuff, but Phil's attitude invites us to make him the target of our frustrations.

The rest of us still resent Phil's claustrophobia and the way he bounds for the entryway every time a large storm wave breaks. John still blames him for kicking the companionway doors out. Phil's prediction of our capsize and his current carelessness with gear begin to convince Rick that Phil is jinxed. He is our Jonah. He's diminishing our chances of getting out of here. We pounce, sucking from him any remnants of his self-confidence and hope, sending him spiraling ever deeper into depression.

When Rick and I discuss Phil, we talk about how he's eating *our* food and drinking *our* water. What good is he? We joke between ourselves that it's time to do Phil in. Even though we jest about offing him, I feel uneasy that discussing it might bring it one step closer to frightening reality. Rick tells Phil quite seriously, "You lose one more thing, you"e walking the plank, mate."

Phil snaps back, "Do that and I'll slit your throat."

Phil retrieves the two five-gallon plastic buckets from forward that contain epoxy, brushes, and rags. On deck, Rick is busy lashing together a gaff when he sees Phil yanking the buckets out the hatch. Rick wishes that Phil would just leave the buckets where they were. He's lost enough stuff already.

"Gives us that chord. I'm going to tie the buckets up," says Phil.

"No, Phil. I'm using it for my job. Go put the buckets back."

"Bloody hell!" says Phil. All he's doing is trying to help, but this is like living in a pit full of snakes. He's had enough. Phil flings a bucket back towards the hatch. It misses, bounces, and plunges into the sea. "You deal with them!"

There's a dead silence while Rick and Phil look at the bucket bobbing along beside the hull. "Go get it, Phil!" orders Rick.

Phil answers, "*You* go get it!"

At the sound of their commotion, I turn around and see the bucket and the two men ready to rip each other apart. They were born just one day and one decade, but worlds. apart. "Come on, Phil," I say, "Look, there's all kinds of things in there. We need that bucket. Please go get it." Phil turns his back on us and stomps away. Leaning his arms on the outer hull, Phil stares out over the endless table of the Pacific. The bucket floats slowly away.

John comes out and hears about the bucket. He too looks at it bobbing just a little ways from the boat. He says wistfully, "Ah, that was my lovely bucket." He turns to Phil. "Way to go, Gunga Din."

The wind is light and we amble onward. No one dives in to retrieve the bucket. We see it for two hours.

Late in the afternoon, Rick and I rest in the cave. We hear John and Phil talk above us. There is also the sound of the fishing reel going *bzzzzzz*, sending out a long silver spoon from the end or our rod—actually two thirds of a rod. Phil tells John that one never knows, one might catch a fish. *Bzzzzzz, plunk, bzzzzzz, plunk.* On the side of the hull comes a new noise, a continuous woody scrape. *"Shit! God damn it!"* It's Phil yet once again. *Bzzzzzz* is conspicuously absent.

In a few minutes Phil slithers in, lies on his back, and goes immediately on ceiling patrol. Nobody speaks for about a minute. Finally I say, "Phil, you didn't lose the fishing rod, did you?"

"Yeah, I sure did, mate," he softly confesses.

Both Rick and I lay into him. "Ah, fuck, Phil! God! How did you lose our only fishing rod? Don't you understand how important that was to us?"

Rick's even, dispassionate, direct voice terminates another short silence with, "Phil, I'm disgusted with you. I don't even want to look at you. Could you please leave? Do you understand what I'm saying?"

Phil nods his head. "Yes, I do." He rolls over and slithers out again.

About ten minutes later John appears in our den. We discuss Phil and how we have to do something about him. We have to do it before he loses any more essential gear. We have to get him back aboard. We have to do it now.

In the remnants of the day's light, nobody says anything while we eat our three spoonfuls of rice, some bits of beets, fingernail full of Vegemite yeast extract, dab of horseradish mustard, and quarter of a saltine, washing it down with a vial of water.

Finally, I broach the issue at hand. "Phil, I think we all want to talk with you. We've all discussed it and I think you know that you've been a liability to us. You keep losing things. Your mind seems somewhere else. We care about you as a person, Phil, and we want you back with us. We need you Phil, we do. We're tired of coming down on you, Phil. We don't want to come down on you. Something has to change."

As soon as I'm finished, Rick begins. He builds on the teamwork theme, almost Outward Bound stuff about how we have to rely on one another if we want to get out of here. He points out that we're depending on each other. "We can't depend on you, Phil, when you're away with the fairies all the time. We need you. After all, you're our heat source." Everybody chuckles. Even Phil cracks a little smile.

John takes his turn next. "Philip, you have to change. Look at that garlic. Think of what that cost us. We could have used that for months. Look, Philip, I don't want to be here anymore than you do. I want to get out of here. I want to go home. But, the point is, you just don't care. You're dragging the chain, Philip, and you just don't care."

Our sermons last a good ten or fifteen minutes each while our sole audience listens. His eyes dart around and his body fidgets. I worry. I feel so sorry for him. And how is he taking this? Are we destroying him? Well, there is no other way. We have nothing to lose. And for once I'm not slinking away from a confrontation.

When we are done, Phil begins to talk. His voice breaks as he tells us, "You guys are right. I know I've been losing things. I *do* care. I do want to get back to Karen and the kids. I'm going to try. I want to be back on the team."

July 13 and 14, Days 40 and 41 Following Capsize

Phil swallows his belches now instead of blurting them into our ears. He quits rubbing his toes against us. Even when he spends hours on ceiling patrol, it now seems that somebody is home. That wispy hair remains like a bunch of feathers tickling our faces, but he can't really control that. Phil is trying. He's really trying. Maybe more than any of us.

We work like slugs under the press of thirst and the first warm days in over a month. To build John's rain shield, we must cut each pipe in half and then lengthwise, so Rick and I begin the tedious hacksaw job. I saw for forty-five seconds before I have had enough. Rick takes a turn while I feed it to him over the cockpit hole. My turn again. Already? One—zip zip—two—zip zip. . . . The sun beats down. Our bodies have no water to sweat. We have no saliva to swallow. My muscles ache. In the heat my head sees only the hazy pipe. Fourteen—zzzip . . . zzzip, fifteen—zzziiip. I collapse. Only fifteen? Rick takes his turn. Hour upon hour we saw, slow, stop. As each pipe is done, we feed ourselves the next, but we feel like very old machines, worn out, in need of new motors. Lubrication—we need lubrication. My mind is in such a fog that I sometimes realize that I have been sawing into my finger. We think only about drink. A cold beer. Water. Anything liquid. I take the next section of pipe. It slips, a slight splash, and is gone. Shit!

In the meantime, Phil and John wage their own weary battle with wood to create Phil's inspiration: a gutter system. With a rusty saw they rip the wood strips in half at an angle to match the slope of the hull. They then plane them smooth.

After Rick and I have ripped all the PVC pipe, we take a hammer and a finishing nail and begin to punch holes. On each edge, at the top and middle of each section of pipe, we scratch an X and then tap the nail lightly to start the hole before finally whacking the nail through it. Rick holds while I tap or vice versa. Sometimes we hammer our fingers. Sometimes we glance the nail and it lifts off into space. Sinking at a rate of a foot a second, the nail will take about three and a half hours to join the piece of PVC on the bottom of the sea. I'm a little envious; at least it will be cool. I don't know how much longer we can keep this up, but we cannot afford to stop. We must be ready if it rains.

A round fuzzy orb is thrust into my face. It's Phil offering me a kiwifruit. I don't care where he got it. "Ah, thanks, Phil."

John and Phil have emerged from the hull bearing gifts. Lined up along the keel, we take an afternoon break, each of us grasping the luxury of an entire kiwifruit. I bite into my plump, full fruit and it bursts in my mouth. It's a sweet, succulent, rich, wet explosion. I wipe the juice from my chin and lick it off my hand. The still air is full of our orgiastic groans. It's as close as we've gotten to sex in some time. I did not know that heaven was green. But it must be. Green fields. The green of land. The green of kiwifruit.

Phil is clearly excited. "You should see all the stuff John and I found in a locker up forward! Stacks of biscuits! Whole trays of kiwifruit! We got boxes of tea, couple bags of instant coffee, and three half-kilo bags of milk powder." In our cave a garbage bag full of these new taste sensations awaits.

"Oh, my," adds John, "I found ten pounds of flour, Jim, and a bag of brown sugar, even a can of yeast!"

All right! Bread. If only we had some heat. "Do you think we could get the gas tanks out and rig up a stove, John?"

"Fat show. The regulator has been under water too long. We'd probably blow ourselves up. Then where'd we be?"

By our next afternoon break we have John's water collection shield and Phil's gutters completed. Rick and I have laced the piping together top and middle with thirty-pound-test monofilament fishing line. We created a wooden spine with two cross braces at top and middle, lashed the shield to it, and tied the entire contraption to the mast. The PVC tubing at the bottom remains loose, so we bundle it together and jam it into a bucket that hangs about a foot off the deck.   John and Phil have the strips of wood glued and screwed down. Two gutters begin at the foot of our mast and run aft, curving outward and down away from the boat's spine. One side ends at our cockpit. They drill a hole to terminate the gutter on the opposite side of the hull and push a piece of plastic tubing into it, which hangs within reach of the mouth of our cave. The sky remains clear, but we are ready.

We feel great. Together we have set a goal and achieved it. We haven't even thought about looking for a ship in two days. We fall into the solid, guiltless, untroubled sleep of men who have done an honest day's work. Our only real need is rain.

By about eleven o'clock at night the stars are eclipsed by cloud. At one it begins to mist. Until daybreak a light rain falls. We are all astonished when we see the results. In the pan in the cockpit under one gutter there's only a bit of water, but the bucket at the mast is almost two thirds full. "Crash hot!" says Rick. I feel like Scarlet O'Hara in *Gone With the Wind*, "As God is my witness, I'll never be thirsty again!" We nod our heads and smile when we look at one another. It's going to work. We are taking control of our destiny. If we can just begin to catch fish and have the good fortune to receive an occasional real rain, there is no question that we *can* survive.

Rick and Phil cram together in the cave entrance, their heads prodding into the hull and their butts jammed tight inside. "What's Harry doing now?" I ask them.

Phil traces Harry the Grouper's movements in a slow-swimming blow-by-blow. "He's over by the dinette . . . and . . . now he's heading f-o-r-ward. . . . Crikey Dick, he's a big bugger. N-o-w . . . h-e'-s . . . gone. Poked into a locker, I think." Typically, Harry makes his entrance, swims through his routine, and leaves within five minutes.

Rick has lashed our only large hook onto a stick. He and I have each tried to gaff Harry several times, bending over with an arm, elbow deep in the water, and taking slow clumsy sweeps, but the hook is set into the side of the handle so the gaff wiggles and sweeps slowly through the water at strange unpredictable trajectories. I can feel John's sardonic smile saying, *I told you so. You'll never catch fish out here.*

I swim through the cabin, gathering gear hammocks made of fishnet. Rick has completed a frame. We cut and stitch the fishnet to complete our landing net. When it's finished, John says, "Looks pretty good, but if you'd . . ." Now that it's done, John has better knots we should have tied, a more effective size, etcetera. Not that it matters because the open ocean is no place to catch fish.

As the packing under our bed shifts, we are compelled to rearrange it. I find my day pack among the soggy stuffing. When we settle again I anxiously spill its contents and find my Sony Walkman. I'm really excited. It still has the batteries in it.

Rick laughs, "You think that's going to work?"

"Well, it's waterproof, Rick."

"Don't count on it, mate." Sure enough, water *resistant* does not water*proof* mean. Okay, so what? What else have I got. Uumm, great! My passport. Never know how sticky immigration will be wherever we land. And here's some good old cash. Twenty-three bucks. Maybe I can bribe somebody for an extra half biscuit. Probably not. Half a biscuit would likely go for about a hundred bucks or more at auction. Well, here now. Four hundred Karl Maldens in American Express Traveler's checks. Don't leave your cave without them.

The only pragmatic item in the pack is my trusty old Buck knife in its leather sheath. Rick admires it. "Nice knife, mate." Rick hates hunting, hates anything to do with killing animals, so I'm somewhat surprised that he's so keen on this outdoorsman's knife. Then again, he hates fish. I've never seen him eat one before, yet he now stalks Harry. It is as if this voyage reaches back and pulls out of us a primordial part of ourselves that we cannot deny.

Perhaps the pack's greatest gifts to us are books: *Yeager, Bury My Heart At Wounded Knee,* and *Arctic Dreams.* Within these books we might disappear for a while, live within other peoples' skins, find how their lives might add to our own out here.

While I'm wondering how to spend my American Express checks, the July–August Bulletin of the *New Zealand Water Safety Journal* reports that the crew of *Rose Noëlle* has drowned in the vicinity of the Kermadec Islands in the Pacific Ocean.

Thunk! "Damn!" Yet once again Phil awakes from a dream or a daze, forgetting where he is and sitting up too quickly, cracking his hairless bean against the ceiling. We all do it now and then, but Phil whacks his head pretty much every day. He hits, gets a stupefied pink elephant look, and collapses again, rubbing his lump-covered pate. With his tattered clothes and wounded head, he looks like he's been in a barroom brawl. Phil scratches and picks at his scabbed noggin and goes back on ceiling patrol while the rest of us read.

Two fingers pluck up the corner of a sopping grayed page and carefully peel it off of the rest. Of the half dozen books we've rescued, John sails off into his ocean adventure sagas while Rick excitedly yammers, unfolding details of Chuck Yeager's memoirs of high speed and high flight. I bury myself at Wounded Knee as Native American cultures are massacred in the name of civilization. Each of us has our heroes.

I can get into Yeager. I have to admit his life is exciting. He came from nowhere, pushed across frontiers, knew how to ride and survive on the edge. John's sailing heros are a lot less interesting. Their voyages seem to be a string of feasts provided for them in each port, women hanging on their arm, the thrill of victory over wide waters, the agony only of putting up with their own ego. My heroes are of a different sort now. They are more like Native Americans who are suddenly caught in life's trying happenstances. They did not intentionally create the adventure in order to conquer it and grasp fame. Theirs was a tragic adventure. Real peril was thrust upon them. My ex-wife, reformed boozers and druggies— common people whom I know or might touch—these are my heroes now.

Rick doesn't understand me. "What are you talking about? Addicts have created their own problems."

Maybe. Yet, sometimes victims and even failures find the courage to face their flaws and yet go on playing life's uncertain game. To me they transcend the intrepid pulp heros of John's sailing books or the fearless celluloid images of Hollywood stars. Those who somehow find the strength to maintain their dignity and compassion, even in the throes of utter defeat, are the ones who soar to the frontiers of human space.

About Mid-July, A Month and A Half Following Capsize

Fine mist from breaking slop against the windward hull wafts across the boat. Sitting alone on the keel as if on a fence rail with my back to the wind, I lick the salt residue from my lips as I look out on the gray chop of our existence. I welcome the feeling of open space. No one rubs against me. No life story in my ear for the tenth time. No limit to my own space.

"Do you mind if I join you, mate?" asks Rick softly.

There's always room for Rick. We sit shoulder to shoulder and feel each other's warmth. We rest quietly for awhile.

"What are we *doing* out here?" he asks.

"Who knows?" I nudge him. "Maybe it's so John can make us famous in his book."

Rick does not laugh. "What a bunch of bullshit. It's Heather and Matthew that are important to me. And you know, they probably don't even know it. I never told them. I didn't even know it. All this other stuff about being the gun—who cares? I had to be the gun of motorcycles, the gun kayaker, the gun photographer. . . . Who cares? *Who bloody cares?*" he says, his arms spread and shaking at the heavens. "I don't even like bloody photography! I did it because I wanted my picture to be better than the next bloke's. *So what?*"

"It's okay to be good at things, Rick."

"Yeah, so people would like me, people would respect me. I had to make a name for myself. That's why I did everything. But what were people liking, Jim? What did they respect? It wasn't me. Just Heather, she always liked me for who I am. She loves me for who I am." He grimaces, looking away to the long empty horizon.

"Don't worry, Rick, we'll get out of here."

Rick nods, but looks no happier. "You know, Jim, I never talked about any of this stuff to anybody before. I never even *thought* about this stuff before. I feel good talking about these things." He puts his head in his hands. "Why here? Why now?"

He needs no answer and I have none to give. His doubts

give *me* answers. All along I've needed Rick, his reassurance, his impeccable logic. When it comes to the boat and the sea, I always know I can ask him anything, no matter how stupid, and he won't put me down. He doesn't intimidate, only accepts. And now I know that he feels the same about me. I actually have something to give him.

Rick turns to me and looks me right in the eye. "We need each other. Jim. That's the only way we're going to make it out of here. We have to be there for each other."

I grit my teeth and choke back my tears. Our hands lock together, our fingers gripping tight. Our arms shake with the energy of our pact. "Rick, I will always be here for you."

Chapter 7
Hall of Fame

"Oop! Harry's back!" declares Phil, ever on the watch for a possible snack.

Rick and I throw our plan into action. We shuffle positions, with Rick and I going toward the entry while John and Phil inch toward the dark side, we become a mangled sandwich of wriggling arms and legs. My eyes meet Phil's as our noses practically rub. "Oh, oh, excuse me, mate," says Phil as his body squirms past me.

Rick holds my legs as I grab our net and pivot to lay askew the plank on my stomach. Lashed to our signal mast on deck, the gaff awaits improvements. For now, maybe—hopefully—the net will be more successful. Even before I can get into position, Harry heads for the exit and drifts out *Rose-Noëlle*'s hatch. "Damn!"

"He'll be back. He'll be back. Take it easy," Rick reassures me. Sure enough, as soon as I get settled in position Harry emerges again. He swims a few feet into the cabin and stops. I dip the net ever so slowly behind him until my leading arm is submerged to the elbow. Rick's hold on my ankles keeps me from falling right on top of the fish.

Phil and Rick chatter away behind me.

"Come on, mate. Go for your life. That's lunch. Come on, Jim," urges Phil.

" Take your time, Jim. Think about what you're doing. Keep your eye on him," coos Rick.

Intense upon the big black shadow, I ignore them, bend, reach, "Rick, hold onto my ankles!" and scoop. I feel the weight immediately as I lift Harry. He feels like a sack of potatoes on the end of a twig. The water falls away from the net. "I've got him! I've got him!"

"He's got him, John! He's got him, John!" shouts Phil.

"Shit hot!" exclaims Rick. "Good on ya, mate!"

Harry seems quite at home in the net, which he fills. He looks even bigger out of the water. The lump of a fish doesn't move. As I crawl backward toward the cave and hold the net high, hoping he won't leap out, Harry just settles into his hammock. Maybe it's Miller Time. Should we offer him a beer? The others make way as I slink inside and pull the net in after me, which awakens Harry from his nap. As I set the net down on the head of the bed, he erupts into action. His bulging eyes look for the escape. "Oh!" says John, "It *is* a grouper." Yeah, a *big* grouper, a good twelve pounds. Harry goes berserk, jumping all over the place, flinging the net and whacking us with its handle.

Never to be put off by food fighting back, Phil leaps into action, throws his shirt across Harry and pins him down, reassuring the fish with "Calm down, Harry. Take it easy. You're going to be well taken care of now. Woah, woah, woah!" Harry bounces even Phil around until Phil sprawls across him. *"Oh, this is a big fish, John. Real big fish!"* There's not enough room in this boat for the five of us. Somebody has to go, and I'll give you just one guess who it's going to be.

In the writhing tangle of torsos, limbs, and fins, somehow Harry is clubbed into submission and we maneuver him over a plastic bag and cutting board. As I set to work, Rick snidely mutters, "Can't catch fish in the ocean."

I push the knife in and air rushes out. I slit down the belly, and Harry's guts fall out on our bed. I scoop the warm mass up in my hand, yank them free of the body, and toss them into a small plastic can. "We'll save these for later," I say.

"Save them for *later?*" Rick and Phil are incredulous—what do we want them for, a possible transplant?—but John and I know better.

Stuffed into Harry's stomach are a couple of partially digested herring with peeled skin and oozing gray eyes. John says, "Oh! Those will be good. Save those!"

"For sure. These will be great!" I say.

Phil retorts, "I'll pass on that, mate."

Rick is more concise. *"Yuck!* You eat that?" He has always turned up his nose even at cooked, choice fish fillets.

The knife verily whizzes as, leaning on one side, I futilely attempt to keep the blizzard of fish scales from falling on the plastic sack. They coagulate in puddles and tributaries of blood that sometimes stream off or flood over our bed. We pay no attention to it. My arms are sequined with scales. They glint off Phil's salt-and-pepper beard and bald head. They sparkle on the ceiling, cling to every nook of our world.

John finishes off Harry with an expert hand. Falling back on skills he learned cutting fish in a factory, he fillets and slices every tidbit of flesh from the ribs, spine, and minuscule depressions in the head. With a flick of his wrist, John's sword scoops out one of Harry's bulging eyes. He picks it up and holds it between two fingers. "Oh, my," he says, "there's a lot of fluid in these eyes. Want one, Jim?"

"Oh, my God, John!" scolds Phil.

John tosses the eye to me. Before I put it into the plastic bin for later, I pose like I'm going to pop it like a peanut at a baseball game in my mouth.

Rick looks mortified. "Ah, *yuck!*"

Our feast is a potpourri of cultures. At John's direction, he and I prepare poisson cru, bringing back memories of his glory years in Tahiti. Our international crew reclines like nobility from the Roman empire in our floating restaurant with the ultimate seaside location. We clutch European spoons. Each possesses his own shallow bowl created by the most contemporary plastics technology. All we need is candlelight.

Before us is our first real meal in months. Marinated in vinegar, one-inch cubes of sea-fresh grouper are topped with onion flakes, sprigs of dried parsley, a splash of coconut milk, and a pinch of lemon pepper.

We stare in near disbelief at our good fortune. Pride, joy, hope, and humility run through each of us. For the first time, we have provided our own food. There is more than we can eat. Harry will last at least four meals. Perhaps this is the beginning of a new stage of our voyage, a voyage that is slowly becoming self-sufficient, a voyage in which men are learning to nurture one another. We are thankful to whatever God or power in which each of us believes. We are awakened to the treasure that is a fish in the sea. The spontaneous silence before our meal is at once strange and completely natural.

Rick speaks first. "I think this is a good time to look at what's in front of us. We've caught our first food. Slowly we're coming together as a team. I think in order for us to make it, we have to do even better than this. But for now, let's be really thankful for what we have."

There is a short silence after Rick stops and then I say, "I really feel like somebody's looking out for us right now. Whatever that power may be, it's real and it's working and I'm real thankful for this meal. I think it's a good sign of things to come."

John adds his own words. "I just think this is wonderful. I think it's fantastic. We're finally sitting down as a crew together for a meal. We're having a good time. I hope we can continue to carry this on."

Phil looks a little uncomfortable but also seems anxious to say something. "Uh, thank you for this food in front of me. I know now that there are fish out here and that we have to keep catching them. Thanks, Jim." He pauses for a moment before he adds, "Amen. Let's eat."

In our own clumsy way, we have individually and together begun a ritual that will precede every meal for the rest of our voyage: We will appoint one of our ranks to say an official grace. As long as I live, I will never eat again without acknowledging my humble gratitude.

Grace serves to acknowledge powers on which we depend, powers greater even than the sea. Grace also serves as a forum. Before a meal, we can talk indirectly about what bothers us, without attacking our mates, with a small uncharacteristic measure of self-control. The rest of our lives are also touched by grace. We know now that we must live with one another. We still argue a lot. Who wouldn't crammed together like this? But now, even in stormy times when we're often ready to rip somebody's head off, within five minutes of a fight we find enough generosity within ourselves to apologize.

The July 22 edition of the *New Zealand Herald* carries a full page story about John Glennie and *Rose-Noëlle,* authored by John's friend Pat Hanning. Pat expresses some hope that we're still alive, but the piece reads like an obituary. Probable cause of death: Hitting a container, being run down by a ship, or being blown to smithereens by our gas tanks.

About the End of July, Eighth Week Following Capsize

Perhaps we have given thanks too soon. We haven't seen another fish for days. Harry is history and so are most of our other stores. John's new theory is that we will only be able to catch the rare fish that swims into the hull. Back on rations, each of us eats three spoonfuls of rice, canned beans, or corn on a typical day. I dress up our Liliputian meals with a pinch of this spice or a grating from one of the rogue apples that continue to mysteriously emerge from the deep and bob about the cabin. Rick, John, and I have all lost a good twenty to twenty-five pounds. Rick's eyes look strangely sunken and hollow. John began the voyage gaunt. His body looks like a skin bag wrapping a package of bones. Phil has lost the most weight—probably thirty-five pounds—but he has never looked better. He has not had any heart medicine to take, but never once has complained, nor has Rick had any asthma attacks.

Without fish to catch, we turn our attention to house-keeping. Again we rebuild our bed and discover lost treasures that have been buried under it. We find a whole head of cabbage pickled in seawater, a couple of apples, a tent groundsheet, Rick's sleeping bag, and my running shoes. I leave my shoes dangling from our mast and hang out the sleeping bag. Phil, Rick, and I lift cushions from the dinette seats and wring them out on deck while John rearranges the base of our bed. He shouts up the berth's dimensions. We slice the cushions to order. John fits the cushions on the platform and covers them with the groundsheet, the edges of which he pulls up high onto the sides of the hull and secures with screws. Now, water from below cannot surge up to soak us. John even leaves an extra tongue of groundsheet sticking out the entrance. On it, we can wash dishes, or we can pull it up in bad weather to ward off waves. With our nest suitably re-upholstered, we reenter to relish our newfound luxury.

Our bed is soft—like diving into a huge sponge. The ceiling is now two inches closer to our noses, but we don't care. It's the difference between resting on stony ground or a surface as soft as a baby's bum. The two-inch rise of foam, as well as the groundsheet, also make it harder for waves from the hull to flood the cave. Even when a now-rare breaker splashes in through the cave entrance, it tends to drain back out. We easily mop the plastic groundsheet, which dries quickly. Slowly the weather outside warms so there is no more condensation on the ceiling of the cave. We are dry. We are cushioned. Our bruises and sores will finally heel. We even have pillows from the dinette. John claims one. The other we trade around, along with Rick's life jacket and a heavy plastic fruit juice "bladder" that we can inflate. We can even use the valve on the bladder to adjust the hardness of the pillow to suit individual tastes.

If we can just keep collecting rain, if we can just find fish, if a ship will just stumble on us, we'll be okay.

Rick's sister believes in parapsychology. She visits clairvoyants near Auckland who see her brother still alive.

Place one cabbage finely chopped, one-third cup vinegar, a half-dozen peppercorns, and a dash of seawater into one of John's two-liter plastic screw-top victual containers. Fill to cover the cabbage with fresh water. Let sit. Grate four apples that are beginning to go brown into a similar container and add the same spices and liquid. In another four or five days, our diets ·will be enhanced with the new taste sensations of survival sauerkraut, or *kapousta,* and pickled apples.

When I finish making the *kapousta,* I crawl out and join John on deck. Under clear skies and a light breeze we drift along. I can provide variety and tasty spiced fare as I draw on *Rose-Noëlle's* stores on which we can rely for days or even weeks. Our nest has become well feathered, fairly dry, and secure. But I look over an open and starkly empty Pacific. My eyes follow rollers that jog past and scurry off into the distance for a half mile, a mile, two, or more until they are lost in the flat endless horizon. Perhaps our small joys are only teasing us. We may never get another real meal. We may never again rest in a lover's soft embrace. We may never reach shore.

John figures we're drifting a whole twelve to fifteen miles a day to the east. That puts us about a thousand miles east of New Zealand and getting farther away all the time. After two months we are probably only a fifth of the way to landfall in South America. And that does not account for the fact that the winds have been mostly from the south. They could be pushing us north, delaying our eastward progress on the ocean's current.

We are sure of nothing. My mates argue. One says the

breeze is from the south, another says from the west, and the third says from the east. "Well, what do you think, Jim?" they ask. Jesus, I'm looking to *them* for knowledge, and they can't even agree about the direction of the wind. "North. We've got the whole compass covered now, okay?"

The best-case scenario seems to be that we will be adrift for eight more months. The truth is, we have no idea where we are and we could drift for years, even decades.

From Lyttelton, New Zealand, in 1890 the eleven-hundred-ton, full-rigged ship *Marlborough* of Glasgow began her fifteenth return voyage to England, a trip that usually took her about 85 days. She carried thirty crew, one passenger, and a load of frozen mutton. Several captains reported that they found and boarded the *Marlborough* again off the coast of Chile, but not until 1913. Missing since her departure, encrusted with growth, her decks rotted, she remained under the command of seventeen skeletons for twenty-three years.

Subsequent research by a Mr. Forbes Eadie attacks one report published in the *San Francisco Examiner* in which a Captain G. Hadrup claimed that he found the *Marlborough* while commanding the ship *British Isles*. Hadrup's tale was full of false "facts" about the *Marlborough*, and the owners of the *British Isles* had never heard of Captain Hadrup. At this time, however, not all reported sightings of the *Marlborough* have been discredited. Even if the case is fiction, such a ghost voyage is rooted in fact.

Derelicts often have drifted across oceans before sinking,

grounding, or being salvaged. Toward the end of the last century, each year about twelve thousand people aboard two thousand ships were lost. About sixteen hundred wrecks remained afloat, were periodically sighted, and charted as dangers to shipping. Oceanographer Phil Richardson has used those sightings to put together a picture of the Atlantic Ocean's currents. Typically, vessels abandoned near the coast of the United States, and strong enough to survive the journey, voyaged to Europe in about ten months. The *Fannie E. Wolston* spent at least three years circumnavigating the entire Atlantic.

Our daily gourmet tidbit rations continue to dwindle and will eventually disappear. Our clothes are already tattered. Our cabin remains a can packed with the backsides of stewing human beef.

Beef? What *is* that smell? John too sniffs at the wind. We detect the unmistakable aroma of cooking food. Phil pokes his head out the cockpit. "You guys smell food?" he asks. It is the downwind fragrance of a cafeteria, a concoction of boiled dinner, fried potatoes, and roast meat.

"Could be a ship out there?" asks John. Our eyes search the horizon until they water, but we see only a starkly flat sea. The breeze soon eases the smell away. The ocean helps itself to, and carries off another serving of our limited allotment of hope.

We lurk in the cave like mourners in a tomb. We wish we had never smelled the food. John is reminded of a fried bread he enjoyed in Tahiti.

"Well, John," I say, "I could make fried bread. We've got the flour, yeast, some sugar, and oil. We have a pan and the barbecue," which is a grate-covered, stainless steel, round dish like a wok. "All we need is something to burn."

"We've got the oars to the dinghy," volunteers John.

The barbecue rests just outside the cave on the plank, safe from the breeze above. "This is going to be great," I say, leaning on my elbows in the entry. The smoke will rise neatly out the cockpit as I flip the bread back to my mates in the aft cabin and wash the pan right here. Smooth city. Just like Dunkin Doughnuts. I set a match to a crumpled bit of chart under the oar briquettes, and it begins to flame, but dies. I try the second match. A little flame. A little smoke. A little nothing.

Rick scolds me. "Come on, mate. That's two matches. We only have a hundred-thirty."

"Look, Rick, I'm doing the best I can. It's just not lighting."

Phil doesn't miss a beat. "Let's pour some kerosene on it and get the bloody thing lit. What do you think. John?"

John concurs. Rick objects. "We have to save the kerosene. The kerosene is to signal a ship." He begins one of his sermons. "You guys just aren't thinking. We don't have a spotlight anymore. The torch gives off bugger-all light. We don't have one flare—"

I cut him off. "Let's vote on it. I vote we use some of the kerosene." All but Rick throw up their hands. Case closed. Next case.

The fire takes hold, runs around the grill—great stuff—

grows, becomes a raging oil-well fire billowing thick rolls of kerosene smoke, *most* of which flows out the hatch. The rest fills the boat. Just as I envision *Rose-Noëlle* metamorphosing into a giant fire ball, the flame retreats and I begin tossing four-inch-long fat cigars of uncooked dough into a sea of sizzling oil. Thickening smog flows into the cave. My eyes sting, my throat aches.

Phil yanks up a corner of the groundsheet and buries his head down in the bilges. "Put the fire out! I got to get out of here! Move, Rick, I've got to get out of here!"

"I can't put the fire out, Phil, and you can't get by me. The fire is right here," I tell him. In less than a minute the neat cigar-shaped breads mutate into grease-dripping bubbled, twisted snakes. I choke, cough, drip sweat, and try to wipe the torment from my eyes with my arm. Phil gasps, "Get me some air. I don't have any air." I flip the first fried bread to Rick who tells Phil to shut up as Rick painstakingly divides it and passes it around.

Phil is suddenly at peace. "Mmm, not bad. This is good!"

Rick tries to roll perfectly regimented breads but cannot keep up. "Come on, Rick. Let's go so we can get out of here." Ten fried slugs at a shot. Ten minutes and I'm done. Spuming superheated steam rises with a curtain of smoke as I plunge the pan and grill into the water. We're out of here.

As we scramble outside, Phil grabs our last bottle of 7-Up, leaving only three bottles of other soda. Gagging, we line up on the keel, our eyes watering, our skin cherry red and feeling afire. One round of the soda bottle drains it. We pass the bowl of heaped breads around. They hurt our throats, but taste great. Success! The grill works. We can now actually cook once in a while. But lighting a fire below was the biggest bonehead move of our voyage. The boat could have ignited. Five more minutes of that smoke could easily have killed us.

Imagine it: In the year 2013, after twenty-four years adrift, the yacht *Rose-Noëlle* is found floating off the coast of Chile. Four skeletons rest in a tiny shelter in the boat, their hands jammed in their mouths. The world wonders what they died of. But John Glennie and his crew did set a new record and should be proud to be installed in the floating fools hall of fame.

End of July/Beginning of August,
Ninth Week Following Capsize

We've barely been out on deck for five days. The weather is total shit, windy, cold, wet. There is no hint of rain, however. Yet again our liquid stores run low. Rick and I split one biking bottle of water a day, John and Phil the other. It's about a half-liter apiece, the recommended minimum daily allowance for long-term survival.

The only reason we go up on deck is to take a piss and have a look around. If you're lucky, a ghoulie won't catch you. If you're not, every time you go up, two, three, even four watches in a row, ghoulies leaps on you while everyone else escapes. Everyone gets his sooner or later. Phil says, "Oh, Jim, it's your turn to roll the dice." He's anxious for me to be caught out, for *someone* to be caught out. His last four rolls have come up ghoulies every time. Everyone *else* got a good chuckle about that. "Good luck," Phil says to me with a smirk.

I leap to the cockpit and, as *Rose-Noëlle* lurches, rubberneck my head at the same time I roll down my biking pants, try to balance on my knees, begin to piss out the hatch, and process incoming information.

Deep in the valleys between waves, I see only the blotted gray sky, the long tumbling crest of the last rolling hill of water moving away, and the oncoming summit soaring up from behind. We rise, rise, rise—five, ten, fifteen feet. The wind buffets my ears, but I still hear the seething sea approaching with the ferocity and roar of an avalanche. *Rose-Noëlle* slews, skitters a bit on sea spew and effervescent foam. It feels as if she's floating in a raging wave of ginger ale. I view a whole world of turbulent sea for a split second before we plunge again.

Sometimes one can anticipate a ghoulie and hide. A dark shape emerges, a giant rising wall of Pacific roller. It rears up near the boat, smashes against the outer hull, spreads out its spectral wings, and smothers the boat. But ghoulies are usually more sordid and sneaky sorts. They commonly arise from the dark right beside the boat, as if solidifying out of a mist, and strike in complete silence. One has but a moment to drop one's jaw, mutter "Oh, shit," and hang on.

I look up at the sheet of cold water about to devour me, then close my eyes and hold my breath. Wham! To keep from being sluiced right out of the cockpit, I let go of myself, grab the boat, and try to stop urinating as buckets of raw sea fill my pants. At least Phil will be happy. From now on I'm pissing inside the hull.

"Coming down!" Conditions in the cave rest in stark contrast to the rugged outdoors. The crisp wind of winter is cut off at the entry and replaced inside with thick, stale, merely cool air. The rumble and crashing of waves and howling wind are eerily cut off.

Phil and John pump me for the details of outer space. "What's it like out there, Jim? Where's the wind from?"

"What do you think it's like? I don't know where the wind is from. God!" I reply while dripping all over the place. I feel like I'm trying to peel off a straight jacket within the smothering confines of our space. Rick helps me strip off my outer layers and wring them. My polypropylene long johns virtually drain themselves, so I keep them on and re-dress with the wrung-out wool.

"Didn't you take the compass with you?" asks John, referring to our radio direction finder. Since finding the little box with a compass like a turret stuck on top we try to keep track of our course and the wind. Since we discovered it reads differently inside the cave than out, we now try to take it out on our watches. Not that it matters. John does no obvious navigation. Maybe he keeps it all logged in that perfect brain of his.

"No, I didn't. I went out to take a leak, not to navigate."

We all still rack out on thin-foam camping pads to keep us off of the slick plastic groundsheet. John and Phil now share the blanket. Rick and I claim the sleeping bag. I squirm down and push my feet next to his in the tapered pocket of the bottom and rearrange the open, wide top over our shoulders. I am starkly aware we are separated from the raging sea only by a thin wall of plastic and each other's company.

The wind and breaking waves are drowned by a dull symphony of locker doors and hidden stores swaying and banging in the surging waters within *Rose-Noëlle's* hull—*gush-ding-thump-bump-claptack-thump-crack-slosh-ding-ting-glump-bumpbump.* . . . The noises create what we call audio mirages. Voices spring from our subconscious, lulling us into daydreams and slumber in which the clamor of our prison becomes background conversations, soft sweet singing, announcers on the radio, the beat of reggae.

I snuggle up to Rick's back. It is as comfortable, cozy, and natural as when I slept with my wife, but there are no pressures, no sexual games to play, no expectations. Our refuge beside one another is unconditional, therefore uninhibited. Sleeping beside Rick is the only real comfort I find aboard *Rose-Noëlle,* my tiny niche of nirvana. Never do we shuffle places with the others without remaining by each other's side. We rest our arms on one another, feel each other's contours and bones, are aware of each other's emaciation and need.

Our collection devices have trapped little in a few light rains. Just a few bottles of soda, a few of water, and a gallon or so in the bottom of the jug remain—a total of about three gallons of liquid or about six days of the recommended survival ration for four men. Phil discovers the shortage with surprising shock. "Bloody hell, mates. We have to start rationing this water."

"What are you talking about, Phil?" I argue. "You're the one who *always* wants water, *always* wants food. Where are you coming from, mate?"

Phil ignores me. "Aren't you guys thinking? We have to go back on the vial today!" The rest of us look at each other and shake our puzzled heads. One thing is for certain. We need rain. Soon we'll need it badly.

After three days of bad weather, our crew's spirits run from melancholy to John's sincere "Aren't we having fun today?" Rick, Phil, and I can't wait to get off of this barge and John talks about fun.

Rick snaps out like a cornered rattlesnake, rolling over to face John with predator's eyes. "No! I'm not having fun today. I hate being here. I don't want to be here. You got nothing going for you back on land, John, but *I* do. You really enjoy this, don't you? You really enjoy this." Rick lays back, still spewing, "Man, this guy's really two sandwiches short of a picnic."

John nonchalantly maintains his stare at the ceiling, giving Rick only an occasional casual glance. "No. I never said I enjoy this here, but we have to make the best of this, Rick. We have to make the best of it. You don't know how lucky you are. You think you'd be alive if you were out there in a life raft or a dinghy?" John gives one of those diabolical and sneering Jack Nicholson laughs, "Ha ha ha! You're warm here. You're dry. You don't know how lucky you got it. You've led a privileged life. You've never had it tough. You don't know what tough is."

Rick is fuming.

I say, "Hey, how about we take that lamp and make something warm to eat?"

During one of his dives, John found tucked into a locker a kerosene light missing only a wick. Rick immediately noted how much like a lamp wick is the strap from his life jacket. He snipped the strap off, trimmed it, jerked around with the lamp's adjustment knob, made the light functional.

Phil suddenly returns from ceiling patrol. "Hey, that's the best idea I've heard today."

"Wonderful. Lovely," says John. "That's just what we need right now."

"No," objects Rick. "We need to save that kerosene." He thinks we've used enough the last few times making custards and bullions.

Opposing views? We'll save five or six ounces to start a signal fire. That's enough. Another vote. Rick loses. Case closed.

Phil begins a small avalanche of goods from our larder. We pick out cream of chicken soup in a bulging can. So what? Let's use it. But then we argue about whether or not we should chance botulism from a blown can containing meat. I know that one should never *ever* touch food from a bloated can, but I still consider eating it.

We open it up, shake a vomitlike gelled blop into a bowl, and stare at it while making our closing arguments, our mouths salivating. John says it's not worth the risk. "We can't afford to get crook," he says. "We have to stay healthy." Phil is for eating it, of course, as is Rick. I just don't know. I surreptitiously slip the end of a finger into the soup and taste it. Not bad—carbonated fizzy stew. But John is right. Then again, it's probably okay. But John's right. But why would Rick promote eating it if it's so dangerous? But John's right. Damn. In the end we pitch the soup. We all stare in disappointed disbelief as the soup hits the water, dissipates into a cloud liberally garnished with cubed meat and vegetables.

We decide to try cooking a "custard," some advertising agency's abstract definition for a concoction of dried cornstarch and vanilla that I mix with cold water in a baked bean can. Rick holds the tin over the small uneven flame while I stir. The lamp wick falls into the kerosene and is snuffed. We retrieve it, trim it, relight it with another precious match. Again and again, the custard picks up a few calories before the wick falls. Forty-five minutes later, it's done. I smother dried Chinese noodles and vegetables from a soup mix with the custard and sprinkle the dehydrated spice and broth over the top.

Every one of us thinks it's great. We talk about the food, dissect each nuance of the bizarre concoction, appreciate the warmth of every single calorie. We share talk about our families, our friends, our homes.

About August 5 and 6,
Between Weeks 9 and 10 Following Capsize

It sounds so trite to say that the little things in life are really the big things, but a few-inch-long strap, a splash of kerosene, and cornstarch over dried noodles can transform our spirits. Water, food, friendship, time . . . things that I took for granted before this voyage now exert an awesome power over us. An apple bobs up from the depths and we grab it, worshiping such a glorious gift, wondering where it has been hiding, praying it will not be our last.

But it is.

Finally we are able to get out of the cabin. The seas have calmed, the ghoulies have vanished, but the skies remain covered in cloud, intensifying the cover of darkness. John shouts down to the cave, "Hey, there's a ship out here!"

We burst upon the scene and huddle on the hull in the ink-black night. A sparkle of white lights rests just above the sea straight off *Rose-Noëlle*'s bow and slowly moves into the face of the wind and waves.

"Let's signal her," urges Phil.

"You can," says John, "but it won't do any good."

Rick and Phil fetch the strobe, flick it on, and hold it up.

"How far away do you think it is, John?" I ask. I have no feeling for distance. The ship's even, slowly moving lights are totally unperturbed by the ocean that bounces us around. It is as if we are part of a movie full of special effects.

"Five to eight miles. Too far away to see us." John's mental gears are grinding, though. "Huh," he concludes, "Wonder what she's doing out here."

What's that supposed to mean?

We watch the lights fade into oblivion, our hearts racing although we know that she is going away.

Back in the cabin we discuss the ship, what kind it might be and where she should be going. John says, "Maybe we're not where we think we are. There's nothing out here. It wasn't a fishing boat. It was a freighter. It had to be going to the islands."

"Maybe it was going to South America. Maybe Antarctica," I offer.

"No, no, no," says John. "A ship just shouldn't be here."

From John's position tucked against the hull farthest from the entrance, the words "It's raining" enter my dreams. "It's coming down harder," says John as my eyes try to focus on something in the dark. "It's really coming down now."

Rick scoots out on his belly, filling the entrance while I pull down empty water bottles and begin handing them out in turn. Rick grabs the gutter tube and this time finds water is constantly streaming out. Rick hands a bottle back to me and I take a hit off of it--not briny at all and refreshingly cool. Phil takes a long slug. "Ah, that's good." John concurs. Let's run with it. Rick hands back another full bottle, filling it in only a couple minutes. John tells us to get a pan under the other gutter in the cockpit. Rick shoots out to do that job while I take over for him. I can't believe how well Phil's gutters work. And so convenient too. No going on deck; no getting wet. Water from the comfort of your own cave. Call 1-800-DRIP. MasterCard. Visa, or any passing ship accepted.

The rain tapers off and we have ten full bottles, which doesn't even include the pan in the cockpit or bucket at the mast. After an hour or so, the rain comes again. I untie the water jug from the end of the plank, drag it aft, and stick the gutter tube right into it, pulling the tube out occasionally and tasting the water to make sure it remains fresh.

By morning the rain has ended, the bucket at the mast is even two thirds full, and we are elated. It seems that every time we run low on water, we are blessed with rain. It is also clear that in fairly calm conditions, Phil's gutter system is even more effective than John's rain shield. From now on, our worries over water will evaporate as our hunger for food intensifies.

Chapter 8
Suspicion

By the First Week of August

When we began this journey, *Rose-Noëlle* contained enough food to feed four men for a few months. Two thirds of that was devoured by the Pacific. We didn't think of rationing until the EPIRB died, cutting our remaining stores to what four men would normally eat in just a few weeks, and we have a third to half of that left. We have now survived for over two months on less than two weeks' normal food rations, plus Harry, of course.

I wonder what all the debate and commotion about that ship really meant? Did it mean that we are not even making any headway to South America? Did it mean that this voyage of slow starvation might last ten years instead of ten months?

At times, as we shift around, we find a lone piece of rice resting between us. We dive for it. More than once, the winner snaps up a small white grain and pops it down his gullet before he realizes it is not rice at all. Often the tiny white pellets are merely bits of paper, soaked and then rolled tight by our bodies. We chow down on pieces of a book.

As we rearrange the sleeping pads, a tiny pale oval is revealed embedded in the foam. John and I spy it at the same time. We pause—it's a peanut!—and pounce. Our hands smash against one another, fumble for the nut, pry at each other's fingers. His hands are strong, very strong. I let go. John leans back and flicks the nut into his mouth. "Oh, lovely," he says.

At first I am on the verge of laughing. Who would have ever thought I would struggle for a peanut? But then I wonder just how far we will eventually go to secure nourishment for ourselves. How long will it take before a mere hand wrestle turns into a fight, and how much longer will it take before the fight turns into something more terminal?

We need to ration, but even more, we need to find food. The sea must give us food.

The annals of ocean survival are full of incredible tales of desperation. There are hopeful tales, such as when Captain Bligh was cast adrift by his mutinous crew of the *Bounty*. In an overcrowded boat with few stores and almost no navigational gear, he sailed thirty-six hundred miles in forty-seven days and led his eighteen men to safety. Only one died, killed by unfriendly natives. But such tales are the exception rather than the rule. Of the twenty-five men who mutinied, eight sailed to Pitcairn with seven Tahitians. After eighteen years, only one man remained alive on Pitcairn. Fighting over women, booze, and territory, twelve of the fifteen had killed one another. Perhaps that is the fate of men who have no competent leader.

Conditions in lifeboats were routinely horrific. Herman Melville listened to one captain's tale in a South Seas pub and from it created *Moby Dick*. In 1820 an eighty-five-foot sperm whale rammed and capsized the whaling ship *Essex*. The crew set off in three boats. One disappeared. Three months later the survivors reached safety. Six had died in one boat and only the captain and a boy remained in the other. Those who perished along the way were eaten. A cabin boy, selected by lottery, accepted his murder in order to feed his mates, calmly laying his head down, saying, "I like it as well as any other."

Cannibalism was so routine in cases of shipwreck that by the Eighteenth Century it was referred to as the "custom of the sea."

After *Mignonette* foundered in a storm in 1884, her crew drifted for a month before killing and eating an eighteen-yea-old boy whom they felt was close to death anyway. After rescue, they were tried for murder and two were condemned to death, but later pardoned. Their only crime was ignoring the protocol of a lottery. Even when the shortest straw was rigged, as long as the crew held a lottery, prosecution was unlikely.

The usual absence of females on survival voyages kept women from confronting their own dark side. After the *Francis Mary* was wrecked by a storm in 1825, however, as the crew died and the survivors ate the bodies, Ann Saunders was elected to carve and serve. After rescue, the captain told how Ms. Saunders was so bloodthirsty that she battled the crew for a double share of blood from the man who was her own fiancé.

The most extreme case of shipwreck terror occurred in 1816 and was made famous by Gerricault's painting *Raft of the Meduse.* After the *Meduse* grounded off Africa, the ship's boat containing the captain began towing a makeshift raft to shore, but then the tow line was cast off. Crowded on the raft were 147 people and too much wine. From the first night, as the raft drifted into the open Atlantic, an orgy of terror reigned. Officers were murdered and people cast into the sea. Although man can live about a month with no food, bodies were being butchered and consumed by the third day. Each night murder and cannibalism commanded the raft. When the survivors were rescued after thirteen days, only thirteen remained alive. No wonder it is an unlucky number.

What is most sad about such survival stories is that survivors probably mistook the symptoms of dehydration for those of starvation. They turned to human flesh routinely within weeks, often days. They drank salty blood and ate flesh, for which their bodies required even more water. Cannibalism might have killed as many as it saved. In 1765, when the crew of *Peggy* murdered their only black slave, one crewman tore out his liver and ate the entire thing raw. He died the next day. The captain, who refused to share the bounty, survived in no worse shape than the rest of the crew.

Even today no real law reigns over these realms to deter us from repulsive crimes. Who is to know what happened if only a few survive to share the same hideous deeds? And even if foul play is revealed, what can anyone do about it? When *William Brown* struck an iceberg, the captain took off in his own boat with ten healthy crew. He simply abandoned half of his sixty-five passengers and left forty-two crew and guests in the other boat. The mate warned the captain that they would have to lighten the load in the mate's overloaded boat for anyone to survive, and pleaded with the captain to take some people, but the captain refused and sailed off to safety. That night, the mate instructed a couple of his crew to begin to lighten ship. In all they cast sixteen people over the side and drowned them. In a tragic irony, the boat was picked up the very next day. Only the crewmen were taken to trial.

These are but a few examples of the harsh realities of survival at sea. And judge not lest you be judged. Who knows to what despicable things anyone may be driven? Who knows when the conditions of the body begin to control the conditions of the mind?

Following World War II, conscientious objectors volunteered to starve themselves in order to see what leaders might expect from the starving populations of devastated Europe. Dr. Ancel Keys at the University of Minnesota directed the study. The experiment first cut the subjects' food until they just maintained their body weight. Then that ration was cut in half for six months. They lost weight rapidly at first. Their entire waking existence, all their thoughts, became centered on food. The subjects automatically became lethargic as their bodies tried to conserve muscular energy. They also became increasingly concerned with themselves. They lost all interest in social activities and had no desire for sex or their girlfriends, who remained in close contact. According to Dr. Keys, "They became essentially isolated individuals in which their whole world was within themselves, and they had no other interest except to take care of that one person."

By the end of six months, after losing twenty-five percent of their body weight, the subjects of the Minnesota study almost stopped thinning. We aboard *Rose-Noëlle* have lost nearly the same portion of our weight. We too have no sexual interest and continually deepen our self-interest. Fortunately, our weight loss is not yet as bad as that suffered by most ocean survivors. Eddie Rickenbacher, famous World War I flying ace, went from 180 pounds to 126 after twenty-four days adrift; Robert Aros went from 155 to 115 in twenty-four days; a woman from the yacht *Spirit* went from 113 pounds to a mere 70 in twenty-two days. Weight loss of thirty percent is common among survivors. What changes must have been created in their minds? Who knows of what acts any of us are capable when we are hungry enough? Perhaps there is no such thing as evil. We may simply be driven to unspeakable acts by our physical as well as psychological addiction to self-preservation. I wonder just how desperate we will get on *Rose-Noëlle* and just how far we will be willing to go.

The government's search and rescue operation is over. *Rose-Noëlle* has nothing more to give us. From now on, we're on our own.

Days grow longer by early August. The peak of winter is past. We find ourselves on deck more often. No one dives anymore. Although the water is somewhat warmer, it remains too fatiguing. Besides, John has cleaned out the useful stores.

To maintain our life, we turn to menial tasks. We take care of how we sit and of how we rest to relieve the wear on our clothes, but still I must patch my pants with pieces of *Rose-Noëlle*'s curtains, using a paper clip as a needle and fishing line as thread. The arm of Phil's synthetic jacket hangs by a string, but Phil refuses to mend anything so I take care of it on behalf of us all. Rick lashes string through the buttonholes of the bear so that we can tie it shut. We routinely sharpen John's diving and paring knives, recheck the knots on the signal mast stays, and dry out our clothes. We tie lanyards onto our kitchen and other tools to prevent their loss. Each task is slow work as we watch, wait, and think of food. Each time I get up to take watch I think to myself, *This is going to be the one. This is the time I'll see a ship to take us out of here.*

Black dots on the submerged portions of the hull are now distinct little gooseneck barnacles, but they're still too small to amount to a meal. Once in a while in the morning or late afternoon, our eyes catch hold of a flash of greenish shadow, the outline of fins. Rick and I finish up the refinements to our gaff, attaching a lanyard through a hole we've carved and beaten through the handle. John has suggested its awkward performance might improve if we fasten the four-inch-long hook against the thin edge of the three-foot stick handle. Rick removes the hook

and lashes it into a new slot that we have carved. We test it. Perfect. Glides right along. But no fish come near.

We eat two meals a day. At breakfast we munch a few spoonfuls of dried rolled oats squirted with a cup of milk made from powder. For a real treat we split a kiwifruit every few days. In the late afternoon we have dinner. We slowly savor every morsel, a teaspoon each of *kapousta* and pickled apples, a few spoons of rice, or a tad of canned goods. A half-liter can of beans lasts a week. Hoping to be satiated, we look forward to the routine of breakfast and dinner, but even as we finish eating, we are ready to eat again. Meals and the warmth of Rick next to me when we sleep are the only good things in my life of which I can be sure, but they are not enough.

We think about almost nothing but food. Glorious meals come to our mind's eye. We cannot stop our dreams, nor do we want to. We bask in the glory of getting at least that close to food, but we fume when anyone else describes the banquet in his head. We just want to be left alone with our own thoughts. We often tell each other to shut up.

John keeps saying, "Isn't it a pity we don't have that garlic? Isn't it a pity we don't have that mutton ham anymore?" Isn't it a pity that the carrots floated away, that we don't have

any strawberries, that the cabbage is finished? Isn't it a pity, isn't it a pity?

"Yeah, John. It's a pity. It's a pity this boat isn't right side up too," says Rick, taking the piss out of John. What a pity.

I wonder how much longer we can go on like this. I wonder why we can't have just a little more. What the four of us decide to ration is sacred. The only thing that makes life tolerable is that there is always something to look forward to, the next microscopic meal, the next vial of water. I never even consider snitching an extra bite of beans or opening up a can, but there are things that conveniently fall outside the arbitrary confines of what I think is untouchable. When Rick and I find ourselves alone in the aft cabin, we dip into the milk powder. We say nothing about our transgression, think nothing of it. We only ooh and aah about the joy of the flavor—like cheese, like the moldy bits of blue cheese. While we are consciously convinced of our innocence, we unconsciously keep a lookout for John or Phil *coming down,* and make sure that the others' beard is wiped clean of powdery evidence. We are like addicts, unable to resist the fix. We are like kids sneaking around doing something naughty.

I am gaining a window into the demons of our souls. Our minds are twisted by fear, insecurity, egotism, the physiology of starvation, and endless rationalizations.

We convince ourselves that stealing to feed our little greed gives us a tiny bit of control in our uncontrolled world. It gives us a choice of action, whereas restraint denies any action at all. The act itself removes us from the situation. We free ourselves from the bonds of rationing and escape, if for a moment. I don't know if John and Phil also steal food. I guess I really don't care. All I know is that this is a special time for Rick and me.

At breakfast, he who is in charge of the milk teat squeezes it over each mate's bowl. None of us is guiltless of giving a subtle, moment longer squeeze over our own. I extend the squeeze for Rick and he for me. Such generosity toward a friend becomes another unconscious rationalization for self-interest—we are not helping ourselves; we are helping our friend.

Before meals, during our grace, while I lie in bed with my hand over my Saint Christopher's medal that I bought at some religious flea market, I say silent prayers. I have run from the Catholic rule book my whole life, but now I find myself dragging it out again and again. Maybe I need something steady to make sense out of the chaos. It is uncanny how, when we have needed rain, rain has come, how our bed fortunately rests a few inches above water, how we all just fit into it. . . . I do believe in a higher power. Maybe it is not a Catholic God. Maybe it is the power of friends, a universal spirit, the awesome unfathomable power of nature itself, but I feel it. And now Rick, too, talks about God.

I cannot argue with basic commandments. Call it what you will, "What goes around comes around" basically amounts to "Do unto others. . . ." Grabbing my Saint Christopher's medal is the same as grabbing a crystal or a book by Descartes, or for that matter, one on theoretical physics. Everybody needs some language, some system, some symbol on which to hang their cosmological hat.

I believe that good wins over evil. But my commandments are not inscribed on stone tablets. They are printed on rubber tires that stretch and twist to the demands of our rocky life. My heros remain noble in the face of horrible realities that are forced on them, but those horrors vary and so, too, does what seems noble or right. Some stand and fight; others submit. Some command; others cooperate. Where is the common thread? How do I know what is right and when it is right?

I calm myself with the notion that no matter what happens, the higher power forgives. It seems little comfort in the face of a commandment that seems so inescapably constant. Thou *shall* be honest. Thou shalt *not* steal. Our God, whatever it is, grants us gifts and I cheat. I ask forgiveness for taking milk powder. But I do not quit. In fact, the drive of my individual needs soon eclipses even my regard for my friend's.

Alone in the aft cabin, I take another spoon of snow when a sudden shadow is thrown across the entrance to the cave. I lick the spoon clean, roll up the powder bag, and tuck both away. Rick's feet, legs, body, crawl into our den. He turns to look at me, "What are you doing down here?"

I challenge his own motives while the dust of milk hangs on my beard. "I don't know, Rick. What are *you* doing down here?"

The seeds of suspicion are sown in the rich fields of our own guilt. Each of us aboard has reason to be suspicious. We know the others are stealing food. We know because we are stealing food.

Chapter 9
Where No Man Has Gone Before

About August 7, Day 65 Following Capsize

"Isn't this great? Out in the fresh air, the four of us together?"

What is John *talking* about? What is this, summer camp? Sometimes I wonder if he's even in the same solar system. Perhaps I'm floating with an entire crew of strange creatures from other planets. *This is the voyage of the seaship* Rose-Noëlle, *its endless mission to explore hostile seas, to seek bizarre perspectives and create an oddball civilization, to boldly float where no man has floated before.* Caught here in the confines of our ship, our personalities become amplified until each does seem alien. Yet somehow, as one day passes into the next and we inch ever onward through this endless ocean space, we create among us some kind of life.

Rick, Phil, and I are unwilling passengers on this mission. At first, from the security of shore, the idea of sailing to Tonga appealed to our need for adventure, but the adventure has become too real, too threatening, too hopeless. Glennie is clearly enjoying it. He has some insatiable need to have such a real adventure come to life. This is the crowning glory to his years of quasi-adventures. I do not know if he even considers death a possible result.

I have to admit, however, that death seems remote as I am awed by the dawn. It seems that every time we hit a low something comes along to lift us out of it—a boat, a rain cloud, a hot meal, the staggering beauty of this morning. We sit in a line on *Rose-Noëlle's* back. Her hull is glazed with the cold dew of night, which soaks the seat of our pants and soles of our socks. Sunlight edges above the clouds, awakening the lavender sea to a multitude of golden hues. A zephyr stirs the multicolored flags that festoon our rigging. The swaying cloths and our faces are alight and warmed by the sun as it breaks the chill of our sixty-fourth desperate night. Long, shallow, ruffled rollers amble across our world, reminding me of Minnesota ranges full of corn, soy, and wheat bending to a gentle wind's sweep, reminding me of home. A lone albatross begins as a tiny speck and grows, rising and falling to the contours of the Pacific, riding the air just a foot above the gentle hills and valleys. I wonder where he is going.

How I wish to be a bird, to have the choice to stay here or move away, to soar confidently with the raging storm winds of the Southern Ocean, or free to seek the shore, mates, and a nest. The peaceful setting before us so belies our troubles that it takes on a strange amplified power. We have come to have a sharpened appreciation for a piece of bread, the warmth of a friend, a scene of such beauty.

Our life here is not fun. It is, however, humbling.

Rick and I, alone in the cabin, fetch the bicycle bottle in which four tablespoons of dried oats have been soaking up half a liter of milk overnight. We spoon it into four bowls. We find a leaking tin of peaches so open it up. We crown each serving with a half slice of peach and an eighth of an apple. It does not even occur to us to help ourselves to a sliver of apple or a flake of oats. Such are the obscure and individual boundaries with which each man unconsciously defines his morality. The food stuffs of our regular communal meals are strictly taboo.

Before we are done, Phil's foot pokes Rick in the nose. He has come down early, overanxious as always. Rick bellows. Phil retreats. By the time we eat they've made up.

After breakfast, the dishes cleaned, we lay back for a moment before launching the daily routine. We first discuss the day's tasks. The fishnet seems too wobbly, so Rick and I decide to re-lash it. Secured to the mast is our Honda generator. If we can get it running again, we can power the spotlight or recharge the EPIRB. Phil and John volunteer to give it a go.

When we perch atop *Rose-Noëlle*, our eyes are about twelve feet above the sea and our visible horizon lies four miles away. Rising to the top of large waves extends our vision by a few miles, but lying in choppy wave troughs correspondingly reduces our visibility to near zero. In calm seas and perfect visibility, sharp eyes might catch sight of a large ship's funnels or bridge rising a hundred feet above the sea when she is ten to twelve miles off, but the watch would not likely sight the ship before her hull hove into view about eight miles away. Smaller craft, like fishing boats or yachts, wouldn't be visible until four to six miles off. When it's calm like this, that is.

Before we take to our tasks, Rick suggests that we change the watch system from hourly to every half hour. He doesn't want to miss any passing ship. I wouldn't know a ship funnel from a flying fish, and I sure as hell don't know if we can spend the energy required to keep a better watch, but Rick has his teeth into an idea so there's no stopping him.

"It takes an hour for a ship to get by us anyway," says John. "I think once an hour is fine."

"It does not, John. A ship comes and goes in twenty minutes."

John returns a snide guffaw. "Not in my experience. I remember when we were in the roaring forties—"

"Hell with the roaring forties, John. That was twenty years ago. Ships were slower then."

"They still take an hour to get from one horizon to the other."

Phil and I glance at each other with raised brows and rolling eyes. We want to stay out of it. It just takes too much energy to get involved. Besides, what do I know? Maybe John is right, maybe Rick is, but who cares?

Rick does. He snorts disgustedly at John's conclusion as if dismissing it out of hand. "Yeah, John, but even if you're right, which I doubt, in a half hour that slow ship will be already past us and headed away."

"Come on, you guys," interrupts Phil unwisely. "Rick, we're already having a hard enough time getting up on the hour."

"You guys just don't want to get out of here. I'm telling you what we have to do and you don't even listen."

That's certainly not fair to Phil who is the most conscientious of us all about keeping a lookout. John probably knows just how hopeless it is to signal any ship with a half-dead, flickering strobe that requires a good rap before working at all. Watches are a joke, good only for morale. They consist of one-time-only, beginning-of-the-hour, thirty-second look-arounds. Without our timepiece, we often miss going on watch altogether. Rick has the absurd idea of making the watches into something actually functional.

John usually ignores Rick, but this time his eyes too are fiery.

"You don't have to throw a wobbly every time you don't get your way. This isn't Outward Bound," he says coolly. "We're not a bunch of teenagers treating you like God Almighty. If you want to be a little Hitler, be one someplace else."

"Look, Rick, let it go. It's not important," I advise him.

"It is too important!" he insists. "We're talking about our lives here. We have to keep a good eye out for ships."

"Stop trying to be the captain," scolds John. "I'm the captain here."

Rick is taken aback both by John's assertion that Rick is trying to take over and by John's sudden claim of command. "I'm *not* trying to be the captain. And you're not the captain either. We're all equal partners here and it's in everybody's interest but yours to keep a better lookout and get out of here.

"Relax, Rick," I tell him. "Let go of it. You're like the last mosquito in a tent. You're just buzzing around bugging everyone."

Exasperated, Rick answers me. "John told us there weren't ships out here, but there *are* ships out here now. We saw one. Don't you understand that?"

I lean toward Rick, stare him straight in the eye, and slowly and deliberately tell him, "Shut up! Just shut the fuck up!"

Phil says to John, "What d'ya think, John, go up and work on the generator?"

"Sounds good to me, Philip."

For the record, on the average day, a slow vessel steaming at ten knots will take about an hour to run the course from our first sight of its superstructure until it passes our position and disappears in the opposite direction; but half of that time she'd be headed away and not looking toward us. A fast ship steaming at twenty knots will run the course in half that time, giving us only fifteen minutes to sight and signal her. Add rough seas, poor visibility, and any course that takes a vessel farther than a few miles from us, and any watch keeping schedule we'll actually use is challenged to capture the right ten minutes, be looking at just the right place at the right moment, and see a ship.

I hold the net as firmly as I can while Rick lays the line around it so tight and smooth that an artist with an air brush couldn't improve the picture of perfection.

He asks me, "What don't you like about me?"

"Well, wha-wha-what do you mean, 'What don't I like about you?' You're my friend. You're all I got on board here."

"That's not what I mean. That's not what I mean. What is it that people don't like about me sometimes?"

"Well, Rick," I say, stumbling awkwardly, confused about where he is going with this and somewhat afraid that if I tell him what I don't like about him, he'll tell me what he doesn't like about me. I can't afford to drive any stakes into cracks in our personalities. I can't afford to jeopardize our pact. But silence too will be a wedge.

"Jim, I trust you. I really trust you. I have to know what I need to do to become a better person. I need to know what my faults are. What do I do that irritates people so much?" he asks, grabbing my arm, making me look into his eyes. He really wants to know. Just like Rick. It's 110 percent energy, trying to attain the summit of virtue like it's a mountain to be analyzed and attacked, dragging me after him in the process. It's as if he's telling me to go ahead and dissect him so he can cure his disease, and never mind the anesthetic. I've wanted to tell some people what I don't like about them, but I've never had anybody *ask* me before. Oh, my God. I don't want him to cut me apart in return. "Jesus, Rick, give me a minute, will you?"

I've never seen Rick reach out like this. He's my friend, but even between friends it is a rare thing for someone to request such honesty. It is rarer yet for someone to welcome, demand, even beg for such honesty from a friend about their own weaknesses, to fling away their armor, to have so much trust. I have never felt closer to Rick, nor has he ever asked so much of me.

Rick closely watches my eyes as I tell him, "First off, Rick, this is really really hard to do. I really like you. . . ." I stumble on with other praise, grasping anything within my mind's view.

"Yeah, yeah, yeah, come on, what else?"

I pause. Oh, God. "But look, Rick, you were a policeman, an instructor at OB, you've had your own business. You've always been in charge, the leader, the person in control." I tell him how I hate the hypocrisy of OB instructors who preach cooperation and interdependence but then constantly fight for control among themselves. "Look, Rick, you're *not* in charge here. We all are. You remind me of John sometimes. You *do*. You think you're right and he thinks he's right. You both think your way is the only way. You're real abusive to John sometimes, Rick, you *are*. Why do you use so much energy constantly battling with the guy? Why?"

"I don't know. It's something to do, I guess." Quietly we return to the lashing.

"You know, Rick, sometimes I'm real abusive to John too and I don't like that. I'd like to stop it, or at least try to stop it."

"I'm going to try as hard as I can just to back off," Rick says, turning to me with sad but firm eyes. "Thanks, mate. I really appreciate this." I feel good, especially since it seems to be over and I have escaped intact. Then Rick says, "Is there anything else you can think of?"

I toss my head smiling. "No, Rick. If I come up with something I'll let you know." We both laugh.

Midmorning, with jobs finished or well under way, we retire to the cave for "tea," which means a cup of instant coffee for Rick and I and Milo chocolate drink for John and Phil who, like most Kiwis, hate any coffee stronger than tea. Like James Bond martinis, our heady drinks are shaken, not stirred, but ours are also milked out of bicycle bottles. Our bodies are so cleaned out that the caffeine is a real kick. Like our chess games, the coffee that Rick and I share provides us with a private space together on the boat, a sort of escape into our own little civilized niche in which we have polite chats about travels and French pastries while John and Phil typically talk about sails and sheets. Although conversation sometimes opens up among all four of us, we are divided by interests and our choice of drinks. They can have their sails and sheets and their Milo too, as long as Rick and I get our cup of mud. But Rick and I have oohed and ahed one too many times the last few days, so today John and Phil declare that they too want coffee. Damn.

"Okay, pass over your bottle." I spoon out the coffee. One for them, one for us, one for them, one for them, and . . . one for them. Rick puts his elbow into my ribs. "What are you doing?" he whispers, his worried voice masked by the slopping waves and banging furniture of the boat outside.

"Hey, trust me," I tell him out the side of my mouth. I finish off both bottles with a teaspoon of milk powder, fill them with water, and hand the loaded bottle of ultrablack speed to Phil who takes great delight in shaking it up.

Phil hands us one smashed up FullOFruit cookie that Rick and I split. I nibble on the edge of mine while Rick gobbles his up, concluding, "Exquisite. Amazing, the taste sensations you get from these things."

There is utter silence from the other side of the cabin. John finally asks Phil, "How's your coffee taste, Philip?"

"Well, I don't know what yours is like but mine is pretty bloody bitter. I don't know how you guys can stand it like this," he says to Rick and me.

"Ah," I say, "I love it. You Kiwis just don't appreciate a good cup of mud." I nudge Rick in the ribs and give him a nod.

"I'm going back to Milo tomorrow," concludes Phil. It is the last cup of coffee Phil or John will ever enjoy aboard *Rose-Noëlle.*

After tea, we go back to work. Rick and I crawl out on the plank and look up to watch Phil bent over the generator, which rests in the cockpit. He's fiddling with levers and wires, spraying LPS anti-corrosive lubricant all over the place, tightening this and unscrewing that. Must be the carburetor. A spring leaps out. It does a triple gainer with a half twist and—plunk—the tiny spiraled diver goes under and never returns. Phil continues to work away as if nothing happened. We tell him about the spring, of which he was totally unaware. Unperturbed he returns to torquing, unscrewing, spraying, hoping. Well, the generator probably never would work anyway. Someday, maybe Phil will find his niche. Everybody is born with some special capability in his bones. Fine work requiring total concentration and care just isn't Phil's. It's something we share.

Rick and I return to our net. Between the hulls the water boils. There must be ten fish thrashing the surface. I yank my socks off, pull up my elastic-cuffed pantlegs, and slide down the side of the hull. Rick hands me the net and I cautiously turn and bend down as if stalking some kind of prey in the woods. I tiptoe to the edge of the near bottomless rectangular pond between the hulls.

These fish are very different from Harry. They swirl around one another like high-speed dancers. I watch flashes of silver, white, and yellow. Until it is fully submerged, I dip the net slowly and then scoop with it as fast as I can toward a swimming form and yank it from the water. I have him! "I have him!" He hangs deeply secure in the net, maybe twenty inches and three pounds of sleek muscle ending in a lemon yellow tail that merges with a greenish silver back and white belly. I thrust the net toward John, who reaches in, grabs the fish under the gills, and quickly carries it off.

In no time John has transformed the aquatic dancer into boneless cubes of food. He breaks the spine with it's attached skeleton into several inch-long pieces. We throw all into vinegar and save the heart, liver, eyes, and stomach in a jar. We are all excited about the prospects for dinner, tonight and for nights to come.

This is no rogue fish. We still see the flashes of its companions as they dart in and out of the ponds and bays of water between the hulls amidships and at the bows. There must be fifteen or twenty of them and they do not appear in any hurry to leave. Where have they been? Why are they here? Why do they stay?

John says, "Maybe they're attracted by those barnacles." The gooseneck mollusks have grown to about the size of a thumbnail now. "You know what we are? We're a floating reef. We'll catch fish now. Fish are always going to be here now," John concludes as emphatically as he used to say, "You'll never catch fish in the open sea." And so it is that a twist of fate, a simple change in his experience, the dance of fish, has broken one man's view of immutable truth.

While our kingfish marinates, John and Phil nap and Rick and I relax in the dull gray light of the cabin that seems to reflect the overcast afternoon skies outside.

Various flotsam has bobbed about within the hull since our capsize. Chunks of *Rose-Noëlle*'s skin from the hatches we cut, empty bottles, pieces of cushion fabric, the Styrofoam top to a cheap cooler, all aimlessly wander on the currents and waves within the upside down cabin like miniature icebergs. We watch with passive interest these commercials for our own television show. They appear, drift off to lodge in a locker somewhere, reappear, disappear completely. I see a bright red rootless island. In a former life the plastic packet contained a rich blend of coffee that Rick brought aboard for us to enjoy once we arrived in Tonga. "Rick, you *have* checked to make sure there's no coffee in that thing, haven't you?"

"Yeah, mate. Long time ago, but I dunno, I just kind o' like to watch it floating around out there. It reminds me of drinking coffee with Heather by the fire."

I wish I hadn't brought it up. I wish I had such memories of special times with Martha, but she was always too busy.

Rick pulls his journal from its hiding place and opens it with the care of handling a priceless, ancient, religious manuscript. He begins to write. It is now a daily ritual. After criticizing John for so long about keeping a log, Rick eventually succumbed to the same need. He did not ask John—probably afraid John would point out his hypocrisy—but just quietly lifted one of John's notebooks and pens. Rick lies on his back with the book propped up on his knees. He protects his words behind a hand. At times I can see memories stir his body to sway or fidget. He pauses now and again and looks into space, a slight smile spreading across his face or tears welling in his eyes. I find myself peering over his shoulder, trying to grasp a small share of what he is writing, what he is feeling. He suddenly glances at me. "Oh, God, I'm really sorry, Rick. I don't mean to pry."

"No, no, no. No worries, mate. Would you like to read it?"

"Really?"

He hands me the open book. Across the pages, Rick's small, tight angular writing is punctuated by dates. He writes with a light touch and with slow care. There are no scribbles or scratched out words. I flip the book to the first page and read "Letters to

Heather." I feel like I'm violating sacred ground, a peeping Tom, but I am too curious to resist looking through this window into my friend's soul. Rick writes to Heather as if speaking, beginning with "Hi Hetty," reminiscing about their travels in Europe together, eating baguettes with cheese in France. He writes about how much he misses Mattie and how he will try to be a better father when he returns. He tells Heather about yesterday's evening meal as if jotting down a note from some hotel room. He tells Heather that he can't stand John Glennie. He does not want to be like John. He tells her that he is becoming aware of things within himself that he never saw before. He tells her of his selfishness. He tells her he wants to prove that he can be more sensitive to her needs, that she and Mattie are the most important things in the world. His words read like a confession. He never writes of fear or of death, but "Letters to Heather" are an epitaph, the only legacy he has to leave from this dark and dismal place.

I envy Rick. I wish I had a Heather to whom I might also confess such feelings. I wish I felt this way toward Martha. I wish I had fond memories of experiences shared. But the one time Martha made time in which we could create such memories, I decided to sail with the guys to Tonga. Not that it would matter. Rick's words make me painfully aware that I do not feel this way toward Martha. I want to, desperately at times, but I know I will never feel this way about her. I care for her, but that is not enough. Yet, as Rick probes himself and lets me look into his depths, I realize that I do care about someone. I am lucky. I am not alone here. I have a friend.

"Thanks Rick." I hand him his book and turn my mind to other things. I pick up Barry Lopez's *Arctic Dreams* and allow him to take me into another world. As I reread chapters again and again, Lopez brings the landscape alive. I become an Eskimo. On the ice, I wait by a seal hole for hours or even days. I come to know the details of my marginal environment. I learn which furs are lightest and warmest, which resist abrasion best, which are the most waterproof, and which shed ice. I combine them to create intricate clothing unsurpassed by modern, synthetic expedition garb. Musk ox horn is more flexible than caribou antler, so I have fashioned the ox horn into the barbs on my fish spear. Bearded seal intestine stretches across the window of my snow house because it is translucent, simple to rollup for traveling and frost free. The animals of this place keep me alive and I honor them for their gifts to me.

How I envy the Eskimo's skill, their knowledge and ability not just to survive but to thrive in such a seemingly barren land. How I admire their humility. Lopez awakens me to the potential of my own hostile world, that we, too, might find our place in it if only we can become sensitive enough to its possibilities. How I wish to be with such men as the Eskimo. How I hope that we can create a world here of such men.

Several hours before dark we switch places. Phil crawls out to take a look around while the rest of us shuffle so I can get at the larder and prepare dinner. Tonight's fare is simple: a half dozen one-inch cubes of marinated kingfish with a touch of lemon pepper and shards of dehydrated onion, a spoon each of *kapousta* and Wattie's baked beans on the side, and daubs of horseradish mustard and Vegemite as garnish. We argue a bit over the small spoon. Everybody wants it. It seems to make the food last longer. Who got it last anyway? Whose turn is it for the small spoon? This is followed by minor bickering about the portions. When it comes to dividing up the food we want justice to prevail. Each of us is a big believer in justice as long as we are the one who are getting more than anyone else. "Oy, mate, kind a light on the old *kapousta* here." Okay, so I give him another dab. Finally grace. Escape into the food.

Because I do the cooking, cleanup after dinner is usually somebody else's burden. That done, we pause for an hour or so of cogitative drifting. I ruminate on the day's highlights, speculate about fishing tomorrow. Rick's sharp elbow jabs me in the ribs and I almost lash out, but pause as I observe how Rick's bones are beginning to protrude. My anger turns to compassion for him and sorrow for us all.

Thoughts that flow through my head soon return to my recurring fantasy. It is just another typical day aboard *Rose-Noëlle* when we see a Japanese fishing boat hauling nets. Our craft drift together like lovers running toward each other across a field of daisies with arms outstretched, slow motion, of course. Cranes on the fishing boat lift *Rose-Noëlle* aboard. We understand no Japanese and they no English, but they pat us on our backs and shake our hands and we bow to them with tears in our eyes. The fishermen lead us to their dining saloon where we ladle down bowl after bowl of steaming rice and wonton soup, and bulldoze platefulls of sushi and other delights down our gullets. We eat from simple white cups and saucers. I sign to the men that I know how to cook and they take me to the galley. Their chef nods and smiles at my intentions. Several men whiz around chopping and tossing food from steaming sizzling woks. I knew we'd get rescued. I knew it. The cook directs me to a steel door with one of those wheels in the middle. The door is three feet high. He spins the wheel, swings back the door on creaking hinges, and points inside to heaped bags.

"Rice," he says. I bend down to enter when the Japanese boat lurches on a wave and I stand up too quickly.

Crack! "Ow!" Phil laughs. Serves me right for laughing at him all those times when he hit his head on the ceiling, I suppose. I hate waking up from dreams.

I might as well get out and take a leak. In the world above, conditions have changed little since morning. The sun has done its day's work and now beds down on the western horizon. It is uniquely alone, a scalding orange ball in a cloudless sky setting the ripples of the sea ablaze. I am compelled to watch even as my eyes water. As the sun sinks, the colors of our flags and *Rose-Noëlle*'s golden makeup fade. On the water, not far from the boat rests an albatross.

There are still no ships in sight.

I hear John behind me. For so long I blamed him for our predicament. Wanting to hate him, I am ironically beginning to feel fond of him. I appreciate his knowledge and skills, his dives to supply us with food that have helped keep us alive. I am coming to admire, even envy, how John accepts life on this heartless ocean. In many ways, of us all, John is most like the Eskimo. And the more I respect and show friendship to John, so he shares more in return. Together we devour the beauty of our surrounds. "Isn't this magnificent?" he says. There is no question about that. There is also no question that I want to escape. I am willing to lose all this, but I also feel for John Glennie. I almost wish that I could see this world through his eyes.

For a moment, I can. "Yes, John, it is magnificent."

John begins to sing a Polynesian love song. His voice is rich and mellow.

In Minneapolis, my sister Cathy writes another letter to a senator, imploring him to lend aid to New Zealand in order to conduct another search for *Rose-Noëlle*. She and my friend Joe bug local papers to keep us in the news, hound politicians, call Heather. Is there any news of us? Still nothing. Before going to bed Cathy steps outside her house. She gazes up to the heavens as she has each day for a month and a half. She feels that, somewhere, I am looking at the same sky.

"Comin' down!" John and I crawl back to our cave. "You missed a good sunset, Rick," I say.

"There's no such thing as a good sunset out here, mate."

I feel enlightened by nature's wonder at the beginning and end of each day, am thankful for the gift, especially since so much has been stolen from us. It is something. We have made it through another day. The sun's rise and fall give me the opportunity to dream. But Rick resents sunrises and sunsets. He feels he will tempt fate if he allows himself to feel that little bit of pleasure. If he enjoys these wonders, it might prolong our journey. Resisting the few charms that are granted us, hating them, is Rick's only way to fight back, his only control over his own destiny.

Before dark, we open a brief and shallow debate about whose turn it is for the first and last watches, and we use the term very loosely. Everybody wants the first or last. The first one allows you to get it over with immediately and fall into four hours of uninterrupted sleep; the last allows a four-hour snooze up front. The middle ones break up dreamland. Who did the final leg of last night's last watch anyway? Whose turn is it for the first one?

We are all tired of the redundancy of our daily tasks, but we are also coming to accept the reality of our surrounds. When Phil begins to turn, we all flip in unison without any warning word. We say less and more often move as one.

It is the end of a typical day aboard *Rose-Noëlle*. We float on, facing as many unknowns as found in distant galaxies. We ride the turbulent seas of this watery wilderness and our own emotions. We have seen beauty and missed the beauty we left ashore. We have argued, struggled, played jokes on one another, and come together. We have survived another circuit of the sun. In myself, I envy the love that awaits my friend ashore. Again he showed me trust and his need for me, equal apparently to my own for him. He showed me his fear, let me glimpse private words that prove his love, in case his body cannot. He has given me something for which to be grateful. I have lapsed into dreams and had dreams shattered by awakening to this reality.

Today we have also recovered hope and confidence in a dream come true. It is a dream that is less cerebral. It is as concrete and essential as the Eskimo's seal. For us it is the dream of fish. Perhaps, they will stay. If we are men enough, we will learn how to use each other as the Eskimo uses different furs. If we are men enough, we will learn when to use that which is strong in ourselves and when to use that which is supple, when to use that which is warm and when to use that which does not frost. Otherwise, we will perish in this place of austere and unforgiving beauty.

Chapter 10
Blow Me Away

About August 8, Week 10 Following Capsize

Phil picks at a tangle of net just forward of the mast. John's casting net would normally stretch out to about fifteen by five feet, but the sea has transformed it into a matted mass about the size of a small backpack. Phil grunts and swears at it as, hour after hour, he untangles an inch at a time and spreads the freed lace out on the hull.

Rick leans over the landing net, redoing a lashing once again to urge it one step closer to perfection. The creases in his hands that grasp the eighth-inch twine are white with tension. If the intensity of his stare could generate energy, it would fuse the line together.

I cut off two thirds of the remaining piece of PVC tubing, pound two nail holes through one end, and secure a five-foot piece of the lashing twine through the holes. Scooting across the keel, I slip into the cockpit and fetch the small, rusted tackle box, taking great care not to drop it. Like opening a jack-in-the-box, a tangle of gear springs out at me. Rusted hooks, nuts, bolts, split shots, swivels, and a few lures rest in bins or cling to an exploding nest of monofilament of various sizes. I unthread a couple feet of the translucent line and tie a swivel onto the end. I choose a four-inch-long lure that looks like a flattened silver icicle.

"Mind if I try the gaff?" asks John to no one in particular.

"Go right ahead," I tell him. As he turns away with the gaff, Rick and I roll our eyes and shake our heads at one another. Yeah, go ahead John. Go take that gaff that Rick and I made, the gaff that has "the hook in the wrong place," the handle that is "too short," and the lashings that "are not quite right," and go out there and catch some of those uncatchable fish that you swore would never be out here.

We all watch John make his way out along the forward beam where he puts an arm on the outer hull. He peers down into the water hole between the bows and waits. After several minutes, John suddenly yanks the gaff—strike one. Another few minutes and another yank—strike two. Again—strike three. *You're out o' there!* I think to myself. I turn back to my work as if returning to the locker room to prepare for the next game.

A brief splash. "Ha, ha!" We look up to find John holding the gaff up chest high, its point neatly through the back of a six- or seven-pound yellowfin kingfish that looks more startled than we. "Just where I was aiming," concludes John.

"Atta go, John!" I shout excitedly. Fans are always so fickle.

About August 10 to 12,
End of 10th Week Following Capsize

The Bear is finally dry. Phil slips on his quite shrunken sheepskin coat that almost fits him now that he's lost about thirty pounds. With the remaining midships button straining but secured, Phil's more ample curves and our usual view of him are altered. His wispy hair blowing in the wind, his salt-and-pepper beard, bronzed face, and corseted upright dignity make Phil look quite regal. Grabbing the gaff, Phil becomes our Kiwi Ben Cartwright (the iconic rancher from the long-time television series *Bonanza*), heading out to the same rich hunting grounds as John, looking to bring home the bacon from the open ocean range.

With the promise of fish, Phil keeps a steady calm stance for hours, lying in wait as long as necessary until they come. When they do, he strikes. Phil has a knack for the gaff. Maybe he has found his niche. Over the last two days, he's stuck a half dozen fish. Unfortunately, every fish has wiggled, flopped, and slipped away to freedom. He may strike one easily, but it seems to send a signal to the others and they all disappear, sometimes for the rest of the day. Phil is getting frustrated, but he keeps at it.

Another day, another hope for deliverance. We are all worn down from this voyage. We move slowly without much enthusiasm for anything except topping up our tanks with food and drink.

Phil strips for a bath, but then sees the flash of fins. Phil spells relief F-O-O-D, so he grabs the gaff, which he calls "the wand," and stalks fish like an Indian in the buff. Rick follows with the net.

Phil snags a fish and yanks it out of the water so fast that it flies off the end of the gaff and lands with a thud on the wing deck sidewalk. Rick swings the net at it but misses. Phil leaps onto the flailing fish, wraps his arms around, and hugs it against his chest. The fish's eyes seem to bug out, like some poor child attacked by an overamorous grandparent. It squirms and thrashes against Phil's pink bypass scar and then squirts out and shoots into the air past his nose. Again it crashes down on the deck and again Phil scrambles after, plucks it up, squeezes and launches it like a bar of soap.

From our perch in *Rose-Noëlle*'s bleachers, we cheer the wrestling match and our hero.

"Go get him, Phil!"

"Come on, Phil, he's getting away!"

"Atta boy, Gunga Din!"

On reentry from space, the fish slaps against the hull, slides onto the wing deck, and appears dazed. On hands and knees, Phil scrambles toward his fumble. The fish whips and slithers sideways, backing away, its eyes round with fear of the pursuing Phil-beast with its mottled brown and milky pink hide, its mangy long white fur, its homemade tattoo called Karen, its pale pinched bum wiggling in the air, and those enraged hungry eyes. Phil's hands close on the fish again and the fish shoots out. Its tail so frantically motors that it ricochets off the surface of the water, hops up, and skitters sideways like a porpoise for what seems like a good five seconds before falling into the sea.

Since leaving New Zealand, we have not laughed aloud together, but Phil's frenzied naked chase and fishy embrace is hilarious. Phil says only "Crikey, Dick! Almost had the bugger."

John says, "Nice try, Gunga Din."

Rick says, "Now *that* was a photo for our calendar."

For once we all find reason to laugh.

As I rest below, Rick takes his turn performing the rite of the great white hunter. Kingfish swarm in the pool between the hulls, thrashing the water. Rick dips his net, sweeps it through the tangle of fish, and pulls it out. The net sags with weight, strains, pops. Rick and Phil grab the net frame before it falls and whoop so loud I can hear them below. I think that maybe it's a ship, so I shoot out of the cabin. "What's going on out here?" I ask, squinting against the light as I edge my head up above the cockpit and look down to Rick's back. He turns to me, holding the net. Hanging there are four small kingfish, a good twelve pounds all together.

"They were swarming. I got them all in one hit," Rick tells me.

"Right," I reply.

I scale and gut while John fillets. The gut jar contains a healthy collection of livers, hearts, and eyes. The remaining organs are too unpalatable even for John and me, so I toss them and the fish heads into a bucket to save as bait. An albatross has been circling the boat all morning and now lands to rest on the water nearby. I toss a bit of stomach and intestines toward the bird. It paddles toward the offal in haste and attacks it with gusto. I test the bird with the next load of guts and it lunges toward them. John and I look at each other. "What do you think a seabird tastes like, John?"

Another meal and another mound of marinated fish cubes. Voting to decide on the size of our feast, we settle on ten pieces per man from our ample stock. We might then afford seconds. We will even treat ourselves to dessert.

Phil retrieves a quarter package of fruit-filled biscuits, but they're a mass of waterlogged salty pulp. We decide they're destined for the burley box instead of for dinner. Normally, burley is ground fish bait. Our burley box is a shoe-box–sized plastic bin that's wedged into the drawer slot at the end of the plank. Into it we have long pitched inedible food like saturated cocoa, old spaghetti noodles, smashed drowned biscuits, and the like. Our intention has always been to save this compost to attract fish, but each of us eyes it more and more, hoping we will not get desperate enough to seek the burley as food for ourselves.

Instead of biscuits for dessert, I make dough balls. With a drinking glass as a rolling pin, I roll out a bread dough on a board, strip it up, and spread jam on each strip. Roll'em up and they're done. Rick calls them "little danishes." To accompany the main course, sometimes I make "savory dough balls" filled with Vegemite, mustard, or both.

Next I instruct my faithful assistant—Rick today—to fetch the chile and garlic bottles. To the dregs of a bottle of Thai hot chile sauce, I have added water. For his trip back to the islands, John's sister stuffed a canning jar with garlic cloves drowned in water. I mix a tablespoon of garlic water and four of its cloves with a touch of chile sauce. Each time we use some of these condiments, we top up the bottles with water again, and as time goes on, we'll drop dried chilies that we've discovered into the Thai sauce bottle. As diluted as the garlic and chile bottles become, they always retain some flavor. Still, I need a little something else. "Hand me the Chinese barbecue sauce," an eight-ounce bottle of thick, black, tarry stuff. A teaspoon of that is enough. Phil happily divvies up the fish into bowls and I measure out the sauce and crown each ration with onion flakes.

John hands me the piece de resistance: the gut jar. "Guts anyone?" I ask.

Phil and Rick give me a "What are you nuts?" look while John is as keen as a panting dog. "A spoonful?" John nods his assent.

"Well, maybe Rick and I should get an extra share of the fish since you guys are helping yourself to the guts," suggests Phil.

"Helping ourselves? Hey, Phil, our guts are your guts. Help yourself."

Phil looks down at a big round eye staring up at him. "Oh, I can't stomach that."

"Well, that's too bad, Phil." I'm glad he doesn't want any. Organs are our best-kept secret treat. They are full of strong, rich, meaty, pungent flavors. The heart is a rare micro-fillet minon. The liver is a sweet paté. The eyes are nearly tasteless compared to the rest, bursting in the mouth like a subtly flavored nugget of cold bouillabaisse. I can't believe these guys won't at least give this stuff a try, but I am as happy as a frugal parent whose children refuse to taste lobster.

In the evening, I crawl out to take my watch. As I pump my bilges over the side, my eyes awaken and I look down. The cockpit is awash in a dim lime light. My heart jumps. What the hell is that? Some beast, some alien intruder has landed on *Rose-Noëlle* and is about to make me into a meal. Carefully I bend toward the source. It lives in the bucket. I slide the bucket slowly towards me, edge my nose over the top. My God! Look at this!

Our fish guts in the bucket are alive with bioluminescence. Funny how I could have been startled by this natural wonder, but maybe natural wonders are what startle us most.

The ocean is full of creatures that produce light without heat. Like fireflies, they release one chemical to mix with a compound and induce a flash, and then another chemical to stop the reaction. Plankton and squid commonly glow when disturbed. They display a natural technology on which chemical light sticks are fashioned. Sailing at night through clouds of sparkling plankton makes one feel as if one rides through a sea of stars.

I'd like to see the faces of a ship's crew if we flagged them down some night with a signal of fish guts.

About 15 August, Eleventh Week Following Capsize

After the feast, famine. For days our brave men have hunted and returned empty handed. Phil remains the undisputed king of the wand, but he just can't hang onto them. Rick has rebuilt his net and dubs it "Cortez the Killer," but when he sweeps Cortez at the occasional fish, he catches only water. He is so intense, so driven, yet so frustrated and fatigued that he often loses his balance and falls on the slippery decks. It does not occur to him to wait behind Phil to land what the gaff snags. The lure dangling from our PVC rod attracts the odd kingfish, but they either screech to a halt and wheel away or teasingly tug on the end and spit it out. It is as if we compete with one another to see who will provide the next catch, to define who is the most essential among us. We are entrenched in the idea that only competition brings out the best in us.

Competition is king, and a very stingy king at that. He's starving us to death.

The only positive development is that the kingfish are constant companions now. They are the only species we see. In the morning and near dusk they play about the surface and nip at the gooseneck barnacles that hang from *Rose-Noëlle*'s aging carcass. During the day, we sometimes peer into the vivid blue ocean to watch the fish, twenty or thirty feet deep, cavorting with one another. Occasionally, one emerges for a second and is gone again. We try to take them prisoner, but fail. Try and fail. They are *our* jail keepers. Their speed, their agility, their freedom eludes and tortures us.

We become despondent. Maybe we were lucky at first and our luck bred vanity and overconfidence. The fish learned quickly about the monsters who lurk above the waves. Now they are wary. Maybe we will catch no more.

Rick's marvelous catch is gone. In the final meal, we eyeballed each chunk with the greatest intensity. We bickered. Which pieces were largest and who got which. It's as certain as tomorrow's sunrise that our stores will soon all be gone. With no fish to supplement our meals, we will turn to eating the condiments and spices themselves. We will soon dip into the burley. I look at John and Rick and realize how skinny and haggard they are. I can now put my hands around my own thighs.

We are weak and weary. It is a slow and arduous task just to crawl out of the boat and relieve ourselves. We are tired, very tired. The idea of sitting in a comfortable chair seizes my mind— just to be able to sit without rubbing against someone, without struggling for space, without having to conform to shapes and surfaces not made for the relaxation of people. I just want something soft in which to relax. I want it as much as food.

Phil and Rick stand back-to-back, shoulders slumped, waiting again for the fish to come and taunt them. Kingfish rarely surface at all now, and when they do, they emerge too far away and defiantly flip their vivid yellow tails at us before running off to freedom. One comes in close, though. Perhaps he has let *his* good fortune go to *his* head. Maybe . . . Phil jerks the gaff and hooks him. The pull on the wand awakens Phil from his near stupor. He drags the fish up onto the beam and tries to pin its writhing body down. "I got one!" Rick wheels around and throws the net down. The fish slips away from the gaff, slides down the beam face, and falls into Rick's rising net.

We celebrate our catch, but we are painfully and fatiguingly aware that this single fish is a precious gift that does not hold a warranty for the future. For once we rein in our pride and our confidence. Rick finally realizes that he must give up some of his precious control. He says, "Somebody has to be behind Phil with the net. That's the only way we'll be able to catch fish." We need each other. Maybe men need to suffer before they realize such simple truths.

Mattie Hellriegel senses the anguish and tension in the air. He wants to be held constantly. Heather goes to bed at night wondering what happened to us. She envisions us drowning, going down, down, down. In her mind the *Rose-Noëlle* explodes in a flash of gaseous flame. Pieces of the boat and bodies rain down. We float, burned and in pain, crying out. She tries to shut the visions out, but they recur. How long will this go on? How long will she hold on to the hope that we are still alive? Until the end of the year, she decides. By then, what kind of a toll will our capsize take from her?

About August 17, Eleventh Week Following Capsize

Despite the rough seas and our inability to fish from the pitching sea-swept decks, we maintain our ritual of tealess "afternoon tea." Today we enjoy a special treat of "Orange Julius," which is a heaping teaspoon each of powdered Vitafresh orange drink and milk per bicycle bottle. While John fills each bottle three-fourths full of water and hands them to Phil for a proper shake, Rick and I pass out the biscuits. "Half or whole biscuit today?" we ask. A whole biscuit by unanimous decision. Democracy at work.

Rick hands a cookie to John and then one to Phil and me. We receive our bottle in return. I feel an ever so slight weight drop on my hip. Oh my, God! In the dim light, I spy a rogue biscuit! Rick glances at me and then quickly turns away. Rick *loves* these biscuits. Naughty boy. Halfway through tea, in one slick motion, Rick's hand falls on my thigh, palms the cookie, and drags it over to his thigh, which he rubs as if it itches. The bugger really has every angle figured out. He draws his hands up on his chest as if resting there, and I roll on my side to screen him from the opposition. Rick's eyes glance down at his hands as they tear the soft cookie in half, making sure he's being *perfectly* fair. He slides one hand back down between us and drops my portion of the loot.

I'm on my own. My heart pumps like a hummingbird. "Oh, I'd love another one of those biscuits right now," says Phil. It is all I can do to keep from busting out in laughter so I bite my lip.

"You're lucky we had one today, Philip. We usually only have a half," scolds John as I roll onto my back again, play the same thigh-scratching game to retrieve my illicit treat, work my hand up to my face into which I slip it, and let the cookie rest therein. Slowly I take a chew, rest, chew, rest, eating the cookie and letting it dissolve.

In coming months Rick and I will play our game a half dozen times. A cookie in our world, a *half* cookie, is a treasure worthy of such plots, deceptions, and risk.

A ghoulie cascades from the cockpit. Rain pelts down. It's my turn to retrieve the bucket of water from the mast before it is polluted by breaking waves. I yank off my clothes and don Martha's rain jacket. Out I go.

In the cockpit, I find that the tackle box has been washed away.

Naked from the waist down I face the raging open Pacific. I still have a hard time believing the difference between the realities of our cave and the outside world, separated from one another by a mere inch of hull. Charcoal black clouds race across the sky. Sheets of spray and rain lash at my face. Spume flies down the face of waves. We lurch over a wave peak. *Rose-Noëlle*'s yellow hull stands in stark contrast to the cold cobalt sea. She is safe and it is the enemy.

I must get up there and get that water. What if the ocean attacks while I am up there? What if it throws me off? For a split second I think to myself, maybe I can bail out, just go back below and ask for someone else to do it, admit I'm too scared.

"How many bottles do you need, mate?" asks Rick from below.

What to do? Oh, what to do? Oh, what the hell? "Give me two!" I yell down. Grasping one bottle in a hand and sticking another in my mouth like an oversized pacifier, I climb out, straddle the frigid soaked keel, and frantically scoot forward, wasting not a moment. Two-thirds of the way there, I stop.

I take the bottle from my mouth and look around. It is all so real. Maybe this is more real than the comfort of the land-bound bed I seek.

The waves and wind and rain remain the same, but now that I'm out of the cave, out of the hull, out of the cockpit, here, totally exposed, I feel strangely calm and no longer afraid. We rise to a crest and I see for miles the ageless restless surface of the world. The screaming wind and thundering waves fill my ears. Yet, alone out here, stripped of all but a rubber coat, I almost feel a part of the relentless and awesome power that I see, hear, feel. The forces that surround me may cause me to slip, to tumble, to break, but like each little wave, my own force is a part of the scene, a contribution to the whole.

Perhaps I have never been so vulnerable, or perhaps I have always been. The cold water that streams down my legs and the wind that cuts across my face wash from me and blow away the grand illusions of safety and security. If the sea has a mind to toss me off the boat and consume me, if the wind wants to blow me away, they will. If the Pacific has a mind to crush *Rose-Noëlle*, she'll splinter under its heel like a bug. In the cabin or out, safely ashore, or caught out here on this half-flooded capsized boat, when our time comes we are all unsuspecting victims, incapable of any real resistance, capable only of the spirit with which we face such raw and strangely beautiful destructive power. It is as risky to retreat as to advance.

So I go forward, for my mates, for my friends. It is my small opportunity to satisfy their need of me. I am thankful for it. Few people get the chance to be needed and even fewer take it. In the face of this raging sea, I am awed. For a moment I think I understand John Glennie, his attraction to all of this, even in the worst of times. For a moment it is almost as if I wear Glennie's skin. Then I fill my bottles and scurry back to the comfort of my companions.

Chapter 11
Throw Another Albatross
on the Barbie, Mate

19 August, 77th Day Following Capsize

The glory of my night's rest is terminated by the voice of a whiny child: "Doesn't anybody want to come up with me to see the sunrise?"

Rick, Phil, and I roll around, our eyes flickering in the dawn of our consciousness.

"Doesn't anybody want to see the sunrise with me?" repeats John. When the weather is fair enough, he usually enjoys his routine at dawn on deck by himself. What does he need us for this morning?

"Ah, God, what is he whinging about?" complains Rick. We ignore John and try to go back to sleep again.

"Doesn't anybody want to come up and celebrate Rick's birthday?"

Rick moans. "Why doesn't he just shut up? What is there to celebrate?"

Yesterday was Phil's birthday and there certainly wasn't anything to celebrate then. "Happy birthday" was about as far as we went. I suppose we tried to make it a little special. I did give him that biscuit.

The scene rolls through Rick's mind. For several days, Rick had pondered Phil's upcoming birthday. We'd been pretty hard on Phil the last couple of months, and Phil had taken it, had come around, had become part of the team. He deserved a little something special. So Rick planned to offer his own share of our precious tea-time biscuit to Phil. When the day came, it was horrible and rough and cold again outside. John distributed the usual ration of a half of fruit-filled biscuit each. Rick had no chance to nick an extra bit, and when he got his share in his hand, he could not bear the thought of giving it away. He looked at it, turned it over, held it like a delicate precious bird that he was afraid to crush. He raised it to his lips and took a wee nibble, let the crumb's sweet-bread taste fill his mouth. The temptation to keep it, to devour it, filled his mind. But he promised. He had said nothing to Phil, but he had convinced himself that he could be generous; he had the strength to give such a treasure away. Then again, Phil would just gulp it down. He wouldn't really appreciate it. Still, Rick promised. And to Rick, a promise to himself was even harder to break than a promise to someone else. Rick held out his gift to Phil. "Happy birthday, mate," he said.

Phil looked Rick in the eye for a while then down at the little bundle of crumbs and jam in Rick's open hand. "Thanks," he said. In that single simple word, Rick knew how grateful Phil was. In that word Phil gave more in return than Rick would ever realize.

That was yesterday. I wonder why John had to wake everybody up to another day in this hell? "Want to see the sunrise? Want to celebrate Rick's birthday?" Christ. Well, we're too awake now to go back to sleep. It must be nice out for a change if John is up on deck enjoying sunrise. "Happy birthday Rick," I say.

Rick just groans.

From on deck comes a last plea. "Doesn't anybody want to come up and see this sailboat?"

There is a flurry of arms, legs, and butts like a crowd of mad shoppers assaulting the narrow doors that lead to the world's bes one-time-only sale.

proud of ourselves. We have prepared for this moment. Today is the day we will be rescued. Today we will eat breakfast aboard a vessel that moves in accordance with the will of its crew.

But the sailboat does not turn. It keeps moving slowly across the horizon with the plodding purposeful zeal of a missionary. I look up at the mast. The smoke rises from the fire in thick plumes, but within a few feet, the breeze has blown it asunder until it spreads into a thin veil across the sky. Nobody is going to see our call for help.

John does not look surprised. Instead he merely observes that the sighting of the boat is more good news, another piece that fits into the puzzle of where we are and when we might get rescued. He says that we can't be where the normal winds and currents of the Pacific would take us. We can't be so far out in the middle of nowhere. "In forty thousand miles of sailing the Pacific, even in shipping lanes, I've never seen boats like this."

To anyone who has sailed the world's oceans it might be hard to believe that a floating hulk, even in deserted waters, would not occasionally encounter the odd vessel, but John's words are good to hear. This time no one says, "Yeah John, but that was twenty years ago." This time no one dismisses him with a wave of their hand because it is just another groundless opinion from the man who assured us that his boat could never capsize and that we could never catch fish in the open sea. *This* time we all need to believe that we have a better chance of getting rescued than we actually should have. The fickle finger of our faith is directed by our desperation and our desires. Our beliefs in John, in each other, in what is right and what is wrong, in where we are, are as variable as the conditions of the sea and sky.

Our disappointment over not being seen is mitigated by the comfort we feel from a vessel passing close by. Rick and I reassure one another, "It's just a matter of time." I turn back to our regular routine and prepare our morning meal. We eat breakfast on the hull while watching the sailboat go away.

When we are done and Phil cleans up, John nudges me and nods his head with lifted brows in a general direction over my shoulder. An albatross paddles nearby. Well, why not? The Maoris eat them. I fetch a plastic spool of monofilament with a three-inch rusty hook dangling from the end. John appears with a piece of rope along which our eyeless, rotting fish heads hang like some angler's record catch that's been marauded by a bear. I choose one of the heads with the care that one might use to select a fine wine. With a head on a hook in hand, I shimmy down the hull toward the rudder, swing the line around cowboy style and let it fly. The bait splashes near the bird, who darts forward, grabs it, and begins to take flight. But albatross are created for high speed gliding. Their wings are too elegant, thin, and long to provide power for low speed liftoffs. To help itself take to the air, it ferociously flaps while running on top of the water, stretching out the length of line until taut and yanking the fish head away. The albatross crash-stops its takeoff, turns and paddles back to the head. This time it picks the head up and swallows, stretching its neck and beak into a line to allow the bait to plummet down its throat. The bird begins to paddle away, accelerates, comes up hard against the fishing line trailing from its beak. I yank the line and the bird goes nuts. It squawks and beats the water to froth with its extended, majestic, tapered wings. "I got it, John. I got it!"

"Oh, my. This is wonderful."

The bird opens its beak, trying to regurgitate the bait, emanating a choking, gurgling sound, but I keep tension on the line so it closes its beak and yanks as best it can while it flogs the water and air. Its feet kick to get a grip on the sea. It's head jerks. Its wings flap. Still I drag it sideways toward the boat. The albatross's flailing wings tangle in the line. I pull it closer and creep back toward the cockpit. As the bird approaches I am amazed by its gigantic proportions.

I tow the bird alongside the hull, yank it, thrashing and stumbling onto the wing deck, and haul the tangle of wings, neck, and snapping beak up toward us. With one hand John reaches down and grabs the albatross by the throat just behind the head. With his other he tries to wring its neck, but the albatross is too big, too strong. "I need a knife," he says. I hand him a diver's knife and John cuts fast and deep across the bird's throat. It squirms and bucks. Its lifeblood gushes. Splashes of crimson fan out and drip over *Rose-Noëlle*'s pristine yellow body.

There is a strange moment of silent peace.

Burritos Albatross

• Take 1 medium albatross, skinned (you'll wear yourself out trying to pluck it), deboned, and cubed.

• Marinate oceanic poultry in vinegar and brown sugar with dash of onion; leave for two hours minimum.

● While albatross marinates, roll out bread dough into tortillas. Save any extra for tortilla chips—roll out and cut into bite-sized triangles.

● In 2 tablespoons oil, combine a little fingernail's worth each of chile and cumin. Stir into oil 1 cup parboiled brown rice.

● Put 1 heaping tablespoon Wattie's baked beans in each tortilla. Sprinkle dried onions on top of beans and roll up tortillas, pinching off ends.

● Combine remainder of beans with cumin, chile powder, splash of garlic juice, and 1/2 cup of spice water (Thai chile water). Save this Mexican bean sauce for later.

● On barbecue, heat two frying pans with light coating of oil; saute marinated seabird in one pan for four minutes over high heat; on medium heat put burritos in other pan.

● Mix Gravox dry gravy with 1/3 cup water and pour over seabird until gravy thickens. Add touch more water and remove from heat. Turn burritos and put on high heat.

● Take seabird and put aside in deep pots or similar to maintain warmth. Put lightly oiled pan back on fire; add rice and stir for approximately two minutes.

● Place burritos on port side of special birthday plates; serve rice to starboard; heat Mexican bean sauce in burrito pan.

● Ladle *precisely* equal portions of albatross and its sauce over rice and Mexican bean sauce over burritos. Take care not to combine the two taste sensations.

● While eating, fry tortilla chips and serve to dip and sop up sauce.

● Recommended beverage: cheap impersonation of 7-Up, vintage Spring 1989 (A very good season).

● Bon appétit.

Under sunny skies and over calm seas, we enjoy our feast. Every one of us is delighted. A boat, a bird, the incredible luxury of a warm cooked meal. Who could ask for a better birthday? Yesterday, during Phil's birthday, when it was so rough and cold and dismal, who would have thought that we would have anything to celebrate just a day later? Now we have so much. This isn't our usual bread and scrape; it's the most food we've had at one time since the capsize. I feel like I'm gathered with a loving family at a Thanksgiving feast. In this strange moment lost at sea, I feel as at home and content as I have ever felt.

"Do you think today, since it's been such a special day for us, that maybe everybody can give their own thanks in silence?" I suggest. Everyone agrees.

Thank you God, whatever you are, for giving us this incredible meal and allowing us to share this together. I don't know what seeing that boat meant, but it gives me hope. I'm treating it as a sign that we will be out of here soon, but I'm not taking anything for granted. I'm just really thankful.

After about thirty seconds I open my eyes and glance up to see Phil eating. He begins to moan in ecstasy. John's eyes open and we look at each other for a second and smile. Rick too looks just so pleased. What a day!

We say nothing as we begin to spoon the food into our mouths. The albatross meat is red and rich. It tastes more like rabbit than like fish and the sauce is thick, sweet yet beefy, and warm. The rice is tangy and spicy with a nut-like crunch to it. The meal is such a barrage of opulent flavors that each of us spontaneously joins Phil in orgiastic moans.

"This is exquisite," asserts Rick. "The *flavors,* the *flavors . . .*"

John groans in a baritone, "Oooaah. L-o-v-e-l-y. Simply lovely."

Phil concludes the critique with, "Not bad. This is okay."

John looks over to Phil. "Ha! Philip, you've never had it so good. This is the Hilton! Look at you."

"Look at *me?* Look at bloody *you,* John." We all can't help but laugh. "Any more gravy over there, Jim?"

Before the fire dies I put on water to heat. Phil fetches the tea from below. He emerges carrying the Bear. As he passes Rick, Phil pauses. He opens the Bear and lays it over Rick's shoulders, like draping a king's cape. Phil pats Rick on the back. "Happy birthday, mate," he says.

Rick's eyes water. "I can't take this, Phil. Your brother-in-law gave this to you. It's family."

"Hey, ya look good in it. It's just the job for ya. Ya had your eye on it for a long time. Besides, it fits ya and I won't fit in it for long when I get back," he declares, patting his stomach and smiling. "It's yours, mate."

"Thanks, Phil." Rick slips his arms into the sleeves and admires himself in the coat. "Shit hot!"

I launch into singing Happy Birthday. Phil and John join in. Slightly embarrassed, teary-eyed Rick slowly shakes his head and grins. When we are through I say to Phil, "That was for you too, Phil."

"Thanks, mate."

"Well, I remember on *my* birthday," laments John with tongue in cheek, "You guys wouldn't even let me have an extra vial of bloody fizz-pop."

Following a moment of silence, Rick pronounces, "Well, John, you just pick a day and we'll have a special birthday treat for you. How's that sound?"

"Okay."

"How about a dessert?" queries Phil.

"Sounds all right."

"Should we have it now, John?"

"No, no, no. I think we've had quite enough today. We'll have it when *I* want to have it, Philip."

Back in the cave, even crammed together like this, we find little about which to complain. We bask in the quiet and calm of our inner and outer peace. Rick speaks. "I just want to say, this has been a real pearler day—one of the best birthdays of my life. I want to say thanks."

"Rick, it was great for us too," I reply.

John takes down his folder of papers. Phil basks in the memory of our meal. Rick opens "Letters to Heather." He writes to her of our good fortune. He writes how he feels really guilty because, although up until now we've had so many shitty times, he had such a wonderful birthday today that he couldn't have enjoyed it any more if he had been anywhere else. He writes, "I shouldn't be feeling this good out here, but I do." He writes how he will remember this great day because there are so few of them.

The next day it is blowing like hell again and the ghoulies await.

Chapter 12
Discovery of Fire

Approximately 20 August,
Day 78 Following Capsize

It is another borderline day. Maybe we can fish; maybe not. A biting southerly Antarctic wind dices the Pacific and scatters it over *Rose-Noëlle*'s sidewalks.

Phil crawls out of the cave. "I'm going to take a little look around."

Some time later Rick says, "I wonder what happened to Phil," and scoots out after him. When he gains the cockpit, Rick looks down to see "the wand" hovering over the water with gaff in hand. Phil swings, strikes, pulls a fish out, but the fish dangles awkwardly, writhes, and escapes. Phil curses. Rick goes berserk. "Phil! Why didn't you tell me you were coming up here to fish? I could've gotten the net around that bloody fish! We got *nothing* now, Phil! We got *nothing!*" Phil rarely misses the fish, but not once has he been able to land one. It is not the first time Phil has set off with his magic gaff alone, but it is the last. Even Phil finally recognizes that we must fish together.

Rick's hands are already numbed by the icy wind, but he unties Cortez the Killer from the mast and slips down to join Phil. As his feet hit the deck, they are washed by waves. The sea actually feels warm compared to the air. Over the last month it *has* dramatically warmed, along with the air on good days. Precipitation is also common. We've not gone back on the vial since we erected our rain collection shield and gutters. Our jugs are all full. We even be-gin to store excess water in the chilly bin that we first wedge against the foot of our bunk and later lash to the plank. As it begins to rain almost daily, we joke that it's like the scuzzy weather in Auckland.

The next time Phil strikes, Rick is ready. Guided by Rick's hands, Cortez nets another meal.

John and I join our mates on deck where I scale and gut while John fillets. John stops his knife in mid-stroke and points above the horizon. "Look. There's a jet stream."

"How do you know that's a jet stream?" challenges Rick.

"That's a bloody jet stream. I know a jet stream when I see it," says Phil, as if defending John.

An iridescent strip of cloud above the rising sun is unlike any other clouds of the day and is clearly the exhaust of a high flying jet. We debate its course, its destination, and speculate on the point of departure of this beacon of humanity and home. Our desire is to believe the jet is an international flight originating in New Zealand. Such desperate wants are the basis of our faith. What we *know* is that the jet's passengers sit in comfortable chairs totally unaware of the plight of four men down here who are but a pinprick to their sight. We envy the secure warmth in which they rest, the certitude of their scheduled safe landing. Within our sight those passengers await, with unquestioning presumption and without any real need, the round of hot meals that will punctuate their day. Within the belly of the flying beast, as we watch, people at rest sip hot coffee. Some might feel a slight twang in their stomach and complain, "I'm starving." How often have I uttered such nonsense without thinking what it really means? As I look around at John and Rick, I now see that we *are* starving. By the time we get back into the belly of our own uncertain, drifting beast, we are all shivering.

My mind turns back to the birthday celebrations that were

such a short time ago yet seemingly galaxies and eons away. How I wish I could retain the comfort and fulfillment of that day, just a few calories of it. Someone suggests we heat up some grub on the kerosene lamp, but the rest of us nix the idea. We have too little fuel left. We do not dare light the barbecue below decks again for fear of fire and asphyxiation. Besides, we have little left to burn in it.

An LP catalytic heater is wedged into the centerboard box outside to keep other gear in place. We think we can remove the heater's rubber supply hose from inside the boat, pinch over the end fitting to make a torch, and control the flame with the supply hose shutoff valve. But no torch will work without fuel.

"If only we had some heat. John, isn't there any way we can get those gas bottles out?" I ask for the umpteenth time, dreaming of hot food, envisioning *Rose-Noëlle*'s LP tanks tucked away somewhere in the wreckage.

"The tanks are hard enough to get out even when the boat is right-side up. How am I supposed to get them out under water?"

"Well, John, can't we just cut a hole and pull them out from the top?" I inquire.

John snaps back, "I will not cut up the boat any more."

Maybe John still envisions saving the boat. Maybe he needs to believe that even *Rose-Noelle* will get out of this in one piece, that this hellish drift is just an intermission between acts one and two of *Getting Back to the Islands*. My suggestion to cut holes into his love and all that he owns is a rape of that dream. But John tells us that the four tanks live in lockers in the cockpit coamings, whatever they are. He'd have to dive deep and long just to get at them. John says that the regulator is likely corroded and the propane has probably leaked out anyway. He reminds us that, even if we got the bottles out, we'd probably end up blowing ourselves up. It is so hard to see the fine line between reason and rationalization.

Later in the Twelfth and Thirteenth Weeks Following Capsize

Most people think we're dead. My friend, Bob McKerrow, who is an Arctic expedition veteran and has worked in the Red Cross Disaster Relief Program, tells my family that he pegs our chances at two to five percent. He thinks to himself that it's a generous estimate.

Soon after we were reported missing, Rick's sister Debbie went to see clairvoyants—two sisters and another colleague. They swung pendulums and read tarot cards. All told her that we were okay. About a week after the search, Rick's mother also visited the seers. Now Heather travels to Auckland. She thinks that she will thank them for their efforts, but perhaps she wants more.

Before they lay out the cards, they warn Heather that there may be bad news. She accepts that. But their story remains the same one of hope. One sees a huge wave, "as big as a house," a boat upside down, floating. One sees Rick wearing gumboots and a cable-knit sweater, sitting with his arms around his legs. One also says that we are on an island, green and rocky with lots of trees, while another is content to conclude only that we will land on an island of twelve letters.

Rose Young, John Glennie's friend who helped prepare *Rose-Noëlle* for sea has a friend who has a recurring dream that we are alive. It might be easy to discount, but the same woman dreamt of an eleven-year-old girl who went missing. At first she dreamt the little girl was being held on a beach, and then she dreamt that the girl was dead. Authorities found the little girl in a shed on a beach, murdered.

Heather does not really believe in these parapsychological powers, but she also does not discount them. She will not rule her life by such predictions, but at this point, anyone telling her that we are not dead is telling her what she wants to hear. Like Rick, she is not certain how to pray, but she does: *Make it true.*

John squats on a forward sidewalk, reaches down, yanks the thick, stretchy neck of a gooseneck barnacle that finally gives way, and drops it in a pan. He retires to the keel with a cupful and pries open each shell that sits like a fat head on the end of each stalk. Opened, the barnacle shells look like black-striped, milky-gray valentine hearts the size of a quarter. John pulls tiny, black-tentacled mollusks that live within and pops them with their necks into his mouth. "Oh, this is lovely," he says, as if enjoying oysters on the half shell.

I finish hanging a bottle of water from one of the mast stays in which two tea bags float and join John's morning barnacle break. "Aah. These are great, John!" The barnacles are succulent and sweet. Phil and Rick are not interested.

We have also gaffed a bit of Sargassum weed that was drifting by and soak it in fresh water for a bitter salty salad. Sargassum is the ocean's horticultural free spirit. It's lacy khaki branches are buoyed by little gas-filled globes called pneumatocysts. It wanders aimlessly on the ocean's currents, housing visiting wildlife like a miniature reef, waiting to be blown ashore or drifting to their death on the open sea—just like us.

Draped across the hull beside John and I is a piece of kelp that we've harvested from where it was tangled up in line and handrails at the bow. It began as a six-inch-wide strop about four feet long but has dried to a curled, bent, rocky crust two-thirds that size. Like cutting leather, I slice it with the diver's knife into strips to resoak later. In fresh water the dried kelp will blow up into instant pasta. Whereas sargassum floats freely, kelp is a wide-leafed stalk that was uprooted from the ocean floor where it usually grows in swaying forests. The biggest plants grow to over two hundred feet at a rate of almost a foot a day. The plant is constantly eroded by storms or pruned by sea urchins and other animals. Whereas the gas-filled pneumatocysts that float Sargassum weed look like little berries, those on kelp may be as big as a soccer ball. Like life jackets, the pneumatocysts raise the leaves up from the ocean floor to reach for light. Kelp is not a deep-water plant. It grows in coastal waters, usually less than a hundred feet deep. Has our instant pasta been delivered from far away, or from a neighborhood store?

Although we are gratified by our harvest from the sea and still catch the occasional fish, our hunger and overall depression continue to deepen. There is no more coffee or Milo for our ritual tea times. We bicker over tidbits so small that satisfaction comes in a package as minute as a peppercorn. To avoid a fight, we deal the black pellets out like cards. As we drift on and on and our supplies dwindle, we desperately need something in our lives to change for the better.

I take the sun tea to our den in late afternoon. We are excited by the deep amber color and the warm bottle. Anxiously we lift our half cup of tea to our lips. It's awful, a slightly bitter, lukewarm, insipid liquid, inferior, I am certain, to anything yet devised by man. "Piss awful! It tastes like perfume," says Rick. It is not the change we need.

"Let's try some of the burley," I suggest. We have shuffled the burley box around from the plank to the cockpit to the keel, where it has been filled and preserved by seawater. The old cocoa, biscuits, sultanas, spaghetti, corn flakes, rice, and other garbage that were too inedibly soaked now nearly fill our shoe-box–sized container. Over several days, I flush the burley box with fresh water. The ingredients have disintegrated into a gelatinous brown mass that we dream into a chocolate mousse. Not only does it look edible, it looks great!

A corner of the burley gives way to my scooping cup with a sound like pulling your foot out of a mud flat. It bears the mild scent of cocoa. Into a bowl I throw the burley and a touch of every spice in our larder. Let's have a wee taste. It's absolutely awful. Maybe more spice will help—something sweet to bring it around— a third bottle of ultra-sweet lemon syrup. Now give it a whirl. Call it Burley Bizarre—incredibly bitter with an underlying sweetness. In goes some beef bullion and a couple dozen kelp noodles. Okay, for better or worse, this Burley Kelp Cocoa Borscht Lemon Stroganoff is done. Let's eat. Phil even says grace—his usual generic family brand.

It's not so bad after all. The Burley Surprise has the consistency of stew, and the kelp noodles are pleasantly chewy and starchy. But after a few minutes I begin to taste only the chalky, bitter yet sweet, rancid aftertaste. The sultanas are nuggets of fermented, bitter-vinegar jellybeans. Everything is good about this stuff except the way it tastes. It's one meal we needn't be thankful for. I don't know why we should expect more; basically we're eating spiced garbage, but I apologize to my mates nonetheless. "I'm really sorry. This meal didn't quite turn out like I thought it would."

John says, "Ah, it isn't so bad," and manages to choke the rest of it down.

Rick says, "I'm not sure what I think of this tucker." Scrunching up his nose, he concludes, "Aw! That aftertaste! What *is* that? Aach!"

"What are you talking about?" says Phil. "This tastes fine. I like this."

Well, there's beacoup burley left that I haven't tampered with. I don't think I'll thank God for that. There's enough Burley Surprise left over for a second meal, but I can't take any more; neither can Rick. The spices set John's body afire. Each night he becomes uncharacteristically claustrophobic, sweating, panting, and clambering in and out through the entryway to gain fresh air. I am embarrassed by my failure, and disappointed by our inability to use the Burley for food. It is obvious that this experiment, too, is not what we need.

Rick has been gone for an hour. I slip out to check on him. He squats on the wing deck, holding onto the stay, desperately trying to induce a bowel movement.

"Are you okay?" I ask him.

He looks up to me with a grimacing smile and waves me off with a hand. "Yeah, I'm okay, mate."

He doesn't look okay. His eyes appear quite sunken and his complexion is a pale gray. After a little while, Rick gives up and shakily stands. He falls to one knee.

"Are you sure you're okay?"

"I just have some pains in my stomach."

I help Rick back up onto the keel. What most people take for granted as a daily routine following morning coffee has become a major concern. None of us has been able to free our system of waste regularly; most of us have had bowel movements maybe a half dozen times in three months. Over a period of days or weeks, peristalsis wrenches our guts with cramps and aches. But nothing happens. We squat and force ourselves until we nearly black out. Nothing. It is a gritty, disgusting, painful process that finally requires the assistance of one's own fingers to pry lose the rock-hard waste.

Rick has had even less luck. He has had only two bowel movements in three months. The whole crew decides that Rick should drink a cup of vegetable oil. Still nothing happens. Of all of us, Rick seems the weakest and most unsteady. He often stumbles. He sometimes slurs his words. Something in our life here must soon change.

At least we are more successful as fishermen. Rick calls our fish pool our little hole in the ice. When the weather is good, we stay out all day and usually catch a fish, sometimes more than one. On rotten days, it is difficult to see the fish through the dull choppy water, and it is cold, so we retreat to our sanctum. To prepare for the days when we are trapped in the cabin, we begin to dry kingfish, stripping them up and threading them on the rigging like wet socks.

Fish that we intend to eat sometime in the near future, we continue to marinate, but, with precious little vinegar left, the marinade is, at best, only a quarter vinegar. Into the fish bucket we toss some bits while eating others. The box is now a near-full confusion of fresh and decidedly unfresh fish. And it does not smell so good.

We decide to clean out the fish bucket before the whole mass goes off. We gorge ourselves, but as we work our way down into the fish box, the pieces become pastier and fall apart in our hands. The rancid smell grows stronger until Rick, Phil, and I have had quite enough, but there's still a pile left in the box. John says, "I'll never get sick of fish. I could eat fish all day long." He eats and eats until he finally says, "Ah, I have to stop for a while."

Within a half hour John makes his way up on deck. We hear him retching for what seems like forever. This is not what we need.

"John, can't we please at least *try* to see if there's any gas in the tank?"

"All right, Jim. Go up forward where the heater was and wait there. I'll give you a yell when I turn it on."

I crawl out, climb up to the cockpit, scoot ahead along the keel to our forward hatch, and drop down into the hull. The frigid water is only up to my knees. It surges along the tunnel hull, careens off the sides and lockers, and jumps about in confusion all over itself as if it, too, is panicky and desperate to escape this place. The water's crinkles, slaps, and thuds echo within the floating sea cave that was once a grand yacht named *Rose-Noëlle*. John's voice is almost lost at the end of a seemingly endless cavern: "Okay, I'm turning it on now."

Immediately, the draped end of the heater hose emits an *ssssss*. I smell the end. "Yeah John, yeah! I can hear it. I can smell it. There's gas in that tank."

John shuts off the gas line while I remove the rubber hose forward. John attaches the hose to the stove connection in the galley, which is fortunately just above water. He pulls some copper pipe from the heater, connects one end to the gas hose, and pinches the other end with pliers, using a feeler gauge to keep the hole slightly open. This is our burner. Within a couple hours John is controlling the flow of gas with the shutoff valve in the galley while Phil holds the torch, Rick holds the pan, and I stir the pot. We did not need our insipid sun tea; we did not need our burley gook; we did not need Rick's deteriorating condition and stomach problems; nor did we need a stockpile of rotting fish that could easily have done in our captain. What we needed was something like this, something as monumental as when we got our cave dry and secure with the ground sheet, something that transforms our world. Now we're cooking with gas! Nobody ever meant it so literally!

Over the next few days Rick and I create a crab-trap stove to John's basic design, transforming a cooking operation that required four men into one that needs only two. We twist the frame of an old metal crab trap into a four-inch-high rectangular stand. Into this we secure the torch. No one needs hold the pot or the torch. The cook only gives orders to his mate on the plank outside in order to control the gas flow.

Although we continue to mark off the days on our calendar with the same lines, the history of our voyage is dramatically divided into Before Heat and After Heat. In those shivering inhospitable days B.H., we embraced *tolerable* moments in life because they were an escape from the norm. Just to get dry for a moment or to warm one's self enough to stop shivering was like finding a tiny ledge of refuge on the face of a dangerous mountain ascent. A.H., we have the luxury of some actual *comfort*, as if we have reached the summit and now find shelter in a cozy lodge, warmed by the licking flames from an open hearth.

Nothing has helped Rick's constipation yet, but there is one thing that we haven't tried. I clutch a glass battery tester that looks like a turkey baster and fill it with vegetable oil. Rick lies beside me, readying himself for his ordeal. "Thanks for doing this for me, Jim," he says.

"No problem, mate. What are friends for?" Neither of us know whether to laugh or cry. "Okay, Rick, you ready to pull your pants down?"

"Hold on, hold on, hold on. I'm going to give it one more go." Rick makes his way to the deck while I wait. In a few minutes he returns with a big smile on his face that reveals success. Oh my, what success! That chucks the last of our major worries, besides getting the hell out of here.

The parachute sea anchor that we set during the storm did not save our asses or increase our catch of fish, as promised in the advertising, but our torch and stove is all we manufacturers could hope for. It has vastly improved our lot and *has* even improved fishing profits. We get up in the morning, head out on deck, and fish until long after we're cold because we know we can crawl back inside, fire up the stove, and swig some boiling tea.

Hot meals are now routine. Typically, I pan fry four pieces of fillet from the day's catch. Sometimes I make fish head and bone soup in which the bones become soft enough to eat, or I stir some gooseneck barnacles into a sauce and pour it over a spoon of rice. We even chow down on the barnacle shells. On days with fresh fish, I stir-fry the organs with a splash of garlic water. Raw, the bitter stomach is so like a tire's inner tube, even the diver's knife cannot penetrate it. But when I throw the three- to four-inch cornucopia-shaped organ in the pan it shrivels, twists, turns, and jumps around as if alive and metamorphoses from near white to charcoal, from a piece of rubber to the chewy fat of a steak. This, the previously inedible intestines, the liver, and the heart create a thick French sauce. Even Rick and Phil now can't wait for the guts, exclaiming, "This stuff is full of goodness!"

Nothing comes without a price, of course. When the flame is high and the cooking a near frenzy, our new torch burns up the oxygen of our space. Headaches, and a patina of greasy soot building over everything, revealing fire's bittersweet nature. But it's worth it. I learn to take air breaks in the cockpit to clear my head. And then it's back below for more glorious heat and its many applications.

Finally able to use our eight boxes of tea, we begin genuine tea breaks. Rick insists on Billy tea to exacting standards: "Come to a rolling boil (nothing less will do), throw the tea leaves in, put the lid on, shut the gas off, let the tea leaves sink to the bottom, and serve." It is so delightful that, when we have enough water, we enjoy tea time in the morning, late morning, noon, late afternoon, and evening. Out of store-bought biscuits now, I make my own with fried bread dough glazed with jam over our glorious heat. When we are done, John and I help ourselves to the spent tea leaves on the bottom of the pot. It is like chewing spinach.

Fire, calories: How monumental it must have seemed to ancient peoples when they discovered the flush, the glow, the incandescent. Fire transcends giving us the ability to cook meat. Just as the cold has pervaded every aspect of our existence, so now has this torch illuminated it, pushed the icy winds back. Now when we are cold and wet from a watch, we slip into our cave and are warmed. Fire is the real beginning of man's wall against the whims of nature, the first step above the mere desperate struggle for survival. How we have come to expect the security of fire-on-demand in our lives ashore. How I now know the magic and miracle of it.

Even at night, we leave the flame turned low, like a reassuring candle or a furnace scaled down to suit our confined abode. There is a gentleness offered by the light. Maybe it is my imagination, but it seems that the talk between us is less tense, more civilized.

Good old bald Phil confesses to us that he is a certified hairdresser. He keeps John's hair trimmed, and John finally breaks down and chops Phil's feathery fronds. Rick and I groom each other. John and Rick departed New Zealand with beards, but now even Phil and I have uncontrollable growth. John's is jet black with a spot of gray under his lip. Rick and I call him Rasputin. Phil's is salt and pepper, contoured and wavy—the Montana rancher look. Rick's growth has such a sharp-edged border and hangs so low that it looks like a fake beard made of shaggy carpet hooked onto his face with wires looped over his ears. Mine is just a hedge of steel wool.

Rick and I sit side by side on the keel with our bodies twisted to face one another. Rick grasps a pair of rusty barber's scissors and carefully trims my mustache, following the arc of my upper lip. "Shit, matey, you've got a lot of gray here in this beard," he kids.

"Ow! Hey, hey, easy."

"Sorry, it's the damned scissors." He continues to clip and tear away. "I'm keen to start cooking when I get back," he says. "Heather's always done all the cooking. I think I'd be interested in doing some cooking."

"Ow! Jesus."

"Sorry." Once again we lapse into talking about bakeries and restaurants that we have loved. "I wouldn't mind doing what you're doing at Outward Bound. I really wouldn't. I could get into that," he says.

What is this tack? I wonder. Rick is not one to give anybody a compliment, but is this his way of saying he actually envies *me?* All this time I've envied the roles of his life. He has his own business, a family. He's a leader. He climbs mountains, paddles kayaks in the sea, takes risks, takes control. Yet he seems self-conscious of his egocentrism, the way his own quests have demanded the altruism of his wife. He feels guilt for demanding her support while barely acknowledging it.

Balance. That is what we both need. A better balance.

After I trim his mustache, we begin to trim each other's fingernails. You can do one hand with the left-handed scissors, but it's impossible to do both of your own. Besides, we enjoy the mutual grooming.

"Well, Jim, how does this sound? When we get back, you teach me how to cook and I'll teach you how to paddle."

He does not know how much this gratifies me. Our friendship will continue. Rick is tough, determined, self-reliant, and competitive. I am soft, unsure, and willing to go to great lengths to avoid conflict. Rick will forge ahead and do what he thinks necessary, verbally bulldozing anyone who stands in the way. I'm so afraid of causing a stir that I do nothing unless specifically asked. He is a man of action; I am a man of compromise. Each of us are too extreme, limbs on opposite sides of the tree of man. But together, if we remain joined at the trunk and grow equally, we will not pull that trunk apart. Together, as we stretch into new air, we *are* in balance.

At times like these I forget that we are even in the middle of the ocean on a capsized boat. Instead, Rick and I are paddling a kayak on the Marlboro Sounds. We knead bread and huddle over a steaming wok. Let's have a taste. As good as those fish guts we had lost at sea? Nah. Never that good. We sit in easy chairs, our feet propped up in front of the licking flames of a fire, cup of steaming coffee in hand. Just outside is the bitter chill of New Zealand winter. The curl of aromatic pipe smoke is in the air. We puff away, overlooking the Pelorus Sound and reminiscing about the days, decades back, lost at sea on the *Rose-Noëlle*.

It does not take a lot of effort to conjure such images. Sitting here in reality, with our fire below, with the sea spread out before us, with the blooming of our mutual need, all we need do is close our eyes and we are there.

A week after our first sighting of a jet, same time, same place in the sky, we spy another. I am not so drawn to fantasies about the passengers' lives now, not so envious. John believes both jets have been heading northeast. If they originated from the same place, we seem to be drifting a bit west. Drifting west. We should not be drifting west. We *should* be drifting east.

Rick has taken the exalted position of match monitor. He deciphers which of our remaining hundred fire sticks are dry enough to store and which need more drying. John and Phil tuck the wet ones away in pockets of their shirts where, between layers of wool and with the help of body and cabin heat, they dry out. Some matches are beyond repair. Some merely smear when we try to light them. Others snuff out. Our stock dwindles. Soon we will be without fire again.

To solve the problem, Phil and Rick center our thoughts on basic technology. Rick urges, "John, we've got to put the screws on to find a flint." Yes, if we had a flint we'd be all set. I ask John how the stove lights its burners. It *is* a flint, but that's underwater. It's too difficult to get at and we're too weak.

Rick's legs have so thinned that his knees are bigger around than his thighs. He cannot even walk the length of the wing deck without stopping to rest. But John concerns me even more. His energy seems drained. His mind appears foggy more frequently. We are all guilty of treating John ambivalently. We may demonstrate little concern for John's emotional well-being, but we show a vested interest in his health. We want him at one hundred percent physically while ignoring fifty percent of his being.

"Ah, I have a brand new hot water heater in a box that I was going to install when we got to the islands," offers John. But he cannot remember where it was stored. It may even be swept away by now. And maybe it has no flint. John says calmly, "Let me work on that one."

A couple of days later, John says he now remembers that the heater is part of the packing under our berth, but he still has no idea if it has a flint or not. Taking up the bed will entail destroying our tidy and dry nest, at least three hours of grueling work, exposure to the elements. Is it worth it? We are so lethargic. Nobody is real keen, but we have nothing to lose. In less than two weeks the matches will be gone. We have everything to gain.

John and I pass the sleeping bags, pillows, and coats out to Rick and Phil on the hull. Next the screws come out, freeing the ground cloth, and I push the mass of plastic up through the cockpit hole. The space below is like a huge bathtub jammed full of drawers, bits of foam, a blanket, rubber boots, two dozen disintegrating toilet paper rolls, and other flotsam. There is, for instance, what once was my brand new $400 down-filled sleeping bag that is now a rotting sponge. After months of being smothered by the drop cloth, the water is black and stinks. John and I rummage through the fetid swamp and soggy debris. Within fifteen minutes we find our quarry. I pass out the heater and we begin the long process of repacking, reattaching the ground cloth, relining our lair with our bedding. We are exhausted, but we must know if our quest has been worth the effort.

From the heater John removes a metal, boxy frame about the size of a half pack of cards. Within the frame there is a spring-loaded, flint-headed hammer. We play with it, urging it to work. We grasp the frame in one hand, pull back the hammer with the other, and let it fly. A fiery shock runs up our arms. Like rubbing our feet on carpet and grounding-out, we receive a strong static-like shock from the hammer every third or fourth stroke. And in the dark, we can see an instantaneous blue flash. It does not matter anymore if we lose all of our matches. As keeper of the flame, Rick ties a lanyard on the flint and carefully stows it away. One unbreakable rule of our tribe is that the flint shall never ever leave our cave.

It is not all smooth flaming with the old spark, however. It is quite a trick to hold it at just the right angle to catch the jet of gas. When the gas is turned too high, our little spark ignites a flame thrower, singeing the hair off the fire starter's arms and leaping past his neighbor's nose.

Then the flame dies. The gas bottle is empty.

John pounds away on the chisel, working a hole into the aft sidewalk that leads to the outer hull. The rounded edges of the sidewalk are now covered with a green slime. John kneels, wearing only a black, wool, sleeveless sheep shearer's singlet against the weather. Waves slosh over his perch and bare feet. Sometimes at knee-height, they break against his whole body as he leans to the work. John has thinned so that his body looks like a bundle of swaying sticks that try to keep balanced, bending to the Pacific, almost breaking, trying not to slip. I await, holding a stay, ready with tools, and grabbing John's hand to steady him when waves strike. I am astounded by his skill and the precision with which he punches corners and chisels the edges of a square hatch. He even fashions hinges, poking two pairs of small holes along the edge of the hatch and stringing them together with light, braided shroud lines from the parachute sea anchor.

When John lifts the hatch lid, one gas bottle rests directly below like a fat white egg. Its twin nests next to it. John obviously has always known exactly where the gas bottle lockers are.

We wrestle the heavy, full tank out and pass it to Phil in the cockpit, where it is securely cradled. We remove the gas line from the stove and empty tank and pull it out, along with the regulator, through the locker. Leading this line from the cockpit into our cabin, we have our source of heat restored within a matter of a few hours and are again reminded of John's power over us.

John's familiarity with his boat and his willingness or unwillingness to act control not only the quality of our lives, but maybe even our ability to survive at all. It is a power on which we depend, but it is also an affront to those among us who cannot stand to have our lives so managed by the whims and qualms of other men, particularly this man. Whenever John finally puts his mind to solving such problems, he often gloats over his success, enjoying his control. We are at once pleased by the results and resentful of them. Why did he resist so long? Why has he fought us? What buttons do we have to push to unlock this strange private man and inspire him to put the same trust in us that we are compelled to put in him?

Poor John. Here I am completely out of my element but am finding a real life within it, while John is in his element yet in so many ways is completely lost.

With our stove restored and an endless supply of sparks, our existence takes on an almost suburban quality. In these cold waters we would not be alive if we were floating in a life raft or open boat. Within days, life raft survivors begin to suffer saltwater sores. In long voyages, the saltwater ulcers often open and deepen until they leave lifelong scars like bullet wounds. Our ability to stay or get relatively dry has prevented saltwater sores, or allowed them to quickly heal. Our water catchment system and frequent rain now keep us so well supplied with liquid that our daily rations are routinely several cups a day, often over a quart. Most lifeboat survivors are extremely lucky if they get two cups a day for weeks or months on end. We have been fortunate to have had such a rich stockpile of food that gave us time to learn to live off of the sea. Even now we have some food stores; whereas few survivors are blessed with more than a few biscuits that last mere days.

Even with the best of luck, only a handful of survivors have returned from more than a month adrift. Only three people, Poon Lim and the Baileys, a husband and wife team, have survived more than eighty days on a raft after their mother craft was destroyed. Few, if any, ocean survivors in life rafts or boats have lived even a week in waters as cold as the fifty-eight-degree sea that surrounds us.

Compared to the usual frantic horror of the usual life raft tale, our problems are longer term and more insidious. As cushy as our survival abode has become, we remain on the outskirts of physical deprivation, slowly infected by it. Our voyage is a chronic terminal illness that drags on and on. We are not in suburbia. We're four men crammed into a plastic prison with little chance of parole. Slowly, ever so slowly we waste away. We have no idea when our imprisonment will stop, or if it ever will.

And if it does stop, will it be in time? We have no standard with which to compare our performance. No one else has lasted this long in an overturned, half-flooded boat.

We convince ourselves that we'll be all set, in Fat City if we can just catch enough fish. With a reasonable quantity of water and a secure fort within which we can ride the seas indefinitely, only a lack of food would keep us from being able to last for years. *Years?* Yes, even I now know we may be out here years.

So, like men reaching middle age, we accept that our voyage in this life is not all that our youthful dreams and ego promised, but we are luckier than many. Maybe we can settle down and accept our life here. But for all that we have, we still need more fish, always more fish. And so we set about the routine labors that will take us from this prison to the survival suburbanite dream.

We have freed the second spinnaker pole from under the opposite wing deck sidewalks and attached it to the fore and aft stays on the side of our mast so that it forms a handrail along the inner side of the fish pool between the hulls. There is enough stretch in the stays that, when you lean on the pole, you sway out over the pool as if on a pygmy trapeze. It's a great support for hunters of yellowfin kingfish.

For weeks we have been untangling the chaotic mass of John's casting net, mending the various holes and tears. Together we have evolved a general plan. Rick and John hone the fine details.

If John and Rick's fights weren't so nerve wracking and tragic, how much the two of them need one another would make their spats comical. In his typical way, John tells us in about one sentence how we should implement the plan. Tie this with a something-or-other knot to the thingamajigs while lashing the whatever to the what-have-you. All extremely confusing. He walks away and returns a few minutes later while I remain standing dumfounded looking at the same end of rope. He slaps his head in frustration when this scene occurs, as it often does. "You *must* know how to tie a bowline," he insists. I suppose John learned these things so long ago that he has forgotten he ever had to and presumes everyone should be as familiar with them as with driving a car. It isn't his fault that I am so ignorant. He was just supposed to take us to Tonga, not be our oceanic mentor for three months, but his impatience is still irritating. While John shakes his head at me in disgust, I think smugly that he does not suspect that people know things about less watery realms of which he has no inkling. It doesn't matter though because, as always, Rick comes along and patiently explains in two sentences, two paragraphs, or two volumes—whatever it takes—what to do and how to do it. Rick makes John's brilliant idea happen.

To the spinnaker pole handrail we now attach one edge of

the fishnet, which we have cut to match the length of the fish pool. Through the opposite edge of the net we thread and tie our remaining length of orange PVC pipe, which also fits the length of the pool almost perfectly. On the PVC pipe we attach four evenly spaced weights. On the keel of the outer hull we screw pulleys. We pass lines from the ends of the PVC pipe through the blocks and back to the mother hull up to the keel.

One of us can sit on the keel with the two lines in hand like the reins of a buggy. Ease out the lines and the weights drop the PVC pipe down through the fishpond and pull the net after it. The huge jaw of the net opens, hanging down six or eight feet. When the fish come, we will quickly pull in the lines, drawing the net's mouth closed and raising it above the water, trapping the fish. This is going to be great. Almost too easy. We won't even get our feet wet. We can catch fish with our eyes closed; we could do it while watching TV. What a plan!

We hang around the fishpond like teenagers waiting for a gorgeous mermaid to emerge, leaning on the pole handrail, gazing into the depths. "There's one," I say.

"Yeah, there are fish down there," answers Phil anxiously.

"Let's drop the net." John and Phil slowly lower the net so as not to scare our catch. Rick and I take the point position to tell them when the enemy is boxed in, when to make their move.

"Hey, Jim, you see any fish?"

No, Rick, but any time now." We wait, and wait. And we wait some more. We pace the sidewalks, glance under the hulls, look back to John and Phil perplexed. "They've gone, John. They're all gone."

We decide to leave the net down overnight. Maybe the fish will get used to it and return for their usual morning frolic in the pool. The next morning we scurry on deck like a bunch of kids at

Christmas. We see nothing. Ah, they must be down there. Let's pull it up and see.

The net rises, perfectly vacant. Goose eggs. Absolute zero.

We persist. The system is too perfect not to work. For days we leave the net in place. Rough weather plays havoc with it, twisting it, tangling it on the outer hull. We yank it free with a rip. Disgusted, we finally roll the haggard, holed net and lash it to the spinnaker pole handrail.

We have failed. We presumed too much. We presumed that fish were not as smart as we. The fish have defeated us; our greed defeated us. We caught nothing. We drove them from us. They are all gone.

Chapter 13
Frenzy

*Beginning of September
and Fourth Month Following Capsize*

"They're back!" *Battle stations! Battle stations!* In the predawn light, in a half-awake excitement, we stumble out onto the keel. Within moments, we scramble to our stations and throw ourselves at the tasks that hunger has drilled into us. We see nothing but the goal. Like dancing on a tightrope, we pirouette around one another on the keel, trying not to slip off. Phil yanks a series of slip knots at the mast, instantly freeing the gaff. He cascades to the sidewalk, urging Rick to hurry. "Come on! Come on, Rick! They're down here. Let's go! Let's go!" Rick struggles with the last bouncing slip knot on a stay that secures Cortez the Killer. John sorts out the sail bag while I clamber down onto the sidewalk to receive it.

Phil quietly tiptoes out along the sidewalk of the forward beam, stalking his skittish prey that may bound off at the first strange noise. He even lowers his voice as he continues to coax Rick, — "Come *on*, Rick" — and then turns his attention to the fish. He whispers, "Oh, God, look at that one. That must be ten pounds right there!" They slide sideways, skimming the surface, their fins cutting the air, and then they nose down and flip their yellow tails at us as they head for the deep. Other mossy green forms emerge from the space-black sea like rockets, somersault at the surface, and shoot off again. Phil coos, "Ooh, come on fish, hop to it. Just a little bit farther. Oh, you're going to be lunch."

Rick, hovering over him, gives a distorted echo: "Come on, Phil, come on. You can do it, Phil." From the bleachers I add to the chatter. John is a silent spectator, calmly sharpening a paring knife that he uses to fillet.

A big kingfish wheels past Phil, just out of range. "Ah! Did you see the size of that one!?" he exclaims. Then there is silence.

Phil yanks the gaff, its point striking flesh with the force of a shotgun blast. He rips the kingfish from the water while Rick slips the net under the fish. Rick and Phil admire their twisting doomed quarry for a few seconds before Rick shoves the mouth of the net at me and into the sail bag that I hold in one hand. With my other, I grab the bottom of the net, tip it up, and push the fish down to seal its fate. I am amazed by Phil's quickness and strength. The hole in the fish from the gaff is so large from the force of initial impact that it is no wonder the fish have routinely wriggled off.

Phil is already stalking a second victim. He scores again before the fish are gone.

Our elaborate net was a total failure and will remain rolled up and lashed to the spinnaker pole handrail for the rest of the voyage. All those hours of untangling it, all our efforts to struggle to the top of the survival heap, all for naught. Maybe that's what we deserve for building expectations. In the society I left behind, people struggle lifetimes to achieve their goals, even when they know that the results always differ from their expectations. In the life of the Eskimo, one cannot afford expectations. One can only hope and pray that one's skills are great enough to fulfill one's needs. In the real world, we are blessed when, one day at a time, we adjust to the vagaries of nature and match the incredible skill of the creatures on which we depend.

In this place, I am aware that we "achieve" little. It is only luck that grants us, together, enough skill to make it to tomorrow. Like parts within each of us, the net was a total failure. We never even talk about it, but it hangs there like a bad conscience. With the net, at least, we knew when to back off, when to cut our losses.

Now, each dawn, as soon as the sun edges over the horizon to light our life, we awake, keen on another day's fishing. Even petty arguments are curtailed when a mate sticks his head in the cabin and says, "The fish are here." We forget about everything and race out to the deck, anxious to get high on the hunt. Then we catch fish, clean it, cook it up, and eat it. Everybody's happy. It is amazing how quickly days pass.

Between brief showers, fish come and we set to work. Phil "the wand" Hofman hooks. Rick nets. I hold the bag. I then gut and scale and John fillets. In time, our arts are refined. Phil learns to use less force with the gaff—just enough to secure the fish and not enough to blast such a big hole in it that it can escape. He hones the point frequently, lays in wait for fish for hours. Rick and I plan a new landing net to replace Cortez the Killer. Utilizing the same handle, we make a new net using wire from the crab trap for a frame, which is thinner and should cut through the water more easily.

Before I gut each fish, I hold it up and admire such a work of art. They are strong and proud fish that I must grasp tightly to keep from escaping. Each one is unique—slightly different in size, shape, color. Inside, too, they differ. Not only does each have varying food in their stomachs, not only are the females full of delicious dull-golden row while the males hold the other half of potential life in milky sacks, but all also differ in the length of their intestine and in the shades of their organs. After I place their organs in the gut jar, the hearts often continue to throb. I do not know why, but when I find eggs inside a fish, I handle that fish with a slight bit more care.

We have never been so self-sufficient before and it feels deeply gratifying. But it is not just our skill that has earned such fulfillment, it is the spirit of these fish that has granted it to us.

Rick too now feels the power of the hunt. He tells me how the thought of a fish wriggling on the end of a line used to make him feel a bit sick. Now, nothing makes him feel more whole. The hunger, the patient stalking, the catch, and the feeding of our hunger touches a primal force within each of us. We are fulfilled by fulfilling our own needs. We may even be gaining weight.

When we say grace now, it seems less desperate. The words sprout spontaneously from some deep and moving place within us. Even Phil finds words easier to come by. It is evident to all of us that, not only are we increasing our own chances of survival but we also have had great fortune to find shelter and water and food when we have needed it. We take nothing for granted.

John and I in particular share a reverence toward our luck. We feel a power, some kind of universal force, watching over us. When we are thirsty and rain falls, or when we are hungry and a fish leaps into our net, John and I look at each other with a nod, or he winks at me. I do not think my God is his God, but we share a sense of power over our lives that dwarfs our own capabilities, a power that has so far been, but may not remain, beneficent. We hope but do not expect tomorrow to be as successful as today.

Rick will not forgive himself. While he was transferring water to the chilly bin on the plank a ghoulie attacked. Seawater sluiced into our fresh water icebox. It seems that water will not be a problem for us now, but one never knows. It was before; it could be again. We must always plan for the future. So we begin to store water, raising the five-gallon jug or chilly bin to the cockpit and siphoning it through the cursed vent tubes into the boat's drained tanks.

Food, water, shelter, companionship—life is complete. It is still difficult to come to terms with the fact that we may not ever reach shore, that I may never enjoy the sound again of children playing, that I may never have a child of my own, or see a baseball game, or be free of want, but that's the way life is sometimes. No one ever gets everything. Like John, we must learn to accept, even thrive in our world as it is; and like Rick, we must never lose hope that we might overcome our adversity and escape, or at least work to make our world a little better.

Even Phil seems to accept our drifting life. In stormy times, he no longer nervously wriggles like a maggot on a hot plate, ready to leap to the entryway. He is not only calm but also enthusiastic. "Just wait to see what we catch tomorrow!"

When it rains at night, we no longer have a light to guide us as we move around and fill the jugs, but it doesn't matter. We know our tasks. When we cannot see, we learn to do without sight. I no longer feel sorry for blind people. When you are handicapped, limited, held hostage, you discover things that you never noticed before. You learn to use things that, even with good eyes, you were blind to, both in the world and in yourself. You can always learn to cope.

One afternoon John, putting one finger to his lips, hands me a slip of paper folded into a nugget like a little fortune cookie. I unfold it, wondering what the spirits beyond have channeled through John to tell me, but the note is more down to earth. Even in the muck you might say. "Do you think we can fry up the burley? Maybe it would taste better that way," it reads. It is an inspiration. I shake my head, "Yeah, yeah!"

I mix burley with flour and fry it up straight. It rises in the pan like little cakes. Throw in a couple spoons of jam and stir it around, and the "burley balls," as we call them, become glazed. They are completely and utterly different from the burley gook that we could hardly choke down. We now enjoy crispy, sweet biscuits that are even better than our old store-bought treats. Burley balls are like found money. They owe us nothing. We did not count them in our food budget, so we eat them over two days in three sittings. Sure it's garbage, but it's really good garbage.

With the help of heat, nothing is wasted. Every part of the fish is used except the scales. We suck fluid from between the vertebrae. The skin is fried to light crisps that we particularly enjoy. Even the bones and fins we boil until they are chewy enough to eat.

Although we would never admit it, in many ways, these are the best days of our lives. Our patience at the hunt, our reverence for our catch, our increasing knowledge of our environment and the raw materials that surround us that allow us to create and refine our tools, and the absence of waste, are all marks of a most valuable transformation. Although we live in a world of water rather than a world of ice, I like to think that the Eskimo would consider us worthy.

Approaching Mid-September,
the Fourth Month Following Capsize

Fish. Fish. Fish. They dominate our thoughts and our desires. They have continued to return to us and we have continued to prosper. Until recently they have appeared primarily at dawn and dusk, but as we drift into increasingly warm waters through lengthening and warming days, they swarm around our raft, at least within sight. I bob for them with feathers and tinfoil wrapped around a couple of steel nuts that dangle from the orange PVC fishpole. Up and down, up and down. They come curiously and follow the lure up where "the wand" awaits with his crooked deadly hook. The more fish we catch the more we are driven to fish. We forget all about keeping a watch for ships. Perhaps we have settled into our hostile environment, or perhaps we have learned greed. We begin to *know* that fish will be there each morning when we arise. We begin to *know* that we will catch all we want.

There is virtually no vinegar left, so we are left with only the sun to preserve a stock. Fish fingers that John calls, "my little babies," we string and hang on the rigging until they are hard. We then weave them through the stove grates and sandwich them securely with a piece of the crab trap. To keep them dry, we take them below at night where they are smoked in the exhaust of our cooking meal. But we are more and more interested in fresh flesh, cooked to order.

At first we catch one, *maybe* two six- to ten-pound yellowtails a day, so we argue over whether or not to have a half fillet (quarter of the fish) each. We settle on a half fillet split in two and eaten in two sittings.

Before long we're capturing three or four fish a day, so we argue over whether or not to have a full fillet each day split into two meals. We're really in the money.

One day we gaff a record five yellowtail kingfish. It's a small step to a whole fish each, and we joke about the day, that will surely come soon, when our pension fund is overflowing with shares of John's "little babies" and we can afford such luxury.

Phil seems transformed. He is a master of his trade now and struts in self-assurance with chest thrust out. We cheer our nautical gladiator as he launches himself into the pit to do battle with Neptune and bring back the spoils. We are gladdened and amused by his proud stance and the confidence he holds in his role as provider. When Phil falls into a general slump, even if he misses a single fish, he pulls up the end of the gaff and inspects the point as if something must be wrong with it.

I, on the other hand, find myself back in the restaurant business, a master chef cooking to order. Food is the center of our essence. Everyone gathers around and stares as I create a common purpose from what we scrounge from the boat and reap from the sea.

Rick tells me he wants it fried forty seconds a side. He times it, tastes it, says, "That's not done. Another ten seconds on each side," and sends it back to the kitchen.

Phil is less picky about his fish. "I don't care how you make it just so it's done." But he detests the gooseneck barnacles. He wants a special soup without them, just for him. We vote him down. It must be the way the barnacles look that turns him off because I sometimes surreptitiously slip a few into his serving and he shovels it down in fine style.

John takes stuff any way it comes and billows an ecstatic groan as he tastes anything I serve up. "We've never had it so good," he says.

Occasionally I poach fish in powdered milk or a sauce made from fish-gut sauté. Rick is impressed with the variety I provide. We can afford little extravagance, but jam biscuits and dabs of tinned food or bits of remaining fruit offer variety. We've dined on another albatross and a smaller bird that Phil and Rick caught. But it is the use of spices and little bits of garnish that make the most difference to our fish staple, sweet one day, savory the next.

Still, I mostly fry our catch. As I lean in the corner with the pan eight inches from my face, a mate holds a screen over the pan to keep the oil from popping out. When we are ready to flip the piece, he pulls the cover off. Sweat dribbles down my forehead, cheeks, and nose. Greasy steam and sputtering oil attack my face and lungs. My head aches, eyes sting, and chest hurts. But the reward is right there. My piece is coming up.

We begin tonight's fare with a teaser of fish jerky: strips of fish woven through stove racks, sun dried, and slightly smoked in the cockpit from the rising fumes of previous meals. The jerky is followed by an hors d'oeuvre of boiled mollusks with garlic and peppercorns, which in turn is followed by an appetizer of sautéed fish guts with Chinese barbecue sauce. Soup of the day is fish head with seaweed. For the entrée we enjoy fresh yellowtail fillets pan fried and cooked to order. For desert we offer fried biscuit cakes glazed with strawberry jam. Would you like a spot of hot tea or cool fresh rainwater, sir?

In brief intermissions between courses, we escape the boiler room of our cabin and take fresh air on the promenade deck, gaze up at the stars, chat about the next course and the way in which the fish futures seem to be shaping up down on *Rose-Noëlle* Street. After the meal we ease back, sated, and fulfilled. Mr. Hoffman suggests, "Ah, Mr. Glennie, about that treat—shall we have it now?"

John just shakes his head. "Philip, you've had enough. Be thankful for what you have."

Despite our success with fish, we still filch unfishy taste sensations from the ship's stores. One day Rick finds me with telltale milk powder on my beard. Another day I catch him. But it is not just us. At night when the light goes out, a waft of beef bullion floods the cave. Rick declares loudly, "I smell beef bullion. I smell tandoori too!" Utter deafening silence. He nudges me and I him in return, knowing the smile that is on each other's face. "I think there are rats in the cupboard around here," Rick teases. We envision John's hands frozen in position just inches away from the cookie jar, waiting to close the lid in the cover of noise, but it remains very, very quiet. After a while we settle back down and the smell disappears. Almost every night we are treated to the routine inspired by a carousel of smells: Vegemite, curry paste, chicken stock, mustard. . . . It can only be John. Phil has always refused the inside position of the dark side in front of the cupboard where the spices repose.

It's one thing for spices and other flavorings to disappear, but our supply of precious kiwifruit has been decimated. We began with almost a hundred, had forty fruit just a couple weeks ago, and now only a dozen remain. I'll admit to taking kiwis several weeks ago, but I know I'm not taking them now. Who is? I'm mad. Rick's pissed. John's angry too. And Phil is livid. Time for emergency legislation.

John, Rick, and I are certain that we three have nicked food, so we are careful not to point accusing fingers. We do not bother to deny what we do steal, but try to cover ourselves with intrepid attacks concerning what we have not stolen. "I don't know what happened to those kiwifruits," I say, "but I counted them two weeks ago and sure as hell there are a lot less of them now." Of course I took them before that, but hey . . .

"Yeah. Somebody's been pulling a swiftie," concurs Rick, eyeing Phil.

There is a cruel irony in our suspicions toward Phil. None of us have any evidence that Phil has stolen a thing, but he is so food oriented that he *must* be guilty, right? Whenever Rick and I have noticed Phil heading for the aft cabin alone, we nod to one another like a couple of store dicks. One of us shadows him, keeping a surreptitious eye on his every move. Who said life is fair?

We toss around the idea of dividing all the remaining stores right now and eating them as we please, but that does not seem feasible. No one would want to consume his whole share immediately, so we would be left with four separate caches that would no doubt become jumbled and lead to even worse bickering. We decide on two courses of action. First, no one is to ever be alone in the cabin. Second, we inventory the remaining stores and choose the essentials: one full jar of strawberry jam, a half kilo of brown sugar, a quarter liter of honey, 250 grams of Marmite, a quarter kilo of bread crumbs, and a half bottle of cheap barbecue sauce. These items we tuck into a locker within the tunnel that leads into our cave. It is exposed to view from the inside and out, and is covered with the folded cushion. It is a virtual vault.

Conveniently for us thieves, we leave the remaining half kilo of milk powder and the spices out because they are so frequently used. Nobody bothers to steal from our half kilo of rice, eight cans of various food, or kilo of flour. We divide the kiwifruits and devour them all over the next couple days to get it over with. So ends our inventory and whatever remnants of mutual trust we may have had until now.

"How about if we all take turns cooking?" suggests Rick.

John declares, "I think Jim's been doing a good job here. He's been coming up with some lovely meals. I'm satisfied with Jim being the cook."

Phil turns to me and says, "Been doin' a bloody good job, Jim. I don't know how to cook anyway."

Case closed. Next case.

We may *accept* our plight, but the only thing we really *enjoy* around here is food, and I control that pleasure. No one tells me what to make or when to make it. *I* choose. I even basically choose how much we eat. I watch the crew gather around the pot while I spin my magic spoon. Their eyes are enchanted childlike saucers awaiting the result. Phil is "the wand," but I am the sorcerer. Maybe Rick is afraid of my power. Maybe he envies it. Whatever. I feel his disappointment in me. The spell that has brought us so close together bends, stretches, threatens to break.

I crawl out of the cave and find Rick working on the new landing net that, together, we designed and were to create in partnership. I flinch, as if slapped. It is one of those minute unspoken things, like walking into a neighborhood store and finding your girlfriend there talking to a man you don't know. Your mind runs with it. Whether you want to or not, within the insecure niches of your brain, your girl and this man roll around in a bed together. I say nothing to Rick and he says nothing to me. He does not even look up.

Another day Rick asks me if he can help me cook. "Sure, if you want to," I answer him. But I do not tell him when I begin to make the meal. John is there. His animated voice and elfish face relay amusing stories about his two-bit catering business in Sydney when he had to debone twenty-five chicken breasts nightly and would throw them in the trunk of his car for delivery. He never made much money at it, but it was fun. I find myself enjoying John's company. John takes a sip of my broth, "Ah, lovely." Rick crawls into the cave and finds us together. Rick stares at me until I look up to meet his cold steel eyes.

Fish, fish, fish, and eat. Fish, fish, fish, and eat. We cannot wait for the next morning and the next round of the hunt. At mealtimes, almost before each piece is cooked, Phil and Rick lunge forward and grab their share like hungry dogs. I'm just a short order cook now. Everybody wants his fish fast and prepared different from everybody else's. Then they retreat to eat their individual dish. As meals become more grandiose, the ambience becomes increasingly ravenous, more isolated, and impersonal. Things just aren't the same as when this restaurant first opened.

Hunting and eating are the only issues of day-to-day living around which our lives now revolve. In themselves they are as simple as going to work in the morning and stopping at the corner store on our way home, but the tentacles of their implications reach out to wrap around every part of our lives. Food threatens to capsize the stability of our relationships.

Phil jerks another kingfish from the sea and Rick is there with his new, wider-mouthed net that glides effortlessly through the water. Phil never really touches the fish until it is prepared for a meal, but now he tells Rick to wait for a moment with the net. He reaches in and pulls the kingfish out, holding it with outstretched hands like a long sandwich. He rotates the fish, admiring it from every angle. "This is a nice one, but I think the one yesterday was a lot bigger." Done fondling the fish, he hands it up to me on the keel where we, the preparers of food, do our job. John shows me his technique of filleting fish and we talk about what we want to do when we get back.

Below us the hunters banter back and forth. "You gaffed that one bang on the right spot, Phil."

"Well, you were right there with the net too, Rick." They discuss their kids and motorcycles and days that they spent growing up in Auckland.

John and I have slowly weakened. Our movements are purposeful but weary. Rick continues to look the most haggard, weaving uneasily as he waits with the net. Phil's as fit as a buck rat. He's probably never been in better shape. He bounces with vitality, twisting and turning like a gymnast. We kid him that his wife won't recognize him. He still has not taken a single heart pill. The medicine bottle is left forgotten in some locker.

The rest of us struggle to climb from the wing deck up to the keel. As if taking pity on us, Phil dives into one of the outer hulls to retrieve a ladder, which we tie against the main hull so that we now have a stairway between our upper and lower perches. While we slowly fade, Phil is eager to take watches, do dishes, check the direction of the wind with the compass. And he is always ready to fish. One morning after a light rain, one of us wonders aloud if it wouldn't be a good idea to check the bucket at the mast, but there is no reply until Phil suddenly bursts, "Crikey Dick, do I have to do all the work around here!?" Before we can crack a tired smile he is out like a shot. What the hell is he talking about? we all wonder.

Phil is so exuberant that he seems to have completely forgotten his forecast of doom, his hundreds of hours of ceiling patrol. Now he is consumed with the life and death of fish and his glorious return to land. He likes this boat now. He likes it so much that he tells John that he wants to buy it when she floats ashore. In the *Twilight Zone* in which we exist, it seems perfectly reasonable, at least to John. They even dicker over a price. How much is this slime- and barnacle-covered, dismasted, half-flooded, torn-apart wreck worth? Well, it seems that John will "let it go" for ten thousand bucks. Phil, on the other hand thinks that's a "bit too high." How about eight thousand? John says he'll think about it, but he also offers Phil a hand in giving the old *Rose* a face lift. I guess it is no unsurmountable task to rebuild a capsized boat once it comes to a feathery rest on a soft white beach.

Like Rick and I, Phil and John also seem to be drifting apart, however. Bargaining over their interests in the *Rose-Noëlle* extends to confrontation. Lying side by side, their noses remaining pointed to the ceiling, Phil and John argue ear to ear. John criticizes Phil's current boat, but now unintimidated, Phil fights back. He details the sturdy integrity of his boat's construction.

"Ho-ho! That thing is going to sink like a stone as soon as a whale hits it,"says John.

"Wait a minute, John. That's a bloody nice boat. That's my home. That's where Karen and the kids live."

"Well, at least you have something to go back to, Phil," John moans. "You don't know how lucky you have it."

"It's pub night, Phil!" interrupts Rick.

"Oh, yeah!" says Phil dreamily, easily distracted from John's morose and dictatorial manner. "I could go for a pint of Speights about now. And a cigarette too."

"One thing I can't stand," says John, "is when people come on *my* boat, bringing beer and spill it all over *my* cushions, smoke cigarettes and put 'em out on the sole."

"What are you getting your knickers in such a twist over, John? Nobody asked you," says Rick. "What's the matter with knocking down a jar now and then? What are you always picking on Phil for anyway?"

"No worries, mate," Phil calms Rick. "I can hold my own with John." And so he can.

On deck, John increasingly confides in me. He tells me how he's never liked Rick, but he doesn't like Phil either anymore. I do not want to listen to it. I tell John that we have to get along if we want to survive and he says, "I know," in the way people accept news that a friend has died. I want to like everyone, try to listen to all my mates and be as much of a friend as I can. I am the ambassador between feuding sides, but more and more Phil and Rick consider me John's ambassador, on his side, against them.

As weeks pass, I still slip in next to Rick under our common sleeping bag, but we begin to bicker with each other about little things. "Hey, hey, give me more space, mate." We grab the corner of the sleeping bag and jerk it to pull it over ourselves in skirmishing tug-of-wars. During the day we talk *to* one another but not *with* one another as we had so many times before. The depth of our conversations are limited to a "Hand me this" or "Go get that."

As John and I await the next fish on the keel, we are separated from Phil and Rick by just a few yards, but the divide seems to be a gigantic chasm. We have our jobs and they have theirs. Ah, screw 'em.

John pulls out a packet of photos of a fabulous family house surrounded by lush gardens. We talk about landscaping and his sister who lives there. John tells me about growing up surrounded by music. He tells me about his brother. He tells me about sneaking into a peach orchard and gorging himself on the glorious juicy fruits. He tells me about his son and how much he misses him, about his daughter whom he has not had a chance to know. He still mentions writing his book when we get back, but why not? He has lost everything. All he owns is this wreck on which we float. We talk about Thailand and our desires to visit it. He asks me about my life and the place from which I came. John becomes much more than the cardboard cutout I thought he might be. He becomes more whole, rounder. John too has something to which to return, a reason to survive.

When John's pen runs out, he commands Rick to give up the pen that has logged all the letters to Heather. I stay out of the middle of that one. Surprisingly, Rick backs off and hands the pen to John.

I don't think that John misses his relationship with Phil, and I think Phil is happy not to be so enamored of the great Glennie image. After all, Phil has now tasted the ultimate adventure, and as we weaken, Phil finds himself the strongest of us all.

But I miss Rick terribly. We have lost each other's trust. Maybe it's not true, but I feel like Rick talks about me to Phil. Maybe he tells Phil all those things he doesn't like about me, the things that I feared he would tell me when, a lifetime ago, he trusted me enough to ask me what I didn't like about him. I keep wondering if I should just approach him straight on, straighten this whole sordid business out, but I just cannot bring myself to do it. I tell myself that it's his fault so he should approach me. He, no doubt, thinks the same. I miss having Rick to bounce ideas against, miss his support, miss giving my support to him, miss our cozy talks at tea. I want to fix it, but there are too many broken parts to know where to begin. It is as uncomfortable as the demise of any relationship I've had with a woman. And here there is no place to run, no place to hide. To be honest, I am sick of looking at him and he is sick of looking at me.

I draw back the cloth that covers the stainless steel deep dish to reveal our evening meal of four fillets. Phil and Rick typically have their nose practically in the plate. Maybe it's my imagination, but their eyes seem more feverish as each day passes. They inspect my every move as I fry the fish and serve the fillets out on the plates.

"Hey, wait a minute," says Phil. "What about that one in the corner there? That one's a lot bigger than this one on my plate. Give me that one."

"Sure, Phil." I exchange the fillets and then hand Rick his plate.

"What about the one in the pan?" he says. "I want the one in the pan."

"Okay, Rick. Which one do *you* want John?"

John and I look each other in the eyes. He smiles a bit and winks at me. John leans forward, his eyes darting back and forth between the two remaining fillets as he continues to grin. "The one on the left is bigger. I'll have that." I begin to serve it to him. "Ah, no, no, no. The one on the right. That's the one I want. That's *definitely* bigger."

The next day John sits on the keel, slicing up our catch. He is incredibly meticulous. He pares off the equal sides of the fish. Each fillet is composed of a thick steak along the back that thins toward the belly and along the ribs. He slices the fillet lengthwise. Like an artist he adjusts, as well as humanly possible, for the difference in mass between top and bottom. The bottom fillet ends up larger but quite thin. Personally, it's the one I prefer because it is sweeter and fuller of fat. The top steak is more of a strip but quite thick. Phil walks up on the sidewalk, his eyes level with the fish. He grabs two pieces of recently cut fillets. "You call these even John!? You call these even!?"

"Look, Philip, if I had a scale here, I can guarantee you they would be the exact same weight."

"Hey, John, I just want to make sure I get my fair share," he says, poking his finger at his own chest.

"Philip, do you want to do this?"

Time stops. "Oh, no no, John." I almost expect "the wand" to come out with "I catch 'em, you clean 'em," but he just says, "You're doing a good job, John. I just want to make sure they're even."

I am so sick of Rick and Phil's fish-crazed eyes scrutinizing everything we do. I'm so sick of their insinuations and suspicions, as if John and I are manipulating the biggest pieces of fish into our own plates. I begin to give them what appear to be the smaller pieces just to get a rise out of them. It's no easy task because John is so good at dividing things evenly, but it's worth the effort just to see them go berserk. It is a great source of amusement for John and I. I hardly get the fish-filled spatula headed toward one of their plates before there is a loud, "Hey, hey, wait a minute!"

But my own game is also turning against me. I find myself less concerned about the sweet belly fillets and more interested in capturing the thick meaty pieces from the back. That is what they prefer so that is what I come to prefer.

It isn't long before Rick and Phil insist that we take turns choosing our own piece of fish. At least that alleviates the basic problem, so we all agree. But how? Who picks first? We try choosing fish sticks. We strip a dried stick into four different lengths. Phil puts them behind his back, mixes them, then holds them out. Longest goes first.

This system doesn't last long. We argue that somebody might just be luckier than somebody else and get the longest ones more often. And maybe this stick isn't really longer than that one. The idea may be okay but this whole process has gone from the practical to the ridiculous.

Finally we decide on a rotating order of age. John, Phil, Jim, and Rick. Next will be Phil, Jim, Rick, and John. And so on.

One would think that we finally have the fish frenzy under control, but wait! Now each person takes his turn choosing a cooked fillet. John and I quickly flip one onto our plates, but Phil and Rick examine each piece, noting every flake and piece of crust. By the time we're done, the food is cold.

So why not choose before the fish is cooked? Now Rick and Phil fondle each piece, turn it around, their eyes burning with intensity as they visually dissect each one. The gears in their minds seem to take offsets from each piece, put them through a complex formula, and calculate probable volume and weight. Sometimes they return to a piece several times before making a final choice. The last guy in line gets a mangled fillet covered with greasy hand prints.

And when I get all the fish into the pan sizzling, there is an invisible tether between each piece and its owner. If I shift the pan or turn it, my barge mates' heads are drawn to the side or twisted around.

Phil becomes particularly annoyed one evening when it's time for fish-head soup. When I make the soup, I dunk the heads into boiling water for a couple minutes to flavor the broth and cook the heads. Then I lay a head into each mate's plate. But out of the four fish heads, which are usually about the size of a baseball, one stands out like a softball. It's my glorious turn at the top of the roster and I tell Phil he should know which one I'm going to pick. Phil frantically objects. "This is a special situation," he complains as he lobbies hard for an amendment to our constitution. But it's clear to everybody that all Phil wants is the big fish head on his plate and there's no real way to butcher the heads for equal distribution. His proposed "special situation" emergency legislation goes nowhere.

John often winks at me during the choosing process before it is his turn. Then he mimics Phil and Rick. He plucks up each piece and inspects it, turning it carefully every which way. Rick and Phil lean toward John, their eyes seriously glued to his every motion until he places the piece back reverently in the plate. Then he says, "Uumm, I think I'll take that one—oh, wait a second, that one seems a wee bit bigger. No, come to look again, that's the one for me." Phil and Rick never catch on. Like zealots faced by a cynical comedian, they merely take his game as confirmation of the seriousness of this fish business.

Finally sick of the whole mess, John suggests we have one dinner of diced fish in a sauce. No way. That would mean that someone might get a cube more or less than the other guy.

During each round, before every meal, John and I are left either smiling at each other and winking, or merely shaking our astonished heads. Sometimes I think I hear him groan with frustration.

Morning after miserable morning, at the first glimmer of light, we launch ourselves from our cabin and begin again to attack the sea and each other. In addition to the fish, we have captured a third albatross and second tiny petrel. The breasts of the petrels are so small that they are like two fingers joined, but we are as keen to eat them as anything else. We eat everything. We will eat anything. Sometimes I have unspoken thoughts. I wonder how long we will drift before we begin to eat each other.

In just a couple weeks, we have traveled far from the spirit of the Eskimo.

About 19 September, Day 108 Following Capsize

After several Mexican meals, four or five rounds of fried breads, and Lord knows how many uncooked dough balls and little danishes, our ten pounds of flour are gone.

In the morning we sight a hazy line of cloud to the southwest and believe it is a contrail. In the afternoon we sight a second jet trail—this one definite.

About 25 September, Day 114 Following Capsize

Rick sits on the hull, his hair tossed in the brisk wind, his arms wrapped around his legs, peering into our fishing hole. He can see no fish.

John emerges from the cockpit for a pee. "Oh. There's a boat," he says in his usual dispassionate manner.

"Where?"

John points and Rick's eyes slowly focus on the shape of sails. John has amazing eyes. Rick calls Phil and me on deck. The boat is too far away to see any smoke that we might generate in this wind, but we delight in its form. Twin masts hold three sails and she moves with the same powerful purpose as the sea itself.

That's got to be *Steinlager*, says Phil. Built to race around the world, *Steinlager* is an eighty-four-foot ketch that flies up to seventy-five hundred square feet of sail. While we drift at a half knot, *Steinlager* would sail a minimum of ten knots in this breeze. We are envious. Just over there a crew works together to harmonize their vessel with wind and sea. She looks so powerful, so strong. Still, I wonder what would happen if she ran into an iceberg in waters south of Cape Horn. How much of a team would her crew be once confined to a life raft?

Steinlager is the only big ketch in New Zealand that Phil can think of that would be moving so fast. She must be out on training for the round the world race. We must be near land! We must be near New Zealand! Rick remains skeptical, but the rest of us are heartened.

On 2 September, over three weeks before we think we have sighted her, *Steinlager* joined her competitors to start the thirty-thousand-mile Whitbread Around the World Race. The starting gun blasted and they were off, down the Solent, away from England, half a world away.

It is the middle of our seventeenth week adrift, 116 days of being cooped up in this cell. At least the weather is like the end of March in the Northern Hemisphere, early spring in New Zealand. There is more rain than ever, but few storms. We seem to have drifted well north toward the equator. In the lengthening, calmer, warmer days, we are able to spend long hours in the exercise yard of our prison. More encouraging than the weather are the growing number of birds and a bloom of bluebottles. In the waters around the boat swim blue-tinged, undulating bluebottle jellyfish that look like translucent, golf-ball-sized hula skirts in action. Sometimes, trapped in the fish pool between the hulls, a few dancers will remain for days. Rick and Phil swear that bluebottles are found only off the North Island, especially in the warmer waters of the northernmost part of New Zealand. We *must* be near land, they say. They are even certain that we must be near Auckland.

A jet rumbles through the sky. We see not only its wake but the whole belly of the beast as it roars directly overhead not more than ten thousand feet above. It *must* be landing or taking off, and the only port possible is back in New Zealand.

"That's as good as a fix," says John uncharacteristically anxious. As Phil has adapted to being here, John has wearied of it. He thinks to himself: *This is enough; we''e been through this experience. We've drifted longer than anyone else. Can we go home now, please?* Like a runner in a marathon, John has completed his goal, proved what he set out to prove. The joke is, of course, that others have drifted longer than we. It is as if someone moves the finish line, the runner crosses it and goes home only to hear that his record has been discounted by the vagaries of fate. And so it should be for anyone looking to set records in this domain.

I want to believe too, however. I want home to be just over the horizon. Everything we see, everything my mates say makes sense, but maybe our hopes are just wishful thinking. We want land too much.

Phil is the only one truly skeptical. He says, "When I see a gannet, I'll believe it." Adults gannets do not venture far from their breeding grounds, several of which are in New Zealand. Within two hours, Phil's eyes catch sight of a bird approaching. Its long, sharply tapered, white wings banded in black, its yellow-crowned head, all confirm that it is a gannet, convincing even Phil that we have nearly arrived. But even as the sun sets, there still is no sign of land.

After dinner below, our torch flickers like a candle. We decide to take a stroll out on the keel to enjoy the star-studded night, the moon, and fresh air. John is the last out. Rick looks down to see the faint flickering glow within the hull. "John, you didn't leave the gas on down there, did you?"

"Umm," John puts his fingers to his head, "I think I did."

"You did what!? What are you trying to do, burn this boat down? You know better than that! You're an *idiot!"* Rick screams.

John sits on the keel quietly. He would like to at least enjoy the beauty that this evening has to offer, but he is knackered. He's tired of this voyage. He's tired of Rick, but he's even more tired of arguing with him. He doesn't bite. Instead, he quietly takes Rick's verbal whipping in silent resignation. He finally just slithers below to keep the torch company.

"Look, Rick. Why are you so fucking hard on the guy?"

Rick is caught aback and thinks for a moment. "Yeah, you're right. I was hard on him, but the boat *could* have caught fire." He pauses. "I'll try to be easier on him."

Phil offers, "I'll stay up here and take first watch."

Rick and I slip below. The flicker of the gas torch still looms in the cave, resting at the head of the berth beside John. John is wedged into the corner with his back against the hull and head brushing the ceiling, looking down at us as I settle in the middle and Rick reclines beside me. We lay on our backs. The dead air is hot and sticky. As Rick struggles to remove his wool singlet, he glances over at John's stony facade. The chiseled nose and deeply furrowed brow cast half of John's face in deep eerie shadow. The other half is starkly lit. Ropy tight muscles clamp his tapered chin on a straight thin line of lips. From within the deep caverns of their starved sockets, his black eyes blaze with the reflected flame.

Rick stops, looks John square in the face, and barks, "What are you looking at!? Just what the fuck are you looking at!?"

Chapter 14
Aotearoa: Land of the Long White Cloud

September 28, 117 Days Following Capsize

Rose-Noëlle eases over lightly ruffled, languorous rollers. Gunmetal waves mirror gray sky. A listless breeze barely cuts the humid midday air. Alone, moored to the keel, Rick sits staring into the dull horizon with his head collapsed into the palms of both hands. His watering eyes bore through the haze toward a smudge on the rim of the world. He does not shout "Land ho!" He does not move.

For days we have seen so many signs of land—the bluebottles, a jet, a gannet, and even a long low bank of pale cloud on the horizon. The Maoris named their land Aotearoa, land of the long white cloud. It *must* be out there, waiting for us. But each hopeful sign of land has been followed by bitter disappointment. Each of us has been so sure that we have spied terrestrial forms standing above the sea only to watch them mutate within twenty minutes into just another lousy cloud. Perhaps this specter in the haze is another apparition, conforming only to our wishful thinking. So Rick does not stir.

I poke my head out, see Rick, and risk coming out onto the keel to sit next to him. I too see the fuzzy charcoal ball on the horizon. I scoot up the keel and stand, hanging onto the spinnaker pole. The spot seems slightly more distinct. I squint, close each eye in turn to make sure it's not a spot in my own tired vision, peruse the whole horizon, and look back to find it unmoved. I look down at Rick and back to the mark that I now feel *must* be land. Down and back, down and back, down again and my eyes contact Rick's, and then we both turn away. Finally I fetch a pot and slip down to the deck to collect mollusks.

John appears on deck and sits next to Rick, who points to the dirty spot. Squatting and yanking barnacles off of the hull under water, I look up. John says, "Yes, it looks like land."

"That's what I was thinking too," I say. Since Rick first spotted it, about an hour has elapsed when Phil makes his appearance. "What do you think, Phil?" we ask, pointing.

"Oh, yeah, shit, that's land!" Phil jumps up and dances to the mast. Hanging on with one hand, he leans forward and pendulously swings from side to side, doing one of those open-handed salute-over-the-eyes numbers. "Fan-bloody-tastic, that's land. Yeah, that's land, John. It's land all right."

All afternoon the dark outline remains, faint on the edges but expanding slightly and becoming clearer. We sit on our excitement. We dare not tempt fate. We dare not get our hopes up only to have a slight change of wind blow us away. So we return to business as usual. John and I collect the mollusks. Phil and Rick snoop for fish. Tea break. But this day, we interrupt our routines every few minutes to take another look. Our deepest hope, our prayer to whatever powers there are, is to awake in the morrow and find it still there. Our dreams dare not progress farther than this.

LIFE IS UNCERTAIN; EAT DESSERTS FIRST reads the door-sized sign in the entryway of Befores and Afters, a restaurant that belongs to a friend of mine in Wellington who specializes in appetizers and desserts. It should also be Phil's motto. Since his and Rick's birthdays, he has constantly ear-bashed John about Phil's Treat—I mean *John*'s Treat. Is today the day? Finally John agrees. Today *is* the day. Still, since first light, Phil has been hounding him. "Is it time yet, John? How about now?" John does not bother to answer.

Finally John says, "How about rice pudding? How about right now?"

"Crash hot!" says Rick.

"Ah, yeah, John, that sounds great," I say.

"About bloody time," concludes Phil, smiling.

After a while John emerges with a steaming pot of rice pudding, which has consumed the last of our rice, sugar, sultanas, and milk powder. With a cup, he scoops and serves the pudding into our bowls and then deals out a few little peach moons and pours out the nectar, polishing off that store as well. To top it off he spoons out the last of our reduced cream. What a feast!

We are finally celebrating John's birthday. It is hard to believe it was nearly four months ago. John was right. We could make it. We've survived longer than I ever imagined possible. With over a hundred liters of water stored in the tanks and our success fishing, if we had to, we could go on for weeks, maybe even months longer.

Fluid turbulence, random action, chance may compose the mortar that glues reality together, but human hopes must rest on a sturdier foundation. Our shelter from harsh reality has been this boat and a grand illusion that we would certainly make it. John's own cocky, pigheaded positiveness, Rick's tool-making skills, my rationing of spices for the morrow's meal, Phil's catching extra fish to dry have all been predicated on the hope that we would survive day after day until we could find land. And here it is. We have lived, not in accordance with the laws of quantum mechanics, but in accordance to the human need for faith in the possibilities of our fate. People have no choice but to act like life *is* certain; save dessert for last.

September 29, Day 118 Following Capsize

Indeed morning light reveals a firm, solid shape still resting directly ahead. The wind has not changed, nor have the seas or overcast sky. The land is still a murky ebony, but its shapes are distinct. There are several islands in sight, tall with mountainous spines.

John estimates that we're about thirty miles out. Rick thinks he recognizes his old stomping grounds. The biggest one he believes is Great Barrier Island that stands guard at the entrance to the Hauraki Gulf. At the end of the gulf, just fifty-two miles away, Auckland, New Zealand's largest city and port, which houses half of the nation's population.

It seems unbelievable that we are here, that we might just drift right into port and pick up a ship's mooring. Rick's parents live in a suburb only a few hundred meters from the sea. Perhaps we'll wash up and be eased down onto that very beach. We deserve it. Why not?

But is Rick sure? Ninety percent sure, he says. He's paddled kayaks in these waters. He's camped on the shoreline. The signs of land all fit. The shapes of the mountains fit. But Rick does not tell us of his fear of Great Barrier itself. It is a fortress island that stands against the pounding sea. There are no real places on which to land, only places against which to be crushed. In my own mind I know no fear. In my ignorance I only see the movie score, the castaways finding themselves on a long strand of white sand.

We are encouraged, but we still fear a change in wind and just hope someone will find us before we are blown back to sea again. There is nothing left to do but to carry on the routine. John begins to store items in watertight containers, however, just in case. By late afternoon we spy several islands to the south and several to the north of the big island that broods right in our path. They also fit into the pattern. They are likely the Mercury Islands to the south and the Mokohinau Islands to the north. Like the butterflies in our stomachs with nowhere to go, we intermittently flutter to the cave only to be drawn back on deck by the promise of land.

Before midnight everything is lost in utter darkness, but from across the sea's faraway plane comes a sporadic, shimmering, faint flash like distant lightning. Besides the occasional slurp of a wave, the atmosphere remains eerily calm. The air feels thicker, more humid, as if a monster lays in wait for us somewhere out there under the cover of darkness.

John blurts out, "You know, I think we have the record now."

What? What on earth is he talking about? "What *are* you talking about, John?"

"The Guinness Book," he says. "A hundred and eighteen days—you blokes are going to be famous. Do you realize that?"

"Who gives a fuck, John?' snaps Rick.

I tell him, "John, I really don't give a shit about any record, personally. I just want to get on with my life. I feel like I just started my life when this happened. If I get another chance, that's enough."

Phil says, "All I want to do is get back to Karen and the kids."

Maybe John knows something we don't. Maybe he appreciates something deeply meaningful that we have yet to see in this horrible reality. But it is more likely that this voyage has merely given him a chance to prove to the world and to himself that he is man enough to master the sea. While Glennie waits and plans for public homage on rescue, I only wish to master myself. My mates and I dream of inner peace or simple escape. As usual, John's timing is dead wrong.

By one o'clock in the morning, the distant loom of lightning has become a regular fifteen-second pulse, perhaps a lighthouse. By two o'clock we begin to see the actual pinprick of the light itself. It *is* a lighthouse and we are plodding along, inching ever closer.

Although we are too keyed up to sleep, we certainly aren't going anywhere very quickly, so we often retire back to our nest for rest or a boil-up of tea. The greasy, fingerprint-infested entry leads to the same dead air, the same fishy stink, the same encroaching ceiling now so covered with soot that the calendar is barely visible. The once orange sleeping bag is now mottled with filth, oil spots, and water stains. A thick sodden brick, *Arctic Dreams* is now dry and feathery, but we don't look at it anymore. From the tunnel of *Rose-Noëlle*'s hull, the echoing slap of water as it dances, the musical thrum of cabinetry swinging in the surge, the clanging of our pots and the stove frame that hang like laundry on a line outside the cave isolate us from the peaceful rush of air and gentle orderly spill of waves of the free sea just outside.

I look at my shipmates and see in our flickering torchlight tattered clothes, haggard faces matted with grease-soaked hair, beards scattered with crumbs of food. All but Phil seem to move in slow motion. Just outside this dungeon is a beacon of hope that we may soon be free, but from within, our world is just the same, and progressively deteriorating. I hope, I pray that this is the real thing this time, that it is not the cruelest of hoaxes perpetrated by a sadistic power beyond our control. Please let us drift ashore.

Finally we decide to kill the flame and try to get some sleep. John slips out. A half hour or so later he reenters our cell and says very matter-of-factly, "A couple months ago we would have been excited and jumped outside to see a boat."

"What do you mean?" asks Rick.

"I just saw another ship, but it's too far away to signal. You can't even see its navigation lights."

"What!?" yells Phil as Rick rolls over unconcerned, accepting John's word. Phil practically bowls John over and scrambles to the deck. "I want to have a look," he says. Almost immediately I hear Phil stomping back across the plank to the cave. He scurries inside, shouting, "Shit, John, that boat is really close! I'm going to signal her." He starts rummaging through a ceiling locker in the dark. There's a clatter of gear flung about, the noise of some of it falling, a wrestling of bodies. "John, John, where's that strobe? We're going to try to signal her."

"No, you're not!" John orders sternly. "It's too far away. You'd just waste your time and the battery. Damn it, Philip, chuck it in!"

By now Rick has joined the scuffle. He'll believe Phil before John any day. "Come on Phil, let's get to it! That ship is probably already getting away."

"Leave the strobe alone!" bellows John.

"The hell I will!" answers Phil.

"Yeah, John, shift your carcass!" orders Rick.

"Get the hell out of the way!" echoes Phil.

"Who do you think you are? The skipper? This is *my* boat! *I* built her, not any of you. That's *my* strobe. These are *my* things. You've been helping yourself to the whole bang lot for four months!

You have no business taking *anything*. I'm in command here! You do what I say!"

"Bloody hell with you, John! You need your head read," Phil challenges. I hear a clutter of grabbing noises and feel bodies shoving and yanking. Phil must win the light somehow because he wiggles back out the hole with Rick on his heels.

John and I lay in the cave for about five minutes that seems like days. I remain as still as a root. I don't care if they signal the ship. I convince myself that we're too close now not to be saved somehow, even if Phil and Rick don't stop the ship. But what is John trying to do now, after all this time, trying to establish his command? But I dare say nothing. John's boiling anger is tangible, like the first light rumble in the ground before the volcano erupts. His body shifts in spasms. He is suddenly gone.

There's going to be a fight. I can feel it. Where is the diver's knife?

Rick and Phil's voices are muffled by John's position in the cockpit. In twenty or thirty seconds John reemerges in the mouth of the cave making a noise that I cannot decipher. He's either chuckling or choking on tears. When he gets in on his back he begins to guffaw. His whole body wracks with sharp maniacal laughter that hurts my ears in this confined space. What is going on? What's with this guy? Is this man, this skin-covered bundle of sticks, about to snap? He struggles to emit sentences between fits of strange gaiety.

"If you want—ha, ha, ha."

"What, John? What's so funny?"

"—see something really funny—" He shakes so with laughter that he can not talk, but tries between gasps for breath. "Ho, ho —you should see—ha, ha—take a look at those guys."

As I poke my head out the cockpit, I see Phil straddling the keel and unsteadily weaving. On his shoulders, Rick perches, hanging onto the mast with one hand and holding the strobe aloft with the other. Off to the north the ship steams. It is alive with light, like a floating carnival. To me it looks only a mile or so off. I see individual portholes. But it is now moving quickly away from us. I have to wonder if John watched it coming all along and never told us until it began to pass by. Why? What is so funny about it? I feel guilt. Rick and Phil have vainly tried to signal the ship while I remained below, but in the confusion of changing relationships these last few weeks, I do not know what to do.

I return to our madhouse dungeon. "Isn't that funny?" John manages to ask between raucous laughter.

"John," I plead, "it's not funny to me." This sets him off into another joyous binge. I feel completely befuddled, lost on a carousel of blinding emotions that is about to be obliterated by the pent-up passions of four desperate men. My tense hope over the last several days intermingles with John's bombastic talk of records, his apathetic reception of a close-passing ship, his intense anger when Phil—who was once John's fledgling clumsy protégé—challenges, ignores, and then casts off his command, and now this unintelligible hysteria. What is going on? How can I get out of here? *When* can I get out?

Phil and Rick finally return below and lie down in the middle between John and I. They are keyed up, chattering between themselves, "Boy, was that ever close."

"Yeah, I was sure they'd see the signal."

"That ship had to be no more than a mile off."

Phil says, "John, you're going berko, mate. We should have signaled that ship a long way back."

"Use your block, Philip. We would have never been seen. It was too far away."

"Crikey Dick, John, I can't figure you out. I think we could even see people on the deck. I just can't figure you out."

Slowly the tense atmosphere in the cabin subsides. We begin to slumber. I get out once to look around. The lighthouse is quite bright now and I see the loom of another to the north. When I report this to my mates there is no response.

We begin to drift off again when we smell garlic in the air. Every time I open the garlic bottle to cook, John emits his long ecstatic groan. But there is silence now, and then a trickle, and then an "Oh, shit, oh, dear. Oh, shit! Oh, dear! I may have just pissed in the garlic bottle."

Rick chuckles. *"That* says it all." As this bizarre sideshow closes for the night, it is our turn to laugh.

September 30, Day 119 Following Capsize

I emerge from the brig to relieve myself and check out the dawn. Fish already swarm the surface, stirring the long low swells. My eyes follow the waves as they roll away to the distance where they merge with . . . oh, my God! Broad shoulders of a monolithic folded island dominate my view. To the north, pencil-thin white beaches meet the oncoming waves. From the distant gray landscape, deep rich green close to emerges from wafts of mist. Color! The color of it! And the size of it! For fifteen minutes I selfishly gorge myself without alerting my mates. I am a glutton. I want the feast all for myself at least for a minute more. Through a carpet of woods, I see the cut of a road leading northward where the hills slope away and disappear into the haze. Behind beaches, the pitched woods are sprinkled with buildings. Dead ahead, near the top of the mountain's chest I spy a lonely, tiny white box.

John comes on deck and sits next to me, cooing, "Oh my."

I feel compelled to ask, "John, are you all right?"

He gazes at the island. Waves of confusion roll across his face. "You know, I'm the kind of person who holds things inside. I got kind of carried away last night. I wasn't sure what I was going to do. I'm sorry."

"You don't have to apologize to me, John."

We sit quietly for awhile. Then John sighs, "Oh, I've lost everything. I have nothing left. At least you three have something to go back to."

John slumps on the keel like some worn-out scarecrow. He wears his black singlet. His legs are threaded through the arms of a dingy white sweater, the body of which is lashed around his waist with green twine. His ducky feet that paddled off to take a last minute shower seventeen weeks ago are covered in tattered wool socks.

He looks beaten, vanquished by the sea, by us, by life. Maybe he thought that he needed only the uncontested command of a boat in the wide open sea to control the path of his dreams. Perhaps we all thought that a masculine voyage to the islands would restore us and prove the integrity of our lonesome flight. It was to be a pure voyage without the complexities of our shoreside give-and-take relationships. But our quest was capsized and, like the boat, is now only a wreck that rests beneath us. We may have lived these last four months as if our survival was certain, but our voyage through life is not. Dreams, like desserts, are best shared, and in the sharing, take on lives of their own. When we four men have shared, this voyage has transcended our mere survival and become much more, but when we have not, it has been much less.

I recall all the conversations I've had with John over the last month. He's told me that I have my whole life ahead of me, that I should use this experience to my advantage. His eyes would sparkle with enlightened fulfillment as if we knew something other people didn't know, that with the gift of this experience we would launch ourselves into a brilliant future. The wreck of the *Rose-Noëlle* would be a new beginning. It was what I wanted to hear, what I needed to hear. He was so confident. "I'm really sorry, John. I know that I've treated you like shit these last four months. But it doesn't matter now, John. It's over. This whole journey is over." I remind him of his own words of confidence and rebirth.

He turns to me, his eyebrows lifted, a sparkle caught in those deep eyes of his. "You're right, Jim. We're really lucky, aren't we?" For the first time, I actually feel like John and I have touched.

The fish boil in their pool as intensely as they ever have. I calmly unlash the net, make my way to the sidewalk, scoop, and come up with a fish. The net bends and collapses under the weight. "That's just wonderful, Jim!" cheers John with a big smile on his face.

"I think we should all have a big meal together," says John, "because we're going to need it." Rick and John may know what is likely to happen to us, but I have no idea. In my mind we're still going to float smoothly onto some sandy beach, carry a line ashore, and tie old *Rose* to a tree. Rick suggests that maybe a "fizz-boat" will roar up to us as we get close, although there's no reason for a small motorboat to be out here. Maybe a fishing launch will cruise by and we'll toss our gear and ourselves aboard while they take *Rose* in tow. I'm ready for a good celebratory banquet.

John doesn't even ask who wants which piece of fish this time; he just dices it and dumps it into the pot. I add the last can of baked beans, a can of corned beef, some water, and boil her up.

The food is warm and there is a lot of it. It helps calm our stomachs as we find ourselves closer and closer to the island. Anxious to return to the deck, we wolf the meal in fifteen minutes. We dream that we will drift to the south of Great Barrier Island and head into the gulf. We can now see details of the rocks and trees. We even see wild goats climbing the slopes. Waves crash into rugged cliff faces and smash themselves into fans of white.

"This isn't going to be a party, you know." Rick's words hit me like an anchor on the head. We *aren't* going to drift south of the island. We're going to crash straight into it.

Ours is a fate met by sailors before. In 1922 the freighter *Wiltshire* smashed into the rocks just south of where we are now. Heavy seas trapped 102 men and the next morning snapped the vessel in half. The island's precipitous cliffs impeded rescuers' efforts, but after two days every man from the *Wiltshire* arrived safely ashore. No rescuers know we are even out here, though. We cannot call for help. Our fate will more likely be like the *Wairarapa*, a steamer of about eighteen hundred tons, which drove straight into

Great Barrier Island at eight minutes past midnight, October 29, 1894. One hundred twenty-one people died and to this day no one knows why. Great Barrier devours the small as well as the large. All that was found of a sailing dinghy in 1984 was debris on the rocks. Booming waves dragged its two crew away forever.

Rose-Noëlle swings down the coast past ridges and seething backwash that serve as landmarks. Our speed seems incredible compared to the apparent stillness of 119 days surrounded only by rising and falling water. We slide south along the island but edge closer to catastrophe by the hour, just a mile or two away now. We will not clear the shore.

We begin to gather gear and put it into whatever we think will be waterproof. Without thinking about it, Rick and I find and share a small plastic container with a screw-top. Rick lists what we will need. "We'll want our life jackets. Get your shoes, whatever you want to bring ashore." I can see by the look in his and John's eyes that both are tense. Rick pulls from his pocket two rolls of film. "You think I should tell John about these?" I shrug my shoulders. "Do you know what these are going to be worth if they turn out?"

Yeah, all our pics for the calendar. There's the one of Phil naked wrestling with his fish, one of us finishing our great net, and another of us looking depressed, John scratching his head and shrugging his shoulders at the great net's failure. We captured John and me cutting the hole through which to haul the LP tanks and Phil and Rick's faces, their eyes bulging in anticipation over fish frying in a pan. The camera caught Phil huddled over the generator with springs popping out and bolts falling in the water, and his gazing toward land like an Indian scout. I recall our laundry flapping in the wind, Phil gaffing while Rick waited patiently with the net, John filleting fish like a surgeon, the four of us around the barbecue like kids around a campfire. In my mind John emerges from the deep with a smile and a hand full of spaghetti and leans against the corner of our cave with the flicker of a flame and an inferno in his eyes. I do not know which we have pictures of, but the images are burned into my memory, enough for a calendar of thirteen months. It was, after all, an unlucky year. Or maybe thirteen isn't so unlucky after all.

I grab the film out of Rick's hand and throw it into the container quickly. "They'll be safe in here." We scurry to gather essentials: "Letters to Heather," our passports, some money, and plane tickets back from Tonga.

Rick takes my buck knife from me and tosses it between his hands, feeling the balance. "Sure is a cracker knife," he says, and then tosses it into the can. The container is full.

John and Phil have also gathered some gear, stuffing some clothes, food, and a couple more plastic waterproof containers into a sail bag. In the plastic jars John has secured the remaining treasures of his life—his notes, boat plans, logbook, articles he's already written for magazines, and his bicycling medals. Phil has donned his foul weather gear and gathered a remaining half-dozen cans of food in a bucket into which he also tosses the diver's knife.

A speck in the sky banks around the northern side of the island, seemingly stops and expands. We hear a faint buzz that grows to the winding grind of an engine at high revolutions as the dot elongates into an expanse of white and red wings and tail joined by a slim fishlike body. I grab the PVC pipe that we've removed from the fishnet and to which we have attached a flag, leap up on the keel, and wag it around like a madman. Phil waves his arms, his white foul-weather bib overalls glowing in the sun that has burned off the haze. Rick grabs Martha's yellow raincoat to flag the plane down. John also waves. Waaaaaooooo, the plane roars above us, beyond us. He must have seen us. We wait for him to circle and make another pass, but he banks again to the west and disappears around the other end of Great Barrier. Would he even know we are in distress? From two thousand feet, with a mast rigged and all, we might just look like a normal boat.

We do not stop to worry about the plane. Maybe he saw us, maybe not, but it doesn't really matter because there's no longer enough time for help to reach us. We hear the breakers, see the smashed water swirl in and out of the rocks. *Rose-Noëlle* rises and eases down again on the swells that grow as the bottom of the sea emerges to meet the surface. As far as our eyes can see, only sheer cliffs drop to the sea. There is no place to land.

As *Rose-Noëlle* skims along, a rocky promontory slips back from view and exposes a bite out of the coast. We see a small beach in the cove. It's been the only break in rock walls for miles. Ah, my beach, I think for just a moment. Maybe we'll drift straight in there.

Other than this distant hope, the danger of land lords over us. Even looking nearly straight up, all we see is a jumble of stone. The air is full of the noise of rushing water, heavy surf, and shouting voices. All but mine are issuing orders. "Make sure your life jacket is on!" Only John is without one.

"Okay, when we get close enough to the beach, jump, and swim for it."

"Does everybody have shoes?" I pull mine from the mast where they've lived for four months. Shoes now feel so strange and confining. Over the open wound that still stands pink and oozing on Rick's ankle, he pulls a pair of socks. I tell him there are some high-top sneakers in the packing of the aft cabin.

He races below, rips the place apart, and comes up again. "No good, I can't find them." But Rick has a life jacket in his hand that he throws to John. "Here, mate, put this on. What, do I have to always be your mum?"

John smiles at Rick as he slips on the jacket. For about three seconds, we are relieved by the unusual lighthearted ambience between the two foes. Then there is nothing left but to wait in our unspoken fear. John and Rick stand on the wing deck, hanging onto the rigging. Phil and I sit on the keel, grabbing the boat's backbone and centerboard slot, already braced for impact. I bite the side of my mouth with anticipation. I get up, climb down to the wing deck, stand for a moment, get back up on the keel again. We hang on as *Rose-Noëlle* rides the growing waves. They break against the weather hull to our back. She surges and we cling to her like riding a giant bronco. She swerves, changing course, heading for a ridge of rocks that is sunk into the shoreline like a cleaver, cutting us off from the beach. We're not going to make it.

We might not even make it as far as the island's ridge. Scattered boulders and reefs stretch a hundred yards to seaward from the shore. The ocean breaks over them. Waves pound through holes that they have punched into the land over millennia. Water floods, back out, eddies, and seethes. Swirling currents grab *Rose-Noëlle*, yank her around, and then twist her back again. "We have to stay with the boat as long as we can," John insists. There's no question now about going overboard. Alone in the water we will be pulverized to bits of scattered flesh. But if we stay aboard, the boat will certainly stop on the ledges. The sea, in a last brutal assault, will rip her apart and leave us clutching wreckage, facing her wrath alone. Dead ahead now is a vast flattened boulder like a tipped table over which rollers wash.

"Brace yourself!" *Rose-Noëlle* quivers. A slow metallic moan emanates from within her body. It is the muted sound of the stub of her mast meeting, digging into, and plowing up the bottom of the sea. A wave lifts us and the noise stops,. The wave then drops us, and the boat shakes as the stick screeches, twists, and folds. Twenty feet before we strike the table reef, we rise and fall again with a shudder as the metal mast rakes the rocks with a muffled unsteady noise of fingernails dragged along a blackboard. Ten feet, eight feet, five feet, another wave picks us up, pausing for a moment. I look down on my mates, on our ship, on the rock upon which we will drop. I jam one hand in the hole in the keel. Rick and I reach toward each other, lock hands, and squeeze tight.

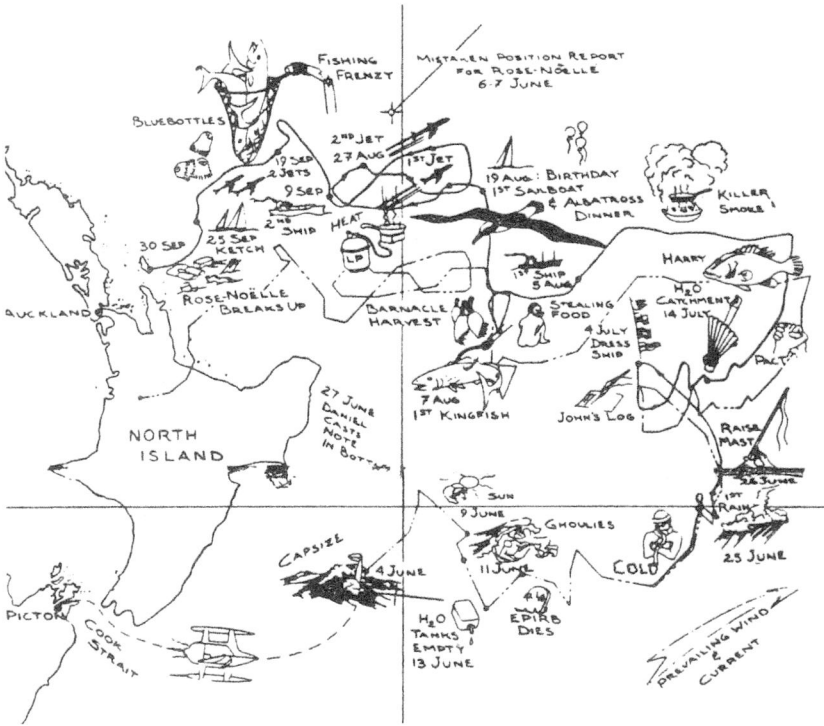

The 119-day drift of the Rose-Noëlle *off New Zealand.*

- - indicates computer-generated drift path generated by Aukland Weather Service, provided courtesy New Zealand Yachting Magazine.

_____ *indicates adjusted probable drift path with dates cited.*

Chapter 15
Adieu

Rose-Noëlle falls. She strikes. Her bones crack and snap. Her skin splits in the shuddering impact of her death. She washes sideways onto the reef, trying to shake us off and almost tipping us over backward as the wave retreats and she comes to rest on the slanted ledge. Each new roller that strikes is shattered against the dropped outer hull that faces the open sea. Booming shields of water sail over the entire boat and land on us. It is frigid, shocking. Phil and I rappel to the wing deck to find small refuge behind *Rose's* main hull. The four of us grasp the rigging, unsure, afraid.

There is no textbook maneuver for this position. *Rose* seems quite stable on this rock now. Nightfall will blind us in just a few hours. Shivering, we listen to *Rose* as she is torn apart by the onslaught of waves. Pieces of her drift around the boat, whirl aimlessly in the eddies. Many are covered with a forest of barnacles. We do not know what to do, so we stand around dumfounded. For an hour *Rose-Noëlle* lurches, smashes down, and works her way more securely onto the ledge.

John shouts to us over the uproar to stay with the boat, but the jaws of ocean meeting stone devour *Rose-Noëlle*. It will not be long before we are trapped in darkness, floating with nothing to cling to. There is so much noise and water in the air, so much motion as *Rose* shakes and smashes down, so much fear and apprehension, that there is no time for democracy. Instinctively we act on whatever sounds like the best idea of the moment. Land looks only a hundred yards away. Maybe we can make a swim for it, but we feel so small, are aware of how frail and powerless our boat is, sitting here under the gaze of this landmass. Rick is keen to get moving. "Look," he says, "the boat is stable. It's getting cold. We're going to start really suffering from hypothermia and it's going to be dark soon. Let's do *something!*"

He suggests we construct a raft on which to float our gear ashore. Even if we're lucky enough to find a tiny break in the island's ramparts to crawl ashore without getting smashed, we'll have a hard enough time just trying to keep ourselves afloat without the added burden of gear. We can use a raft to add to our buoyancy and to cushion us while landing. Rick and John direct us to take the chilly bin and clamp the lid closed, gather the five-gallon water jug, the orange fish buoy from the masthead, some old clumsy life jackets, water bottles in a sailbag, and some drawers, and bundle it all up with rope. Our bags of gear, even a sleeping bag and blanket, we bind to the makeshift raft. Under the raft's ropes, Rick jams the bear.

We begin to push it overboard, but it tumbles into the fish pool between the hulls. When the waves retreat, the fish pool drains and the raft sits on a rock bottom. If *Rose* lurches forward on another wave, she might override the raft and crush it when the wave withdraws. We must get the raft in the water, floating free, but already it is a soggy, cumbersome, ragtag, lump. John ducks below to see if there is anything down there to augment the raft's buoyancy, but all he finds is debris crashing around in a cabin with its top ripped away by hammering rocks. Waves tear the dinette table from the hull and smash it into the side. It's too dangerous below.

Our weary muscles strain as all four of us yank and pry the raft out of the fish pool. We roll and coax the raft to the top of the outer hull, but there it sits like a mutated amoeba, saddling the keel and going no farther. John and Rick hop off the boat to pull it from the other side. The raft gives way and plummets to the rock. Rick and John roll it into the water and set it adrift.

We gaze at it for about five seconds. Rick stands about ten feet away on a small summit; John at the boat's side. A tremendous rumble fills the air. *Rose-Noëlle* pitches, rises, groans, breaks, and surges forward on a turbulent sluice toward John and Rick. Rick clings to a pinnacle but John is knocked off his feet and disappears in a thick soup of sea marbled with foam.

Fortunately, the wave carries him forward faster than the boat so he escapes *Rose-Noëlle*'s onslaught as she comes to rest with a tooth-smacking slam. Fifty feet away, John emerges in a confused puzzle of whirlpools. He pirouettes one way and then the other, is swept away and then pulled back. His head rides the currents, his eyes wide as fried eggs. The life jacket, which is unsecured because Rick used the ties for our kerosene lamp, forms a puffy yellow nest around his head. A hundred feet from him, in its own pool, the quickly deteriorating raft wheels around, pieces of it strewn out on the water, bubbling up, being sucked down by the oceanic Jacuzzi.

My mind conjures frightening images. First, *Rose-Noëlle* drifts away, leaving Rick on the reef to face the open sea alone. Then, *Rose* is back on the rock when a huge roller plucks her up and drops her on top of Rick. "Get back on the boat! Rick, get back on the boat!"

He seems not to hear for a moment, but then turns. Dazed, he stumbles to us and we yank him aboard. Another wave jolts the boat, and another. *Rose* slews and twists in agonizing contortions. More chunks of her flesh join the clutter of our raft and John in the surrounding maelstrom.

Then we are free, floating off again, edging forward, then being carried back toward the open sea—advance, retreat, advance, slew left, whirl right. . . . Our gear is on one side of us, John on the other. John does not seem to be swimming, just going round and round. If he is yelling, we are made deaf to his pleas by the booming waves and the destruction of his love as we all drift shoreward. Rick finds a line with signal flags tied to it, maintains the presence of mind to carefully coil it, swings the coil forward and back—once, twice, on the third lets fly. The line sails toward John, unwinding as it goes and lands short of him. Another throw lands to the side. Each time Rick pulls it in, coiling, collecting data instinctively, recalculating. The third toss drops the line almost over John. He grabs it and we begin to pull him in. He seems to struggle against something caught around his legs, but he gets it free and we haul him aboard. He's been in the water about fifteen minutes.

John is clearly out of it, shaking wildly, unable to get up. "Oh, thank you, thank you," he says. "Oh, I'm sorry, I think I shat in my pants," he adds embarrassed. This voyage has destroyed this man's entire material world. It has starved and strained him into a ghost of the confident boastful Captain John Glennie whose boat could never capsize, whose dominion over his god within could never fail.

Slowly *Rose-Noëlle* works her way through the counter-currents and rocks until she grounds for good within fifteen feet of a couple-yard-wide strip of flattish stony ground backed by steep cliffs. "This is it. Let's go!" says Rick. He leaps off the boat into chest-high water. "Come on, Jim!"

An image permeates my brain. In it, I drop into the water when another wave lifts *Rose-Noëlle* and drops her six-ton carcass on top of us. I fight the fear. Take control, I tell myself. Follow Rick. Do it! Now! I focus only on the dry rocky beach, lower myself, and grab Rick's hand. We wade ashore as fast as we can, but the water is as heavy as lead. Receding waves sweep around our waists, hold us back, pull us toward *Rose-Noëlle*. Oncoming waves push us forward, and so too they lift *Rose* and send her leaping forward, snapping at our heels. She stretches her leash to the bottom, comes up hard, and settles back again. It is a long thirty seconds before we reach the rocky ribbon above water. As we stumble away from the wreck, Rick and I clutch one another. One of us loses our footing and then the other, but one of us is always there to support our mate. We can only hope that Phil and John will follow without being crushed. They are on their own now.

We stagger from boulder to boulder around the tiny peninsula that stood in our path and robbed us of a softer landing on a pebbly beach. Behind us, Phil and John make their way ashore among the increasing debris of the disintegrating boat.

Refuse from our equipment raft swills among the rocks, the core of it in a confused lump. John's eyes are drawn to the remnants of his belongings. *Rose-Noëlle* is doomed. John has nothing left of any value save the bucket with his bicycling medals, log, writings, and boat plans, but he is too weak to retrieve them. Phil wanders among the wreckage, bends over to the bulk of the raft, and cuts a bucket loose. It is not the bucket that contains mementos of John's past glories or hopes for the future; it is only the bucket containing food for the journey ahead. It is all John can do to get up and follow. In his pocket he holds identification, useless outdated credit cards, and, printed on soaked little rectangles of heavy paper: *John Glennie . . . Adventurer by Choice.*

We stop at the point of land to wait for our comrades and look back to see Phil and John approaching. The walls of the peninsula are too steep to climb, which would allow us to hike around to the beach just twenty-five yards away, but we also cannot bring ourselves to plunge again into the cold water. When Phil and John arrive, we remove a few cans of food and the knife from the bucket and drop them into our pockets. A few tins of food and a knife are all that remain of John's beloved *Rose-Noëlle*. As she is ground to bits, John looks back. It is time to say good-bye to her, to the men we once were

Phil says, "See you later," and plunges into the little lagoon. We watch him for a minute or so as he surges across and pulls himself onto the opposite shore. We follow, holding onto one another for support. Once across, I struggle from the water while Rick helps John to his feet in the surf, but John can hardly stand, much less walk. When I return to help, a wave catches me off guard and I fall, striking Rick's legs from the side and knocking him down. He yells with pain. As we flounder to our feet, John teeters, plummets, strikes his face on golf-ball–sized pebbles. With his legs still in the water, he doesn't move for about five seconds. Rick and I reach down and peel him off.

It is getting dark and we would like to lay down forever right here and now, but Rick knows that we have already lost too much body heat and says, "Come on, keep moving." John wants to remove his clothes, but Rick scolds him to keep them on. Time and again John begins to strip, but each time we force him to remain clothed.

Once away from the beach we are out of the wind and make our way over a grassy slope and then into a gully that increasingly steepens. Our goal is to mount the hill's spur and follow it to the single man-made structure on this end of the island that we spotted before the crash: a box sprouting a TV antenna twelve hundred feet up. Our footing is quaky, our balance destroyed by four months at sea. Stumbling over roots and bushes, weaving around small trees, we fall frequently, but we get up and proceed with our bush-bash until darkness hides the trees and other visual references. We spend more time on our knees and butts than walking. We must halt.

We jam the knife into a tin of corned beef. Grabbing chunks of the salty meat, we wolf it down like it is some kind of elegant roast. For the 119th night, we nest like spoons to try to stay warm. We shiver, suffer from bruises and cuts, are miserable even before the light rain. We listen to the rolling surf as it clatters rocks, rends man-made things. For a brief moment we long for the comfort of our dry secure little cave that now lies crushed below. Every time we get comfortable and begin to fall asleep, one of us has to get up to relieve himself. Somehow, though, perhaps because we bask in the security of even this miserable piece of ground, perhaps because we are so dogged tired, we sleep more than the moment we think and the night disappears in a seeming blink.

"It's light out," says someone.

"Nah, it's just the moon," answers I. But no, it is another day.

October 1

John D., the director of Outward Bound, looks at the row of his staff's message-mail pigeonholes. He hesitates for a moment, as if his act betrays the hope that we are still alive somewhere, and then removes a nametag. Jim Nalepka is gone.

Outside the school, students grunt and groan as they bend and stretch and then take off on their two-mile run in preparation for awaiting adventures.

We were lost at sea for four months. Now we're lost in the bush. We decide to make for a northern settlement rather than for the lone house cresting the hill. At first we take a step and fall to our knees with vertigo; then two, then three, until finally we walk in a weaving unsteady line. We argue about going this way or that, turning right or left, heading up or down. We still operate an uneasy democracy, but this is tempered by our trust in Rick. Even John keeps saying, "This is your territory. You be the leader."

Rick tries to steer our band to its goal, but the bush gets too dense. Finally Rick says, "Look, we have to turn around and go back. From the hill at least we can see where we are and any settlements." So we thrash our way back to the spur and labor upward again. After four hours of pointless bush-battling, we cross an almost imperceptible dent in the foliage. Possibly, just maybe, it is the shadow of a path. We follow it until it becomes clear that it is a human-created track.

A Nikau palm attracts Rick's eye. Guiltily, he cuts into the revered native Kiwi tree, slicing pieces from the trunk. We eat the yellowish-white, melonlike chunks composed like congealed masses of pasty, dry, fish eggs. The sacred tree yields our first harvest from the blessed earth and I want to enjoy the meal more than I actually do. I want this tree to be a sign that our survival trek is over. I want its bounty to be succulent and sweet, releasing us from the necessity to do and eat whatever we must in order to gain the strength to move on. But like insipid cereal with just a hint of sweetness, the beautiful tree provides bulk, nothing more. We still wear the masks of weary, desperate, lost men. Will we ever get out of this? Will the bush now trap us as the sea has done?

We carry on until the path finally opens onto a wide, clay road woven with tire tracks. We whoop and holler, slap each other on the shoulders and backs. We have returned to humanity!

Turning to follow the road up a weaving incline, we soon pass a *bach*, but the small cabin is empty. A hundred meters further a second bach is also deserted and locked, but outside stands a greatfruit tree with eight glorious, luscious, juice-filled fruit. We're so keyed up that even as we stop to look at the tree we keep marching in place, but the greatfruit tree is too much for us; it draws us like steel to a magnet. We have not seen fresh fruit in over a month. It isn't even floating in saltwater! We grab one and slice it up. We doff the skin of the first, grab a second, slice it in half and dig in; rip off a third, peel back the skin, split it up, and push our faces into it. Then a fourth. Juice covers our noses, cheeks, and chins. We wipe it off with our hands, lick our fingers.

Wait! We've had enough. We decide to leave two fruits. We give the absent owner our apologies and thanks and move on.

A cold drizzle clouds our view, but looking up we see our goal. We pass several small outbuildings, but everything is locked and deserted. Finally we arrive on the summit, at the door of the house on which we gazed just a day ago while so full of fear. It too, however, is empty and locked. We are spent. We decide to break in, spend the night, and walk out in the morrow. Fortunately, we find a window with a broken latch through which we tumble into our new nest.

The house is composed like a jumble of boxes. The inside is still under construction with wire ends sticking out of the walls and boards stacked in the living room. The phone and electricity are dead, but the gas stove works just fine. The place is commodious and dry. What else could one want? What's more, the place is stocked with food. Somebody must spend a lot of time here. But we are in too much of a hurry rifling the cabinets to care about the decor of the place or worry about its owners.

It is not long before we are full-flung into an orgy of food. Someone shakes a huge jug of milk powder into solution. John piles so much museli and dry cereals into his bowl that they begins to cascade over the lip and onto the floor. As if mesmerized, he continues to spoon it on until I snap him out of it with a sharp, "John, stop it! You can't get any more into that bowl." The rest of us are no better than marauding bears. We tear open bags, rip the tops off boxes, spin off jar caps. The table is piled with sultanas, nuts, peanut butter, Marmite, honey, sweet biscuits, cereal, dried fruit, milk, Milo. . . . We do not even bother to light the stove until we are sated. Then I brew up coffee, real coffee, hot coffee.

We sit in real chairs with real cushions. It is like sitting in a womb. The joy of clutching a steaming cup, of *not* rubbing against someone else, of having no fear is indescribable.

I look up to find a man staring at us from the top of the stairs. He's bronzed of skin, clean shaven, and stands there stately in a white cardigan topping stylish white pants. He begins to float down the steps, a model about to emerge onto the runway. "My God, Philip, you look like a million bucks!"

"Ah, thanks, mate."

"Where'd you get the slick threads, mate?" asks Rick.

Phil tells us that the wardrobes upstairs have plenty of clothes for us all.

We wash in heated water poured into a shub—a shower-tub that is like a bathtub cut in half. We take turns alone in the bathroom. Looking into a mirror is a strange sensation. I find there a skinny body with long beard and hair. I've lost twenty-five pounds or about sixteen percent of my weight, but I have retained good muscle tone. Phil has lost a good forty, maybe fifty, pounds but now looks great. John and Rick are the most haggard, but none of us, once washed and newly clothed, look like we've just crawled out of Auschwitz. We have no telltale saltwater sores that are the trademark of life raft survivors. We have not lost a third or more of our weight that is so common to survivors of shipwreck who spend half our time adrift. We are incredibly fortunate.

Meanwhile, Phil leads John outside to have a go at starting a generator. Phil can't wait to kick back, put his feet up, and watch TV. John begins to help him, but then thinks it's best we leave the generator alone. With all the disconnected wires, two voltage systems, and our ignorance of the setup, we could easily blow up the system or start a fire. Phil is persistent, but John is just as reticent and finally convinces Phil to leave it be.

Sitting in the living room with another glorious cup of coffee in hand, I gaze out a large window onto the open Pacific Ocean, it's expanse unbroken by land until, five thousand miles distant, it washes up on the shores of South America where in theory we should have drifted.

As the afternoon wears into evening, the drizzle outside becomes rain and the wind begins to rattle the windows of the house. It is not a raging gale, but it is blustery enough to hammer home to me once again just how lucky we have been. We landed in the nick of time.

Perhaps we were *un*lucky to be on a boat that huge storm waves can turn upside down and that will not reright itself, but that is true too of many boats with single hulls. It is also true that more conventional craft, if holed, sink with all the determination of a rock. Thousands of ships of all kinds that faced the same conditions that sealed our fate have been overturned, broken, flooded, and lost. The sea does take prisoners after all, but one also cannot underestimate its power to destroy.

Nor can one underestimate the power of men to create. In the aftermath of disaster, we made a life on a boat that could not sink. There we were blessed with food and water, with the expansive exercise yard that life rafts lack. And when it came time to crash ashore, she brought us safely in; whereas a more fragile rubber raft would have been rent by the sea and rocks too far away for us to swim against the eddies. *Rose-Noëlle* gave us a chance out there and somehow we found the strength in ourselves and each other to survive. Sometimes we even shared more than that. Rick says, "We became part of the elements out there," almost as if we became kingfish or albatross.

Now that we are clean and dry while the rain streaks the pains of glass through which I view trees whipped by wind, I wonder, have we lost something, or gained it?

There are too many mysteries to ponder. Why was it that we were able to clamber ashore just before night when we would have been entombed by the deadly sea? Why was it that rain fell every time we really needed it? And why did we not drift that five thousand miles east, instead coming to rest back against the breast of the place we departed? The answers do not really matter. Everyone will provide his own. The questions themselves help me to recognize and appreciate the richness in just being here, in just surviving, in being granted more time. Time: That is the only commodity of real value.

We are like Romans retreating for brief moments between endless courses. For the evening meal, however, we are more patient than we were in our earlier ravenous attack. I make spaghetti with asparagus. We lay out a table under candlelight, with personal serviettes, forks, and knives. I uncork a bottle of red whine and pour it into fragile, tall-stem glasses.

Each of us takes a turn giving a brief, glassy-eyed, heartfelt thanks. We speak calmly, slowly, as we first did when we made old Harry into *poisson cru*. Then we raise our glasses and propose a mutual toast to life and to each other. We eat patiently, enjoying each bite, relishing each nuance of flavor. No meal has ever gratified me as much.

A mild romp to Tongan beaches was our adventuresome dream. The road we traveled was through hell—sometimes we have put each other through hell—but demanding as it was, it was also fulfilling. We all sense a unique feeling of accomplishment. Now there is no tension over what tomorrow will bring. All of our past arguments, misery, judgments of one another have been drowned and swept away. We sit in the flickering, romantic glow of the candlelight and bath in the radiance of each other's spirit. I do not yearn to be anywhere else. I am totally satisfied and content here with my mates.

In some sense I feel completed by these men. I would like to think that we needed each other to survive. We needed John's single-minded self-confidence, Rick's perfectionism, Phi's steadfast consistency, even my diplomatic need to be needed. I would like to think that no other group of four people would fit well enough to survive our experience, but when I look within, I see more clearly now that parts of everyone's souls have a place within my own. Survival is not so much a matter of what strengths are peculiar to the four of us. Rather it is a matter of discovering how much like anchors peoples' personalities are. Sometimes while we struggled to survive on the deep blue sea, the way in which we solved problems and managed our relationships with one another kept us safe, but at other times even our greatest strengths became dangerous weights snagged round our legs. Just one little slip and at least one of us may not have made it back alive. It is so difficult to know when and how to stand up for yourself and when to back off and lean on someone else whom you might not even like.

None of us are heros. We are just men, as flawed as any men from any age, struggling along the indistinct line between self-interest and altruism, hoping to survive. We are not unlike other social animals in that respect. If we stole from one another, so we were at times generous. It will be no different next year or next decade when we decide just how to manipulate our taxes, as if the money will not eventually come out of somebody else's hide. We then will turn around and give a wad of dough to charity. If we are evil men, so too is civilization until that day when, out of the goodness of its collective heart, people everywhere drag out all their goodies and divide them equally. My mates and I rationalized all right, and we fed ourselves before we fed our mates, but *within limits,* as vague and variable as they might be. I do not know if it would have been so in another month or another year, however. That doubt, like my awareness of unanswered questions, makes me appreciate our good fortune. We did not have to confront deeper demons within.

The voyage is over, or so we think. Time for home. Phil desires the feel of Karen and his kids beside him. Rick craves a chance to forge a new life with Heather and Mattie. John and I . . . well, I at least wish to find out if Martha and I can learn to enjoy mutual need. But this jolly crew is in no hurry now. It feels good just to rest on solid ground, looking out on the torn ocean, listening to the windows rattling in the howling wind, feeling safe.

After dinner we settle into separate spaces in the house. John writes a letter to his journalist friend Pat who helped him write *Playboys of the South Pacific* and who surmised that we were likely blown up by our propane or run down by a ship. Rick, Phil, and I lay under the light of candles or kerosene lamps. I hear John getting sick somewhere.

The last few days, the last few months have been exhausting, but I do not sleep. I roll this way, flip over that way, and get up. I thought I would cherish being alone, but it feels too strange. I sit on the side of Rick's bed. We try to put into words our feelings about how wonderful it is to be back and how we are glad not to be out there at sea tonight. We are filled with excitement, completely empty of apprehension about tomorrow.

On his way to the bathroom or outside, John periodically

pokes his head into the room as we talk and says, "Oh, isn't this wonderful?" Sickness is preferable to drifting, I suppose. Eventually we all gravitate back to the kitchen where we brew more tea or coffee and wait for the next day.

Rose awakens at 4:44 A.M. She has had her own dream this time. In it John stands on his boat and yells to her, "Here I am." Later in the morning she tells John's sister about the dream.

In the United States, my friend Joe shuffles the piles of papers on his desk and discovers my last letter to him.

Over coffee and rice pudding, we enjoy the breaking of a new day. Wind and rain matter not a whit. Looking out onto the white-capped ocean, Rick says, "Shit, if we'd come in today we wouldn't have made it."

Phil slips out to diddle with the generator again and John takes after him fuming. Again Glennie lays claim to his captaincy. He insists that Phil leave the electricity alone; if we start a fire, John says he'll be held responsible. After what has become a typical confrontation between Phil's new-found energy and Glennie's old-time command, Phil stomps off up the hill.

Phil returns saying, "I hear a phone up the hill." I trot up the road with him. We break in through a bathroom window and find a crank phone. Spinning the crank, we can't figure out how to work it when a three wheeler roars up carrying the first outsider we've seen in four months. He is short, handsome, looks gentle and quite perplexed as we buffet him with cacophonous jabber about a capsized boat, albatross, ships, crashing against rocks, bush-bashing. . . . I expect him to grab us like long lost friends, but he merely nods, politely listening, shakes his head slowly, and calmly punctuates our chatter with an occasional Swiss-accented, "Aha. Unbelievable." It must be unbelievable. It was his friends who sailed the dinghy into the rocks of Great Barrier four years ago and were never seen again. Before we slip off to our new friend's macadamia nut farm and his home for a hot meal, he connects us with the police and Outward Bound.

"You have a collect call from Jim. Will you accept the charges?"

"Who?"

"Jim Nalepka."

"Nobody named Jim Nalepka works here. Uh, wait a second." I hear a hand cover the phone and mumbled voices. After about twenty seconds the director of OB picks it up. "Hello," he bellows, "Jon D. speaking."

"John, this is Jim. Do I still have my job?"

There is a pause, then a "Jim! Jim!"

I tell John just to stay still while I talk for a couple minutes. I tell him what's happened and ask him to call our families. He keeps insisting we must be on Great Barrier Reef in Australia, that we must be confused. Yes, we are confused, but we are not in Australia.

A mud-spattered four-wheel drive slides to a stop out front. Shane Godinet, constable at large and the entire police force of Great Barrier Island, confronts us as we lift the garage door to let him in. Hands on his huge, burly, two-hundred-twenty-pound frame, Shane's push broom mustache, his curled bush of hair, the crow's feet at the edges of his eyes make him look like a young Samoan Albert Einstein on steroids. He accuses us: "So you guys are the ones who broke into this house!"

"Well, yes, sir. Were glad to see you," I say timidly.

He laughs. He's a bit taken back by Phil's clean-shaven, smartly-dressed appearance, but he checked out our story on his way here and seems to accept it. Graciously, he collects the whole crew in his vehicle and says, "Let's go to my place and have a whiskey." We roar off down the hillside, bouncing and swaying over the slippery mud road. "Just got this rig," says Shane with a smile. I am petrified—much more scared that on *Rose-Noëlle*. Shane cracks jokes, pumps a tape of Jean Pitney love songs into the machine, and whips up the volume. He skids to a stop in front of a store. "Okay, what do you guys want to eat at my place?"

Half in shock, we gaze at one another. I say finally, "Bacon and eggs?"

Phil adds, "Oh, a loaf of white bread."

John wiggles his eyebrows and says, "Couple of chocolate bars?"

Before you know it, we're spilling out demands for ice cream, juice, *real* milk. . . . Shane disappears. People timidly wander out of the store, bend down to gaze in the windows but keep their distance like we're some kind of wild, exotic, unpredictable animals. The doors burst open, Shane bowls out to the car, tosses a box of grocs in the back, and we speed off again.

At his house we shower while his kindly wife, Teresa, takes individual orders. We breakfast on bacon, eggs, whiskey, and ice cream. A bit odd perhaps, but quite palatable. Phil leans back and lights up a cigarette, the first in years. He is in ecstasy.

Within an hour of arriving at Shane's place, the heavy-thudding whir of helicopter blades overshadows our talk and then dies. Shane greets three men at the door who come in and wander around us silently. One carries a paper pad, another a camera. Over several uncomfortable minutes these secret agents approach and withdraw in waves—looking in their direction draws them to us, but as each of us timidly looks away they withdraw. The guy with the pad finally introduces himself as a reporter from the *Dominion*. Would we mind answering some questions?

They need no bright light in our faces. Right away, Phil begins to spill the beans. Urged on by the exotic torture of a clicking camera, Rick and I join in. John is conspicuously quiet, offering only minimal answers to pointed questions, stroking a cat into oblivion, waiting for Pat, his own friendly reporter, to arrive.

The phone rings. The agent without the camera or pad says, "We have to go." I have no idea where we're going or why, but I really don't care. We thank the Godinets and file out to the heli-copter. Agent number three jumps into the pilot seat. There is a confusion of shuffling bodies as we try to pack the chopper. The four of us climb into the back seat, which appears to be designed for three. We scramble after the ends of the seatbelts and finally settle, crammed in together. At least we are together, off to take a heli-copter ride, off on another voyage.

The long blades of the chopper begin to rotate, spin with glee, whir. The air is full of noise and anticipation. A man comes running across the lawn toward us. I don't know how I know, but I say to John, "Hey, John. I think that's your friend."

John glances out, unsnaps his safety harness, lunges forward. Confused protest spews from the front seat. That's what the phone call was about. Another helicopter has landed. These reporters have tried to scoop us away all to themselves. They're pulling a swiftie on their competitors, just like Rick and I did when we nicked an extra sweet biscuit. I swing the door open and John jumps down.

"Okay, okay, let's go" the reporter says. I swing the door shut. We tip forward and begin to rise. John runs away from us, runs to his friend.

Chapter 16
Swept Away

While our helicopter soars across the Hauraki Gulf, John clasps his friend, Pat, thinking, *At last, I have a friend with me.* How different things would have been out there for him with a friend like this, someone who would understand, someone he could trust. In the glow of reunion, John and his friend board their own chopper and bolt away to a future that is free of us.

Rick leans forward and shouts to the pilot over the noise of the mammoth eggbeater, "Hey, my parents live in Walsford Bay right near the beach. There's a little path down there. Any chance of dropping me off down there?"

The pilot turns to look at the reporter for a moment, but we can't see the conversation between their eyes. He twists his head a bit more toward us and bellows, "No. We can't do that," and then turns back to business.

Why can't he? we wonder. After all, we never really left New Zealand. Technically we shouldn't have to clear back through customs or anything. Who knows? Maybe the powers that be have got our friends and families together someplace for a reunion. We settle back and enjoy the ride.

We land at Mechanics Bay in Auckland, are hastily herded into a cavernous garage and toward a bunkerlike office. Rick's parents appear, embrace their son, shake my hand, and are pulled away again by an irresistible stream of confused motion that sweeps us into the office. Interests of the state still take precedence over interests of the heart.

Around an oval table, Rick, Phil, and I sit while a group of medics and a couple of cops stand about eyeing us. From across the table, Captains Bowen and Lyon, who represent the Maritime Transport Division of the Ministry of Transport and the Mercantile Marine, respectively, begin to debrief us. They probe us like a couple of insurance auditors looking for a fraudulent chink in our story, hoping to trip us up. I suppose, with our new clothes, absence of sores, and fairly meaty physiques, our interrogators have a right to be suspicious. How could we have been adrift for four months?

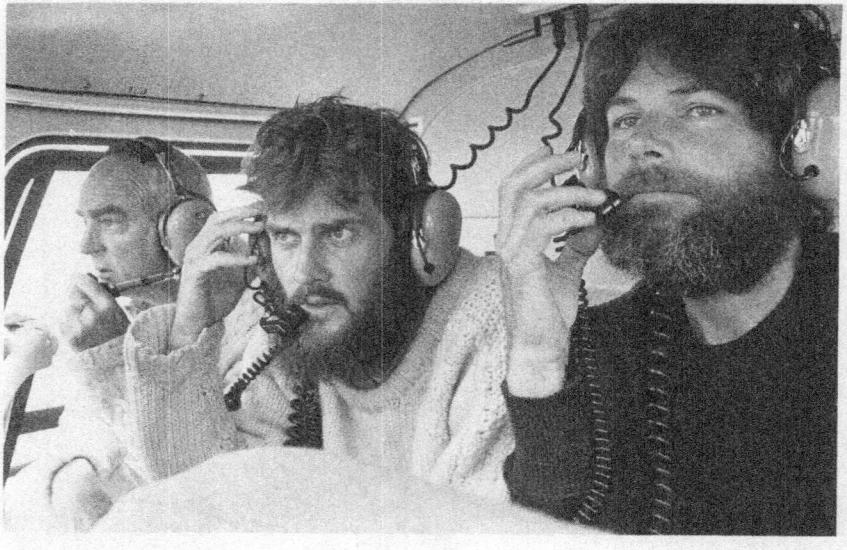

Phil, Rick and Jim lift off to a separate future, Glennie having leapt out of the helicopter to embrace an old friend.
(Reproduced with the permission of Dominion, Wellington)

But why would we want to make up such a story? Phil seems happy to answer every probe, but I just want it to end so I can go home. I never asked for all this hoopla. I quickly become irritated with the questions that drag on and on. Their twenty-minute interview seems to last days.

One of the policemen says to us, "Look, there are a lot of television reporters and newspaper people out there who want to interview you. I would suggest that you talk to them now for ten minutes and get it over with. Then they won't bother you again."

We take his advice. It's just one of many mistakes we'll make as we become immersed in civilization again. I feel lost, vulnerable, as powerless as I felt when *Rose-Noëlle* flipped over one early morning. For one hundred nineteen days we struggled to find our own potential; for seventeen weeks we battled the sea for control of our destiny; for a third of a year we created our own little society out there on the edge of the world. Now humanity bundles us up like helpless babes, yanks us over here, pushes us over there, stuffs its face into ours, coos gibberish for its own entertainment, and assumes that we are likewise entertained. We have no choice in the matter, have nowhere to run, nowhere to hide. I feel smothered. Control over my own life has vanished and I resent its theft by people I do not even know.

Gathered round a television set, Martha, Heather, Mattie, and a host of friends cheer as they see the first concrete evidence that we are alive. They hear that we have landed on the forested Great Barrier. As the psychics predicted, it is an island of twelve letters, and when our friends see Rick step out of the helicopter, he wears gumboots and a white cable-knit sweater.

Our flock is rushed back into the hanger and corralled between five chairs and a host of camera-, paper-, tape-recorder-clutching reporters. We sit with the nation's star of TV chat, Paul Holmes. Lights flood the impromptu stage. On tall, spindly legs, a video recorder's unblinking eye stares, steals our image, and spits it out to the world. Voraciously packing the rim of televised space, careful not to cross the invisible boundary, a mob of reporters eagerly waits, looking like they're ready to bid as Pat Holmes auctions the livestock.

Holmes' questions are typical—"How did this happen? What did you do for food? For water? Where's your skipper, John Glennie?"

"We don't know. He took another helicopter."

"Did you know where you were? Did you think you'd be rescued? What did you think about?"

Jesus, what did *you* think about over the last four months? You think we can sum it up in a sentence? You think it's that simple? Do you assume we're brain dead, or are you?

"In all that time that you were out there, did you ever despair?"

Rick looks Mr. Holmes straight in the eye and returns a question, "What do *you* think?" It probably isn't fair. Holmes is just doing his job. And he has recently returned from an air crash in the sea in which one crewman drowned. He's been out there too. Yet we just want to be left alone.

The interview done, we are ushered to an ambulance and whisked away to the hospital. There they test our blood pressures, feel our bones, take our urine, suck our blood—just like the press. In fact, when I go to the can, a reporter follows me like a puppy, yapping questions into my ear as I bend over the urinal. "Look," I plead, "please, won't you leave me alone?" He backs away from my snap for a second, but then dogs my heals until the doors of the examination room swing closed on his face.

Rick's parents and Phil's daughter arrive. Within minutes the nurse says, "You're free to go." Waiting in the lounge behind swinging doors, a pack of reporters pace. "We'll go the back way," the nurse says, leading us down the maze of hallways to a door. We are set free in the sunshine.

Sitting in McDonald's on Queen Street, Auckland, I am entertained by the activity of hundreds of people. Punkers with spiked purple hair and chains punched into their ears, stumbling and drooling drunks, a Maori biker with a hundred tattoos layered on arms that hang from massive shoulders like sides of beef, business people in pinstripes, students with bags of books, kids running around and screaming at each other, and two ocean survivors compose the cast of this street theater.

I don't even like this food, but Rick and I have talked about it for so long that we crave it. For the next two weeks we will stay with Peter and Helen Hellriegel at their home near the sea. En route, they have obliged our fanatic whim.

Heather and Martha arrive shortly after dark. In a huge bathtub I float, with ears underwater, doing ceiling patrol. Martha's face fills my eyes. Her lean athletic frame, long sandy-blond hair, and big brown eyes fit perfectly in my dreamy memory of her natural beauty. I give her a huge hug and get her all wet.

We talk about what we went through. She does not hesitate to tell me how hard it has been for her with only Heather to lean on. It strikes me how much turmoil we have caused in other people's lives. I am sorry for it, but, of course, it is not my fault. It is great to see Martha, but it is one more thing I must deal with when I need rest. I *want* to be tremendously excited. For months I have spun a dream of a wonderful reunion full of passion and intimacy, but something is wrong. I hide it from her, hide it from myself.

At Outward Bound, the community celebrates our return with a potluck dinner washed down with champagne. The yachties in Picton around Phil's boat throw a bash that lasts long into the night. We are home. Isn't life great?!

I want so much for Martha to fulfill the romantic dream that I created and anticipated, but I have no strength to be an equal partner with her, and it quickly becomes obvious that we both are overwhelmed, exhausted, spent. At night when we sleep together, I now miss the more familiar comfort of Rick by my side, who expects nothing of me physically or emotionally. I do not want to sleep with Martha, I want to sleep with Rick.

I climb up the steps to the pantry to snoop for a snack. While trying to keep the hinges from squeaking, I slip out a box of biscuits, the same biscuits we used to steal on *Rose-Noëlle,* and I carefully separate the cellophane to keep it from crackling. A hand lands firmly on my shoulder. I jump and turn to find Rick. We laugh, sit down to share our pilfered treat and some milk. They don't taste as good as they used to.

When Martha urges me to return home with her, I resist. I don't want to go. Rick and I feel an obligation to tell our story to the people who want to hear it. We give the press three days. Maybe it's really an excuse because we need a few days to wean ourselves from each other. The government meanwhile decides to appoint an independent investigator to conduct a preliminary investigation into the incident of the *Rose-Noëlle.*

We receive telegrams, phone calls, and visits from friends and relatives. Some people who drop by the house are people I don't know at all. Under the press of family obligations, Rick is clearly getting worn down by the redundant questions.

Rick and I take turns answering the phone. Telephone interviews find their way into radio, print, even television. We receive attention that I never dreamt I would get. At first it feels so good that I see potential for another addiction. But the task is absolutely draining. Media requests and polite questions soon evolve into demands. Everybody wants just a little piece of us, but there are only so many pieces to give. We have little left for our family and friends who really deserve it. One television reporter imports his traveling show into Peter and Helen's basement and conducts an hour-long segment. The interviewer wants to tape all of us separately now and again together a year from now. I can see the glee in the reporter's eyes just thinking about it. What a concept!

One night we're particularly amused, however, when we flip on the box to find Phil in a 45-second spot going into a bakery. He stands in front of a legion of cream puffs, grabs two or three, and puts them on a plate. He stuffs one about halfway into his mouth. The camera zooms in. "AAAH That's good!" he exclaims.

"How's it taste, Phil?" asks the interviewer.

"Ah, it was worth the wait!" he says.

Rick and I fall right off our chairs and roll around laughing so hard that I begin to see stars.

Three days pass before an Australian live radio interviewer asks, "Do you still stand by your claim Mr. Hellriegel?" Stand by our *claim*? Rick cuts the interview short and slams the phone into its cradle. It is the first of a new barrage of probes. No longer are we asked about what we experienced. Now we are challenged to prove we experienced anything at all.

Was it real or was it a hoax? They speculate that maybe we were running drugs and smashed into the island. Maybe it was a huge publicity stunt for Outward Bound.

Rick and I are both pissed off about the entire affair. Who asked these reporters to cover this story anyway? Now they turn around and accuse us of doing something sleazy. Maybe it's *them*! Maybe they milked our survival as long as they could and now the suggestion of a hoax gives them an extra teat to yank. Maybe it's people in the government embarrassed by failing to find us, then writing us off for dead, now angry that we have the bad taste to show up alive. John Glennie's theory is that the Aussies started the rumor because they can't stand New Zealanders getting anything over on them. They have to kick sand in our faces whenever they can. Whoever it is, they're idiots. Do they think that Glennie would destroy everything he had worked for nineteen years to create just to fashion a story for the press? Get real.

Little do we know about the false reports of our positions, the rumor of seeing us in Tonga, of the lie that Heather received a post card from us, most of it thanks to the Bramwell grapevine.

Two guys from the Ministry of Transport rap on the door and question Rick. Two days later they interrogate me. They want details of the entire event. Leave no boat unturned.

Just a hundred yards from Peter and Helen's house a beach spreads out to the Gulf. On clear days I peer out over thirty-five miles of water to Great Barrier Island. We almost cleared it. We *could* have ended up right here, fulfilling my naive dream of washing onto a nice soft beach. What would the skeptics think of us then, riding up easily to safety within 100 yards of one of the crew's family homes? At least the investigation will eventually satisfy the press and the authorities and let us get on with our lives.

Rick has no interest in seeing John, but I do. About a week after our arrival, Peter drops me off across town at the home of Penny Whiting and Doc Williams, old friends of John's who have offered him refuge. John is as animated as he was before we left on *Rose-Noëlle*, fitting into Doc and Penny's family like another one of the kids. The twinkle in his eyes has returned and he's putting on weight again. He does not seem put off by or angry at the skeptical press. Instead he says, "Oh, I've been giving interviews all over the world. Look at my feet. See how they're swelling up," like an amused and curious scientist observing someone else's elephantiasis.

In this setting John seems almost to have never been away. He looks comfortable, at home. I confess to him that it's difficult for me to be around Martha right now. He in return tells me that he's trying hard not to surround himself with people who demand things from him.

We sit down to a bountiful feast. "Isn't it wonderful to be sitting down again to a lovely meal?"

"Yes John. It really is nice."

In early November the Ministry of Transport releases its preliminary inquiry into the capsize and drift of *Rose-Noëlle*.

So why didn't we drift East to South America? The investigators acquired weather reports for the area throughout the time of our drift. These showed that the wind patterns were relatively unusual this year. The New Zealand Pilot notes that ocean currents in the area are variable and quite influenced by wind. The New Zealand Oceanographic Institute further notes that our projected loop of drift lay inshore of the stronger and more consistent offshore currents, that information on currents in the area are sparse, and that information in recent years concerning variable currents has enlightened oceanographers to unexpected flows. One example is an ocean-current drogue deployed in 1978 that flowed West *against* the presumed current near North Cape at the top of New Zealand, not far from the last leg of our drift. If *Rose Noëlle*'s drift was controlled by weather and weather-driven currents, she would have first drifted generally eastward, curved to the north, looped west, and dipped southwest. At the request of New Zealand Yachting Magazine, Greg Reeve at the Auckland Weather Office plotted our exact course, assuming a half-knot drift in twenty-knots of wind. It is an uncanny mirror of our tale. Although Reeve's plot shows the loop of our drift going beyond Great Barrier Island through Auckland, it begins to the southwest of our assumed position of capsize. If one adjusts for that and subtracts a minuscule fraction of a knot, the track would land us virtually on the same rock.

Although these findings indicated that we *could* have drifted back to New Zealand, *did* we? Investigators returned to the landing site with John to dredge up pieces of the wreck. From the sea, divers pulled anchors, line, plastic tubs, our water jug, the twisted frame of John's bicycle, his garland of plastic flowers . . . Scraps of John's sail bag were as close as they came to finding his log, medals, and mementos of our itinerant society. Of *Rose-Noëlle* only a spray of chunks remained, few more than a yard wide.

Professor Brian Foster at the Department of Zoology, University of Auckland analyzed the marine growth clinging to the deck. Three species were studied. Their type would have begun growing in offshore waters south of thirty-nine degrees South

Latitude. Their size was consistent with a growing period of 60 to 90 days. Professor Foster further concluded that many barnacles were damaged, probably by impact upon landing, but that some barnacle "decapitation could have occurred while adrift (e.g. biotic removal, including human harvest)." I think about our barnacle soups, barnacles on the half shell, and sauteed mollusks. Biotic removal indeed!

A final bit of evidence that supports our claims comes from children. "Hi Daniel," the letter begins. "I found the bottle that you sent a message in . . ." The letter is signed, "Write soon, Karen Shrubshall, aged 16." Karen found the bottle on 21 September about fifty miles north of Auckland. It was cast into the sea about 120 miles northwest of our capsize and due west from Greg Reeve's calculated position for *Rose-Noëlle* on 27 June. Daniel Bramwell tossed his message overboard from his family's voyaging yacht. It, too, floated opposite the charted currents, drifted in a loop similar to ours, and landed nine days before we did and just to the North of Great Barrier Island.

It is indeed ironic that Daniel's father, Jim Bramwell, had so long confused the search and rescue efforts by his mistaken reports of our position and other rumors. Now his son with a bottle game, proves him wrong. James himself finally wrote a letter clarifying that he never positively identified the senders of the mistaken positions as *Rose-Noëlle*.

The inquiry makes us even more aware of all the efforts that were spent on our behalf. The government of this tiny country with limited resources, charged with searching nine-and-a-half-million square miles of ocean actually looked for us. Many larger governments routinely refuse to search even a square yard of ocean unless they have a confirmed SOS/Mayday message or EPIRB signal to track. New Zealand held an extensive search with extremely limited information. My sister Cathy and friend Joe Shierl from Minneapolis joined our New Zealand friends, families, and interested parties from the boating community, to create a formidable coalition. But in the end, for all of us, offshore and on, it was a painful waiting game.

The inquiry's findings are a relief, take a load off our backs. In a letter to each of the crew, Minister of Transport, William Jeffries concludes, "You and the other members of the crew have been an inspiration in your achievement." With a stroke of a pen, he causes us to metamorphose from liars to heros. In a press release, he further states, "The miraculous voyage of the *Rose-Noëlle* is testimony to the benefits of a sound vessel, ample provisions, and the determination and courage of its crew. If there was ever any question that the *Rose-Noëlle* was not overturned and drifting for 119 days, then this investigation dispels those doubts." Even cabinet ministers will not argue with a note in a bottle.

The media, of course, milks this new turn of events for a couple more days, but then disappears like a bad dream.

Our drift accomplished at least one positive thing. Until now, New Zealand has relied on aircraft to pick up EPIRB emergency signals. None were within range of our pleas for help. Since late in 1983, however, satellites have been capable of acquiring EPIRB signals, but they need to beam the message to a receiver on earth. Most rest along the Atlantic Ocean rim. New Zealand decides, in the wake of *Rose-Noëlle*, to install a local user terminal and join the international distress reporting system, known as SARSAT for Search and Rescue by Satellite. The system will cost one-and-a-half-million kiwi dollars.

Phil returns to Picton, Karen, the kids, Friday nights at the pub, and his boat with no name. He will dub her *Toroa*. Eventually he will buy a trimaran.

John hits the lecture circuit and begins writing *the* book with co-author Jane Phare.

Rick and I return home to the Marlborough Sounds. The hospital in Auckland found that we were all only a bit anemic, but Rick does not seem to bounce back as well as the rest of us. After battling one brain tumor into remission and then being lost at sea, Rick returns only to learn that another tumor grows in his head.

I must get back into the mainstream again. Hoping everything will fall into place if I just force myself to get used to the motions of normal life, just as I got used to the motions of the sea, I re-turn to work at Outward Bound in December. As I walk by the garbage area, a hand grabs my arm. Bill Hathorne's tanned, handsome face is somber. "Hey mate," he says with a soft, low, mournful voice, "I'm really, really sorry for what I said to you before you left."

"What? What are you talking about Bill?"

"Remember when I said that I'd get your pushbike if you didn't come back. I didn't mean anything by it. I really didn't."

Everybody seeks connections to our experience. If they had a dream, if they prayed, if they sent us thoughts, if they gave us up for dead, or if, like Bill, casual words tempted fate, whatever their contact with us or our voyage, they feel compelled to create a link. They helped to cause the disaster, prolong it, save us from it, or divine its true meaning. Maybe they are right, or maybe there is no connection. There were plenty of wrong dreams, visions, predictions, and irrelevant coincidences. No matter what happened, how it turned out, there would be people with connections, faiths that reality would justify. Even now, maybe forever, people tie themselves to our experience with the most fragile umbilicals. They were involved. They grieved. They need to find something of meaning in it, just like I do.

I've never seen Bill serious before. I tell him it's no problem, his words were no curse. In fact, I sell him the bike. I tell him he's getting a heck of a deal.

I do not get back into the swing of things, however. I never got so used to the sea's motions that I could forge a normal life there either. I'm useless. I seem to spend a lot of time aimlessly wandering, letting my coworkers carry me along.

I don't want to see anybody. I feel like I'm hibernating. Everyone I see seems to expect me to tell them my story. People introduce me as one of the guys who floated around on a capsized trimaran for four months. I hate it! Martha is going back to Canada. I realize that she made that decision while we were out there at sea. She had already grieved and gone on with her life. Meanwhile I feel I'm clinging to her. I have needs. She has nothing to give me. Maybe I didn't give her enough before I left. We're trying to piece together something that was never whole in the first place. Am I crazy? Am I okay?

Rick and I begin to visit psychologists. They tell us we're okay--just post traumatic stress syndrome. Sounds official. Doesn't feel any different.

Physically I feel stronger all the time and recognize that I am slowly coming around, settling on solid ground. "See you later Martha."

She does not look up from the typewriter as her fingers fly across the keys, typing yet another report, letter for Amnesty International, article for Youth Hostel magazine, her application to grad school in Toronto, or something. As long as there are Marthas in this world, there will never be a real energy shortage.

I step out of our bunkerish cellar flat, and am blinded by the late afternoon light. Standing outside the highest house in the settlement, my eyes adjust and open onto the panorama of Queen Charlotte Sound. I can see all the way to the end of it. The same lush mountains ring the same cold waters, but now that it's December and summer, the landscape and the settlement's gardens are in full bloom. Hills are covered with Punga trees and gorse, which sprouts enticing yellow flowers from its thorny branches. Sailboats and the Outward Bound cutters hang like toys to moorings about a thousand feet below and a half-mile off. From this perch one could have witnessed *Rose-Noëlle's* ill-fated departure half a year ago. Miles up the Sound, a bright white ferry turns to head up Tory Channel. Perhaps it is the same ferry with which John took such joy in playing chicken. I take off down the winding paved road.

Now it is summer. No frost lies upon my path. It's a lousy time to run. The air is hot, thick, full of glare, but I feel a tremendous sense of freedom. It is a joy to feel each muscle tense and relax, the trickle of sweat. It is as if my mind rides a churning human locomotive, slipping easily into daydreams as my legs rhythmically pump, always pushing on.

At the bottom of the winding road I turn onto a long straight stretch that splits a valley of pastures and cows. I see Rick and Heather's white station wagon turn onto the stretch and drive towards me. For twenty or thirty seconds I see their car grow. Heather is driving and we both slow as she approaches. We greet each other happily and I wave to Mattie. "Hi Rick!"

Rick does not answer. From the far front seat, he leans against the outer door, his head cocked to stare at me from under the top rim of the car's window. His eyes are incongruous with his slumped body. They are sunken but wide and burn with some kind of anger. Heather continues to roll forward, but Rick's eyes fix upon me, his head swiveling to keep me in his sights as they move off.

Martha leaves in January. My stint at Outward Bound stretches on to March. I often visit Rick and Heather, but my visits with Rick are hit-and-miss. Some days he is warm and responsive. Other days he is cold and distant, almost lifeless. The doctors tell Rick and Heather that the brain tumor is medically inoperable. He can't tolerate any more radiation. They search outside New Zealand, to Australia and the States, but the news is no different there. The tumor is growing and there is nothing anyone can do. With the help of a local doctor they try alternatives like visualization, herbs, color therapy, and continued psychological therapy. Rick remains adamant that he will beat this again. He's a perfectionist. He's in control. Control is the one thing of which he cannot let go.

By March Rick spends most of his time in bed. It is difficult for him to walk. By May he rides a wheelchair and his condition is diving rapidly. The right half of his body is nearly paralyzed. He can barely see or hear from his right side. His head aches. The doctors give him six months.

I think back to our days on *Rose-Noëlle*. Perhaps this tumor began even then when Rick seemed to become clumsy, to stumble and fall a lot. Photos of him in the helicopter upon our rescue show his right eye drooping.

Occasionally, Rick and I revisit our voyage together. We laugh, remembering Phil wrestling with his fish, the way he always wanted to eat and drink everything in sight until we were low on water when he'd suddenly shock us with his pleas to ration. We laugh at the vision of Phil chowing down cream puffs. Phil was predictable, reliable. Even when we sat on him like the low man on the totem pole, Phil always took it in stride. Once he snapped out of his pessimism, his lightheartedness and honesty were a relief. Things rolled off of his back that would have crushed us, and in the end he became the strongest of us all. Phil needed no Glennie heros; he had enough of one within himself. When we see Phil, we all have a good time.

Rick does not want to see John. Maybe John was a step out of synch with the rest of us because he's a man of another generation, forged into society's mold to quest for success, victory, and control, just as women of his age were compelled to support such quests and nurture families. And maybe that mold for both sexes is well outdated. But John also found something special out of sight of people, some kernel of excitement and fulfillment in the company of nature, even when nature is hostile. He shared that with me even though he does not suffer fools gladly and I was the fool on his ship. I remain grateful to him. Maybe Rick doesn't want to see him just because they're too much alike.

Yet they are also different. Rick absorbs the meaning of our voyage, struggles to face the failures in his life, begins the arduous task of rebuilding his relationships with Heather and his son. John, on the other hand, seems as egotistical as ever. He introduces himself to my sister with, "Aren't you going to thank me for saving your brother's life?" He might have been kidding. Who knows? He is partly right anyway. We wouldn't have made it without him. But there are whole truths that he seems to have completely missed out there. All of us were weak and vulnerable until we learned how to lean on one another. Glennie's bravado kept him in command of his own mind and gave us the needed reassurance that we would make it, but it appears that he still does not see that such strengths were, at other times, also weaknesses.

Rick and I have been like brothers, but now, other than an amusing reminiscence, he cannot stand to let me get too close. He must rely on other people and he hates it. My strengthening body bounds off to enjoy reunions and a future while he is more trapped and as adrift as ever. He hates to watch. We no longer know how to take comfort from each other. He grows distant, shuts me out, voids the pact we made upon the wet overturned hull of *Rose-Noëlle*. We are no longer there for one another. We try, but it is too painful.

I have not yet seen the rest of my family or the friends I left behind in the States. It is time for me to go home and to do something different. I'll make a trek to Africa, a journey that was always on Rick's old list of things to accomplish.

In Rick's room, the curtains are drawn to keep the sun from assaulting his sensitive eyes. Over the right one he wears a patch. Today, Rick is excited for me and upbeat. "I'm jealous. I wish *I* was going to Africa," he says.

"Don't worry, I'll be back and tell you all about it." We discuss how crazily things have turned out. "God, Rick, I feel really bad. Here you are on your back and sick again and I'm feeling good and going home. I feel guilty about that."

"Guilty!?" he snaps back with his muscles tense, his thinning body nearly leaping out of bed. "I'm going to get better!"

"God, I know you are Rick. I'm sorry. I didn't mean to insinuate you weren't."

He lays back. "I know, mate."

I lean over my friend and give him an embrace. He in turn puts his left arm around me and pulls tight. We hold each other for a very long time. Finally I let go. I stand. We reach for each other's hand.

Mattie roars around the house just outside Rick's door, seemingly oblivious to his father's condition, or just accepting it as children are apt to do.

Heather walks with me to the car. She and I also linger in an embrace. She whispers in my ear, "If he dies, you don't have to come back."

Chapter 17
Odyssey

October 1990

"Don't expect him to look the same as when you left," says Heather when I return to New Zealand. His looks are the least of my worries. I've never been around anybody dying before and I'm as nervous as I was when Rick drove us to Picton for a blind date with *Rose-Noëlle* and an adventure of a lifetime. Do I have the right foul weather gear to accompany Rick on this, his final voyage? Will I know what to do? He overcame one brain tumor only to get lost at sea and got ashore only to find another tumor filling his head. And here I am, running around, able to dream about my future, a torturous reminder of what he was, all he had. How can I face his understandable anger and impatience? My nightmare is that he will turn to me and say, "What did you come back for?"

So much has happened in a mere year since Rick and I made our pact on the back of *Rose-Noëlle*. Yet our voyage did not end on the rocks of Great Barrier Island. Rick drifts on.

Heather drives me to the hospital, looking good, even happy, her hair teased by the breeze sneaking over the top of the car window, her hand casually thrown on the wheel. She astounds me. After a decade of Rick's traumas and a year of singlehandedly caring for him and two-year-old Mattie she still awakens at 4:00 A.M. to get through her daily chores. Recently, Heather's best friend died from encephalitis and, after struggling 22 years with multiple sclerosis, her father also passed away. Maybe, without time to grieve, she runs on a stream of adrenalin. Heather brushes aside fatalism like a bit of dust. She tells me Rick's spirit is high. He's going to get better.

My heart pounds as we reach Rick's room in the hospital's Hospice ward. My eyes behold a wraith. Rick's five-foot-ten frame supports just 100 pounds. The thickness of his wrists and upper arms are the same. A gauze patch is taped over his right eye. He cannot move his right limbs or hear through his right ear. But his creamy porcelain skin stands in striking contrast to his black beard, wide eye, and sharp, crooked smile. He is still a handsome man.

Despite anti-spasmodic drugs, Rick's right arm and leg begin to twitch as I rush to him. His head jerks. He gasps, as if hyperventilating. His eyes pool with tears. I bend over and we grasp each other. Rick's good arm wraps around me and pulls me tight. We are both afraid to let go. "It's great to see you mate," he tells me.

With our hands firmly entwined, joyously staring into each other's eyes, I tell him about my travels as if they are journeys we made together. Achieving Mount Kilamanjaro's summit at sunrise after a light snow, we peer over oceanic plains spreading out below. It feels like we can see all of Africa. Among mud and dung homes, we sip tea with handsome, almost arrogantly proud Maasi villagers who wear beads around their necks, bright cloth around their slim bodies, huge holes in their ears. An oversized sun sets in an orange ball, silhouetting zebra, giraffe, and gazelle as we ride a 1930s British railway car from Nairobi to Mombassa. I can see in Rick's eyes that he is there with me.

Within minutes I cease to notice Rick's emaciation. His twitches calm and seem as normal as a yawn. Listening carefully to his slurred words, I still sometimes ask him to repeat, but soon it is only like deciphering a foreign accent. He takes slow, deliberate care to talk and I take care to listen. It took months for us to adapt ourselves to the crippled *Rose-Noëlle*, but I effortlessly accept the mere shell of Rick's body that is broken only in contrast to what it once was.

Rick says he's happy to be here in Hospice. It is easier for Heather. "The food is the pits though."

"Hey mate, that's why I'm here. I didn't come 10,000 miles to cook you ordinary food!"

Every few days, Heather and I exchange places at Rick's side. We brush his teeth, rub his feet, prepare his meals–everything but give him showers or sponge baths when he is even too weak to be assisted to the bathroom. Nurses are willing do everything, but it feels good to live with Rick again, to give Heather some relief, to give. I note how the nurses feed him, move him, brush his hair. I have never really appreciated these multitudinous heros who do not move mountains or order armies around, but painstakingly move from soul to soul, changing bedpans, one at a time.

Crowning Rick's left ankle is a dark-purple, thickly calloused scar, the remains of his open oozing sore from *Rose-Noëlle's* capsize. To Rick it is insignificant; the tumor in his head is even beatable still. As his body weakens, his determination strengthens. He challenges everyone. "You told me I had to take one of these pills yesterday. Why two today? What are these things anyway?" Without the strength to move himself, he commands us to exercise his arms and legs, rub his feet. He especially likes a nurse who mockingly calls him "Your highness."

Visitors become a hardship. Rick awakes, feeling good, but then a compassionate, well-meaning guest smothers him with tears. How skinny he is, they note. Rick flinches, as if pity is a knife with which they carve his flesh to feed themselves. He must reassure them, support *them*, when he can barely muster enough energy to keep himself alive. When visitors leave, he feels shattered. Rick asks us to screen callers. By November he wants to see almost no one except Heather and I.

En route to the hospital, I feel like a fresh horse prancing. I am in Rick's exclusive club. Heather and I do not pity him to his face, imply that he is worse today, or that he will die, even as I think that he must. Instead, we create a life within the wreck, accepting tomorrow's uncertainty, enjoying small things, meals, today. Rick and I reminisce about being adrift, or chat about Phil's recent weight gain and his new baby girl whom he named Phillipa Rose of all things.

Rick believes that he has manifested this disease in himself. In the face of mountain peaks and raging seas, he was fearless, but he never pushed the frontiers within himself. As if creating an image chiseled after some archetype of noble manhood, he drove himself to achieve goals, but never to face his failures and softer side. Stand tall. Stand rugged. Do not bend lest you break. Rick now thinks that pressures between his outer strengths and inner weaknesses caused a crack in which this tumor took seed.

I ask him about what he wants to do with his business and he tells me, "I don't know. I don't care." All his past conquests and future pilgrimages–the photography book, adventures, building his business–mean nothing. "All I want to do is go home and live in my house, live a simple life and paddle the Sounds with Heather and Mattie."

When we first got off *Rose-Noëlle*, I asked Rick if he felt humbled. He said, "Shit no," and looked at me like I must be mad. But this disease *has* humbled him. He appreciates a simple foot rub and the turning of each day. Instead of bitching about his bad luck, Rick tells me, "I'm happier right now than I have ever been in my life."

Rick's condition and our emotions ride a roller coaster. Sometimes he hasn't enough strength to feed himself. Then he can hardly breath. Thinking he'll not live to the weekend, Rick asks us to call his mother. Two days later he tells us to call her back. He thinks he'll make it.

Rick cannot chew, so we blend his meals smooth as baby food–oatmeal and fruit with yogurt for breakfast, rice with peanut sauce or maybe lasagna for dinner, even torts for dessert. Then he demands tomatoes without the skins and gets picky about the food's temperature. I get pissed off at him, but then I try to feel what he is feeling. Food is all he's got.

Increasingly I appreciate the unspoken intimacy of brushing Rick's hair, brushing his teeth. Each day issues a new challenge and crisis, and I become aware that I need him simply because he needs me. I reap power from my control over his life. Still, I dream that he will get up, walk out of here and prove everybody wrong. "Wouldn't that be great?" I say to him.

His eyes light up and he says, "Yeah!" But only I get up and walk out.

Before Heather comes, Rick gets all worked up and gains a special look in his eye. Together they speak affectionately, make kissy faces. "Move over," she orders, knowing he can't move. So she pushes him aside and hops in bed with him. He slings his good arm around her shoulder and rubs her arm up and down. The more I see of Heather the more I see what Rick loves. She quests only to build relationships. She exudes fun and an inner peace that evades the restless Rick. They have fights, but for once, Rick and Heather are content. I want to be committed to somebody like that. I want to tell them to shove over as I hop into their death bed, or I want them to hop into mine.

In December, Hospice finally boots Rick out. It's time for

him to be around dogs and kids, to make a home life as best he can. His home, however, is not well-suited for long-term care. Heather's mother, Gloria, offers her custom-built house with its wheelchair-wide doors, a handicap bathroom and all.

The house looks like a country club on the edge of the sea, next door to good old Outward Bound. OB students run by in the morning. Rick lives in bed, but even he can hear them grunting and yammering. Gloria often tells Rick, "There's a group going out on kayaks now," or "They're heading out on one of the cutters." Sometimes a group scales the rock face just outside his room. He never responds.

Somebody must sleep in Rick's room to empty his pee bottle or help him to the bathroom. Rick's confused hearing makes it too hard for him to concentrate on more than one person's voice, so he refuses to watch television or listen to music and we spend his waking hours talking or reading to him. Although he sleeps fifteen hours a day, between the feeding, medication, washing, entertainment, physiotherapy . . . Rick is a 24-hour-a-day job.

Sometimes we cannot wrestle him into the wheelchair and get him into the bathroom quick enough. I want these months to be a celebration towards the close of Rick's life. I want everybody to feel close to one another, to be selfless, but sometimes we become so fatigued and irritable that we celebrate only our time off. Sometimes terminal illness is only as enlightening as scraping human waste off of the floor.

Family funds must be scratching bottom, but Rick tells me to fetch his checkbook. He directs me to buy Heather a hundred-dollar gift certificate to a fancy local restaurant, something she can enjoy away from here with a friend. He dictates a card: "Heather, I realize that I love you more than anyone. You're the one who keeps me alive. Thank you. I love you."

On a bright, summer, Christmas day, boats glide past on a light breeze that wafts up from the Sound, bringing the smell of cut flowers. Excited children babble, keenly showing off their presents. We hear neighbors at their barbecues or shuffling off to the beach. I enjoy the family, turkey, glasses of wine, lounging, the change from being tethered to Rick's side, but he calls out. His dim room is laced with a stale smell. He sits propped up on a pillow looking like a dead man who speaks. A napkin tucked under his chin is smeared with food. I feel like I am climbing back aboard the *Rose-Noëlle*, back to days with little hope, minuscule pleasures, monstrous fears, and aching yearnings. I want to escape, to run back outside and sip sherry, forget all about Rick and this room. Just one day. But what can I say? "See you later Rick. I have to go catch some rays?" I try to cut the conversation short, but he drags it into a long reminiscence. Slowly I settle, sit down, rest. I despise his wrecked body with which we endlessly drift; I miss the bright carefree light of normal life, but I am happy enough to feel the love of my friend. He has so little besides memories.

As January turns to February and February slips into March, May, and June, Rick still never whines about his disease. He never says, "Poor me." But we are Rick's slaves. Whenever we pass his room, he inevitably calls us. "Pull my shorts up a bit. No, no, down a little. Over to the side. Not so much." The food is never right. It's too hot, too cold, too mushy, not mushy enough. Sometimes he sends it back five or six times. Heather finally blows up at him, but Rick just lays it on thick in return. "If you give up on me, I'm going to die," he threatens. In his mind, the little details are essential to his survival and cure. To climb up a notch and rest on a slight plateau, he works so hard monitoring his drugs, his food, his breathing, even his waste. Miraculously his speech clarifies. Then he comes down with the flu, or his joints swell, or he gets an infection. Sometimes he sleeps for a day strait. When he is well enough, he drives us mercilessly to pay as much heed to every lump of broth or twist of cloth as he does.

Heather seems to know what words keep his spirits up. Or maybe he just puts on his brave face for her. One day with me, however, he breaks down and weeps. "I'm scared. I'm so afraid right now. I'm afraid of dying," he confesses. I don't know what to say. "Thank you," he continues. "Thanks for being here. I really need you and Heather." I massage his feet. He closes his eyes and sleeps.

When Rick gets diarrhea, it's like everybody gets it. We all struggle to get him to the toilet, clean him up, clean ourselves up. He yells at Heather, "Come on, come on! Get me in there. I'm crapping on the floor!" The phone is ringing. Mattie steps into the room pleading, "Mommy, mommy."

"I wish you were back in the Hospice," Heather says exasperated. She picks up the phone.

"How's it going?"

"Rick's got diarrhea."

"Well yeah, but how's everything else going?"

"RICK'S GOT DIARRHEA. DON'T YOU UNDERSTAND?"

"Heather?" Rick yells. "I have to go again!"

After a while, outsiders get the message. Then they call up and ask "How's the diarrhea?" But by then it's something else.

With increasing fatigue and tenseness, Heather, Rick, Gloria, and I stumble on from day to day. Heather and Rick constantly bait each other and are eager to bite. Neither can understand how hard it is on the other. As his condition worsens and our work load increases, everybody's tempers flare more frequently. I try to say something positive only to smash my good intentions with the slip of a single word. "Hey Rick, I read this article where this person who was dying, too, finally recovered . . ."

"Fuck you!" screams Rick.

"What? What did I say?"

"You said they were dying *too*."

"I didn't mean it Rick."

"Yes you did!"

I know Rick must begin to deal with reality, but I still feel lousy. When he feels a bit better, we make up. Wanting to mend fractured fences with Heather too, he has me roll in a phone and we hold a three way conversation with me serving as everybody's mouthpiece. "Tell her I really, really love her."

"He says he really, really loves you Heather."

"Tell him, me too."

"She says, 'Me too.'" That twisted smile creeps across his face.

Heather continues, "Jim, ask Rick if her remembers that time back in France, that night when we . . ."

"Heather!"

"Oh go ahead and tell him." They both make me feel special. It's almost as if I'm inside both of them.

Once in a while I bring in a couple beers and pour him a glass. When he drains it he says, "Man am I bombed." We joke together, return for a bit to a normal existence, taking in stride what nature has dealt us just as we did while trapped in an offshore cave. Phil visits a few times and we all have a good laugh with the spirit of a bunch of blokes gathered at the local pub.

Rick spends so much time quiet, just thinking. I wonder what he fills the hours with. Sometimes I know he drifts to a different world where, with a healed body, he returns to the calm waters of the Sound. He puts his kayak in the water, slides into the cockpit, dips his paddle, and moves away. He works on his dream world like a master artist until it becomes as real, even more real, than this dismal place to which he must return. The drip of water falling from the lifted paddle blade, the smell of foliage, the feel of the breeze. Soon, I hope. Soon, let him inhabit forever such a world of dreams.

Rick mixes Valium with antispasmodic medication, sleeping pills, bowel stimulant, asthma inhalant, and massive steroids that help reduce swelling of the tumor but bloat his face. His arms hang like twigs. Over his barrel chest, a patina of muscle stretches. Only his stomach protrudes, like some gigantic melon.

There are occasional good days, but they are rare enough to shift one's perspective on good and bad. On a good day, Rick makes out his will. He bequeaths a couple coffee cups and some clothes to me, his kayaking stuff to his partner. Most of the rest goes to Heather and Mattie. He has little to leave, but the act is a message to us that he is finally letting go.

Mattie and Heather run into Rick's room mornings, jump in his bed, and throw covers over themselves. Gloria comes to look for them. "Oh where can they be?" Mattie loves the game.

Sometimes Rick calls Mattie into the room and Mattie hops up in bed beside him. Rick looks on his son and tears begin to drip down his face. "Daddy loves you," he says.

Mattie looks up into Rick's face. "Why are you sad?" he asks. "Is daddy sad because he's sick?" He pats Rick's cheeks with his little hand. Rick weeps.

Heather looks ragged. None of us look forward any more to spending time with Rick, and we feel the heavy burden of guilt for it. Once we are in the room with him, it is okay, I enjoy my time, but it takes an increasing amount of steam to get through that door. There's nothing more to say. Nobody has a life. Nobody has a choice. There's no relief in sight.

The only real option is long-term permanent care in an impersonal open ward. "I wont go to one of those places. I won't do that! Would you want to do that?" Rick challenges.

Anger wells inside me. I am angry with Heather for not taking care of herself. I am angry at the disease. I am angry with Rick. How can he be so blind to all that everyone does for him? But when I sit down beside him, and grasp his frail hand, the anger slips away. I climb aboard with him, try to slip beneath his skin, feel his pain, his frustration, his yearnings. Sometimes it works. For a moment I am actually there. But it is too horrible.

Up and down, up and down. Just when we think he will pass away, Rick improves again. He speaks more clearly, swallows more easily. On Heather's birthday, he invites visitors to his room. He sits up and eats cake with his wife. They kiss.

This voyage with Rick has lasted twice as long as the one we took together on *Rose-Noëlle*. I want so much to be here for the end of this thing, to be a part of it, but when does it end? I want so much to fulfill my commitment to Rick, to myself, but will it ever be fulfilled, even upon his death? And I honestly don't know anymore if he will die.

Will Rick think I have turned my back on him if I leave to write about our odyssey together? Shaking with nerves, I reveal my plans. In quiet resignation, Rick reaches deep inside himself, summons up courage and dignity from I know not where, and lets me go. He fortifies me, telling me that this new quest is a really good thing. He is so grateful that I have been here for him these last eight months.

A couple weeks before I leave, Rick tells me, "I'm really really tired. I've just had it. I'm tired of trying. Just sick of all this." His knees and ankles are so swollen that the skin is starting to split. He is in agony that medication only partly subdues. He has no muscle tone, only the tone of bones.

In the last few hours we spend together, Gloria reads us the last few chapters of Barry Lopez's *Crow and Weasel*, which I have shared with Rick many times. Each sentence triggers so many memories and feelings in us. Crow and Weasel trek into a northern wilderness where none of their tribe has traveled, to extend the eyes of their tribe, to face in themselves what that journey reveals.

Rick and I, too, have voyaged far away, seen things that none of our tribe have seen, felt things that only such a journey could inspire. I suppose all people make a similar trip as they pass through the corridors of death, if not before, but like Crow and Weasel, Rick and I have shared a special track. Our souls have crossed, lingered, become one.

After their trying journey, Crow and Weasel gaze into the heavens and wonder if those with whom they shared parts of their odyssey are witnessing the same beauty, and hope it is so, just as my sister did while we were adrift. "In the silence that followed, Weasel said very softly, 'It is good to be alive. To have friends, to have a family, to have children, to live in a particular place. These relationships are sacred.'

"'Yes,' said Crow. 'This is the way it should be.'"

As Gloria reads, our eyes fill with tears. Rick can no longer cry. His eyes can only water as he fidgets and groans and breathes in rapid short gasps.

We hug each other for several minutes, unable to let go. "You take the book," he tells me. "I want you to have my half." He says it's like the gift that Mouse gave to Crow and Weasel after they spoke about the difficulties of leading a good life: ". . . to be truthful instead of clever with people, to live in a community where there is much wisdom." Mouse then gave his friends a flint that made Weasel feel a part of something much larger than himself. "He felt he could carry on a long way now, no matter how dark or heavy the forest might seem."

Slowly I back out of Rick's room, taking him all in, hoping I will always remember each curve of his face, the exact turn of his bent smile. I want to take him with me, but even now, the remains of his breath and the heat from his embrace begin to fade. The wound on his ankle is now just a slightly discolored memory. Moisture from his tear against my cheek dries.

On the way to the ferry I think about how bizarre the last couple years have been–from a city road crew, to Martha, *Rose-Noëlle*, Rick. How easily events can change you. How easily you can set them in motion. How difficult it is to live wisely.

On July 5, 1991, three weeks after I left New Zealand, Rick Hellreigel died. He is my friend.

Jim and Rick.
(Reproduced with the permission of
Dominion, *Wellington)*

About the Author

In addition to being the author of *Capsized* and the 1986 *New York Times* bestseller *Adrift: Seventy-Six Days Lost at Sea*, Steven Callahan is the principal at Steven Callahan & Associates. Based in Maine, Steven and his col-leagues provide a variety of marine services from design, construction, and consulting to equipment testing and boat deliveries. Steven maintains a special interest in offshore voyaging, safety, seamanship, and survival. Since 1977 he and and his associates have also been involved in most aspects of the communications industry, especially publishing and television. Recently, Steven has been consulting on feature films, most notably *Life of Pi*.

Steven's memoir *Adrift* has been translated into 16 languages, and remains in print some 26 years after its initial publication. KIRKUS described the book as "a riveting tale of survival. ... Callahan is, besides being an adept sailor, a fine writer." *Newsweek* called the book "utterly absorbing." And the *Wall Street Journal* hailed *Adrift* as "a fascinating tale. ... A clearly written ocean yarn in which the stakes are high and a brave man wins through."

stevencallahan.net

Printed in Great Britain
by Amazon